本书得到以下项目或机构资助：

浙江省哲学社会科学规划课题（24NDJC125YB）、浙江省软科学研究项目（2023C35101）、国家自然科学基金项目（72203200、72141305）、国家重点研发计划"文化科技与现代服务业"重点专项（2022YFF0902000）、全国统计科学研究项目（2023LZ040）、浙江省统计研究重点项目（23TJZZ08）、中央高校基本科研业务费专项资金（S20220165）；

浙大城市学院数字金融研究院（Institute of Digital Finance, Hangzhou City University）；

浙江省哲学社会科学规划课题（23NDJC078YB）。

RCEP区域
跨境电商发展研究

周闻宇　吕佳敏　陆嘉骏·著

RESEARCH ON
CROSS-BORDER E-COMMERCE DEVELOPMENT
IN THE RCEP REGION

ZHEJIANG UNIVERSITY PRESS
浙江大学出版社
·杭州·

图书在版编目(CIP)数据

RCEP区域跨境电商发展研究 / 周闻宇,吕佳敏,陆
嘉骏著. —杭州:浙江大学出版社,2023.11
ISBN 978-7-308-23986-8

Ⅰ.①R… Ⅱ.①周… ②吕… ③陆… Ⅲ.①国际贸
易－电子商务－研究－中国 Ⅳ.①F724.6

中国国家版本馆 CIP 数据核字(2023)第 120130 号

RCEP区域跨境电商发展研究
周闻宇　吕佳敏　陆嘉骏　著

策划编辑	吴伟伟
责任编辑	陈思佳(chensijia_ruc@163.com)
责任校对	李　琰
封面设计	雷建军
出版发行	浙江大学出版社
	(杭州市天目山路 148 号　邮政编码 310007)
	(网址:http://www.zjupress.com)
排　　版	浙江大千时代文化传媒服务有限公司
印　　刷	广东虎彩云印刷有限公司绍兴分公司
开　　本	710mm×1000mm　1/16
印　　张	17.75
字　　数	320 千
版 印 次	2023 年 11 月第 1 版　2023 年 11 月第 1 次印刷
书　　号	ISBN 978-7-308-23986-8
定　　价	88.00 元

前　言

本书基于阿里研究院和蚂蚁集团研究院提供的相关数据,针对 RCEP (Regional Comprehensive Economic Partnership,《区域全面经济伙伴关系协定》)区域内跨境电商的发展现状和未来趋势开展了一系列相关研究。本书主要涵盖以下三个方面的内容:一是 RCEP 区域内跨境电商发展水平的衡量;二是 RCEP 区域内跨境电商的发展现状;三是 RCEP 区域内跨境电商的未来发展趋势。

针对 RCEP 区域内跨境电商发展水平的衡量问题,本书立足于跨境电商大数据,构造了 RCEP 区域中小企业跨境电商(B2B)指数、RCEP 区域跨境电商进口(B2C)指数以及 RCEP 区域跨境电商支付服务指数,分别用于衡量 RCEP 区域内跨境电商在 B2B 和 B2C 层面的发展水平,以及相关支付服务的发展现状。这三项指数均反映出 RCEP 区域内跨境电商及相关支付服务在过去 3 年内得到高速发展,且仍保持稳健的上升态势。

针对 RCEP 区域内跨境电商的发展现状,本书搜集和梳理了 15 个 RCEP 成员的社会经济和跨境电商发展的相关信息,并对各成员的跨境电商和一般贸易的发展状况进行了横向比较。相关分析显示,RCEP 区域内跨境电商的发展空间巨大,但各成员的发展水平仍存在较大差异。与此同时,本书梳理并分析了全世界范围内一系列有关跨境电商发展的经典案例,以此梳理出 RCEP 区域内跨境电商及相关行业未来的发展脉络。

基于全面的数据研究和案例分析,我们相信,随着 RCEP 的正式生效,区域内跨境电商及相关行业将迎来更为广阔的发展空间。但与此同时,我国企业在 RCEP 时代也将面临更加激烈的竞争与更大的挑战。为了促进我国跨境电商行业在 RCEP 时代下的繁荣发展,本书提出以下六点建议:第一,强化企业引导,借力 RCEP 增强我国企业的核心竞争力;第二,积极优化地方政府营商环境,助力企业适应并对标 RCEP 的高水平规则;第三,积极实践更高水平的跨境电商规则,落实 RCEP 的部分重要条款以保障企业和消费者权益;第四,优化企业经营生态,支持跨境电商平台建设与专项人才培养;第五,完善我国数字监管立法,并制定更为健全的跨境数据流动机制;第六,综合强化跨境电商发展韧性,在提升抗逆性的同时促进可持续发展。

Abstract

Based on relevant data provided by AliResearch and Ant Group Research Institute, this book provides a series of related studies on the development status and future trends of cross-border e-commerce in the RCEP region. This book mainly covers the following three aspects of cross-border e-commerce in the RCEP (Regional Comprehensive Economic Partnership) region: (1) the measurement of the development level; (2) the development status; (3) the future development trend.

In order to measure the development level, three indexes are compiled based on the cross-border e-commerce big data in the RCEP region, namely, RCEP Cross-Border E-Commerce (B2B) Index of SEMs, RCEP Cross-Border E-Commerce Purchase (B2C) Index, and RCEP Cross-Border Payment Service Index, which are used to measure the B2B and B2C development level of cross-border e-commerce companies and the development status of related payment services in the RCEP region respectively. These three indexes reflect that the cross-border e-commerce and related payment services in the RCEP region have developed rapidly in the past three years, and still maintain the steady upward trend.

In view of the development status of cross-border e-commerce in the RCEP region, relevant information on the socio-economic and cross-border e-commerce development of 15 RCEP members are collected and sorted out, and the development status of cross-border e-commerce and general trade in these countries are compared horizontally. Correlation analysis shows that there is huge space for cross-border e-commerce development in the RCEP region, but the development level of members differs considerably. At the same time, a series of classic cases about the development of cross-border e-commerce around the world are compiled and analyzed, so as to sort out the future developing venation of cross-border e-commerce and related industries in the RCEP region.

With all the comprehensive data research and case studies, it is believed that with the entry into force of RCEP, cross-border e-commerce and related industries in the region will have broader development space. However, at the same time, Chinese enterprises will also face more fierce competition and greater challenges in the RCEP era. In order to promote the prosperity and development of China's cross-border e-commerce industry in the RCEP era, this book puts forward the following six suggestions: (1) strengthening enterprise guidance and leveraging RCEP to enhance the core competitiveness of Chinese enterprises; (2) actively optimizing the business environment of local governments to help enterprises adapt to and benchmark the high-level rules of RCEP; (3) actively implementing higher-level cross-border e-commerce rules, and improving some important provisions of RCEP in China to protect the rights and interests of enterprises and consumers; (4) optimizing the business ecology of enterprises, and supporting the construction of cross-border e-commerce platforms and the cultivation of special talents; (5) improving China's digital regulatory legislation, and formulating a more robust cross-border data flow mechanism; (6) comprehensively strengthening the development resilience of cross-border e-commerce, improving resilience and promoting sustainable development.

目　录

Contents

第一章 综 述

2022 年 1 月 1 日,《区域全面经济伙伴关系协定》(Regional Comprehensive Economic Partnership,RCEP)正式生效。目前 RCEP 的 15 个成员包括中国、日本、韩国、澳大利亚、新西兰和东盟十国,覆盖人口约 22.7 亿人,GDP 总量超过 26 万亿美元(约占全球的 33%)。我国对 RCEP 其他 14 个成员的进出口总额超过 10 万亿美元(约占我国外贸进出口总额的 30%)。相较于同时期的《美墨加协定》(USMCA)、《全面与进步跨太平洋伙伴关系协定》(CPTPP)、欧盟(EU)等,RCEP 覆盖的人口最多,成员结构最多元,经贸规模最大。RCEP 的生效将为区域合作的深化和发展创造崭新机遇,为世界经济的开放融通注入强劲动力,为中国经济的持续繁荣提供强大引擎。

为了更好地理解 RCEP 对区域内跨境电商(cross-border e-commerce)发展所产生的深远影响,浙江大学国际联合商学院联合阿里研究院和蚂蚁集团研究院,通过严谨、细致的数据分析,对一系列有关跨境电商发展的重要问题开展研究。基于全面的跨境电商大数据,本书主要回答了以下三个方面的问题:一是如何科学地衡量 RCEP 区域内跨境电商的发展水平,二是 RCEP 各成员的跨境电商发展现状如何,三是 RCEP 区域内跨境电商未来的发展趋势如何。

针对 RCEP 区域内跨境电商发展水平的衡量问题,我们构建了 RCEP 区域中小企业跨境电商(B2B)指数、RCEP 区域跨境电商进口(B2C)指数以及 RCEP 跨境电商支付服务指数,分别用于衡量 RCEP 区域内跨境电商在 B2B 和 B2C 层面的活跃程度,以及 RCEP 区域内跨境电商相关支付服务的发展水平。基于全面的跨境电商大数据和科学的计算方法,这三项指数分别从三个不同的维度揭示了 RCEP 区域内跨境电商发展的现状和趋势,从而共同构成了用于衡量区域内跨境电商发展总体水平的"晴雨表"。

针对 RCEP 区域内跨境电商的发展现状,我们搜集、梳理了协定所涵盖的 15 个成员的社会经济和跨境电商发展的相关信息,并从国别和商品类目两个维度对各国的跨境电商与一般贸易情况进行了对比。针对 RCEP 区域内跨境电商的发展趋势,我们整理和撰写了一系列与跨境电商发展相关的案例,用以揭示跨境电商在不同国家和地区中的发展进程与演变趋势。具体而言,这些案例涵盖了五个不同的方面,包括数字跨境贸易平台、物流服务、跨境支付、微型跨国企业以及政府创新管理。除此之外,本书还就我国在跨境电商发展过程中可能遇到的问题和挑战,有针对性地提出了相关政策建议。

RCEP 将为区域内跨境电商的发展注入强劲动力。跨境电商作为互联网、大数据、云计算等新技术与经济社会发展深度融合的结晶,能够通过拓展贸易的主体和范围,使更多的国家和人群分享人类经济发展的红利。针对区域内跨境电商的发展,RCEP 进行了一系列有针对性的制度安排。协定在强调跨境电商传统规则的同时,在消费者权益保护、网络安全与数据隐私、对话与争端解决机制等方面均制定了相应的条款,进一步规范了跨境电商的组织形式与流程体系,以促进各国线上消费市场的融合,推动跨境电商的繁荣发展。

近年来,随着信息技术和物流模式的快速演变,跨境电商的商业模式也在不断创新,并在全球范围内迅速普及。对于中小企业而言,跨境电商使它们可以在"足不出户"的情况下融入全球市场,实现"天下没有难做的生意"的美好愿景;对于消费者而言,跨境电商让他们享受到来自世界各地的优质商品和服务,极大地提高了消费者福利。更重要的是,跨境电商自身具有高度的普惠性。具有不同自然禀赋的国家和地区,可以通过跨境电商融入全球价值链,共享人类经济发展的成果。正是这样的普惠性,促使大量的企业和消费者在过去的 20 余年间向线上迁移,而这一进程在新冠疫情暴发后更是得到了进一步加速。随着 RCEP 的正式生效,区域内与跨境电商相关的行业也必将迎来更为广阔的发展空间。因此,对于任何国家(地区)和个人而言,把握其中的时代机遇都显得尤为重要。

　　本书的具体结构如下:在本章的余下部分中,我们将简要描述 RCEP 区域内跨境电商的发展现状,并对协定中与跨境电商相关的条款进行分析;在第二章中,我们将提供三项指数的构建方法,并对指数进行分析;在第三章中,我们将提供一系列与跨境电商发展相关的经典案例;在第四章中,我们将依照国别对 RCEP 各成员的跨境电商发展状况进行描述与分析;在第五章中,我们将对区域内跨境电商未来的发展趋势进行展望,并针对我国企业可能面临的挑战,提供相应的政策建议。

第一节　RCEP 区域内跨境电商发展现状

　　第一,RCEP 区域内跨境电商规模大、增速高。根据 Statista 公司以及各国统计局的数据,在全球范围内,RCEP 区域具有较大的跨境电商规模。具体而言,RCEP 各成员 2020 年的跨境电商总体规模约为 1.8 万亿元(约 2850 亿美元),占全球跨境电商总体规模(5950 亿美元)的 47.9%。其中,我国 2020 年的跨境电商总规模约为 1.69 万亿元,占 RCEP 区域总和的 93.8%。这一数字在 2021 年进一步攀升至 1.98 万亿元,增速高达 17.2%。在图 1-1 中,我们列出了全球不同区域的跨境电商规模。

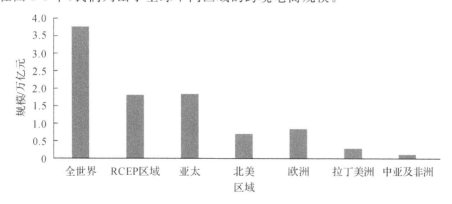

图 1-1　2020 年全球不同区域的跨境电商规模

数据来源:Statista 及各国统计局。

3

第二,RCEP 区域内跨境电商较一般贸易增速更快。根据 Statista 以及各国统计局披露的最新数据,RCEP 区域内跨境电商规模从 2016 年的约862 亿美元,增长至 2020 年的约 2850 亿美元,其间的年均增速高达 34.8%(见图 1-2)。这一增速远远超出同期一般贸易增速,以及各成员的国内贸易增速,并且保持了稳健的增长态势。值得一提的是,RCEP 区域内跨境电商规模高速增长的很大一部分原因在于我国消费者对于海外商品的需求的快速增长。本书测算得出,2018—2021 年,我国跨境电商总体规模的年均增速均高于 30%,且占 RCEP 区域总量的 85% 以上。

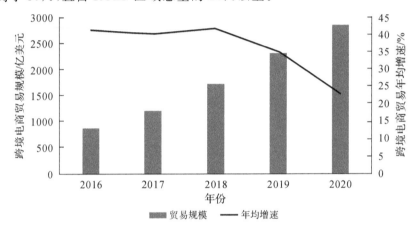

图 1-2 RCEP 区域内跨境电商规模及年均增速

数据来源:Statista 及各国统计局。

第三,RCEP 各成员的跨境电商发展程度差异较大。RCEP 15 个成员的经济发展水平具有显著差异,其中:第一梯队的澳大利亚、新西兰、日本、新加坡、韩国在 2021 年的人均 GDP 均超过 3 万美元;中国、文莱在 2021 年的人均 GDP 则在 1 万美元左右,处于第二梯队;第三梯队的马来西亚、泰国、印度尼西亚、越南、菲律宾、老挝、缅甸、柬埔寨在 2021 年的人均 GDP 均低于 1 万美元。各成员在经济发展水平上的巨大差异也反映在跨境电商的发展程度上。根据联合国贸易和发展会议(UNCTAD)和各国统计局披露的最新数据,处于第一梯队的 5 个发达国家 2020 年的数字贸易总规模(含跨境电商)占 GDP 的比重均在 4% 以上(见图 1-3),而全球平均水平为 3.8%。

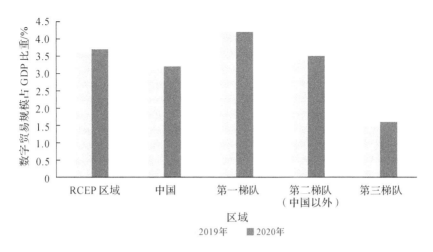

图 1-3 RCEP 区域数字贸易占 GDP 比重

数据来源：UNCTAD 和各国统计局。

第四，RCEP 各成员的数字基础设施发展水平差异较大，在客观上存在数字鸿沟，但总体情况正逐步改善。跨境电商的繁荣发展离不开数字基础设施的支持，但目前 RCEP 区域内仍存在数字基础设施发展不均衡的问题。根据世界银行的数据，2021 年，RCEP 区域内的 5 个发达国家的平均互联网普及率高达 85% 以上，而余下的发展中国家的平均互联网普及率仅为 66%，其中，我国的互联网普及率为 71%。值得一提的是，这一指标在发展中国家内部也存在较大波动，其中马来西亚的互联网普及率高达 80%，而老挝的互联网普及率仅为 25%。类似的数字鸿沟也反映在智能手机的普及率上。RCEP 区域内发达国家的平均智能手机普及率为 80%，这一指标仍显著高于发展中国家的 64%。但 RCEP 区域内发达国家与发展中国家在智能手机普及率上的差异要小于互联网普及率，这也反映出移动互联网自身所具有的相对普惠性。值得一提的是，RCEP 区域内的数字基础设施也正在日趋完善（见图 1-4），这将有助于区域内跨境电商的长期健康发展。

第五，RCEP 区域内企业加速布局线上业务，推动跨境电商供给端不断完善。在过去的 10 余年间，随着全球范围内跨境电商的快速发展，RCEP 区域内的企业也在持续布局线上业务，而这一进程在新冠疫情暴发后得到了加速。在新冠疫情的冲击下，RCEP 区域内企业面临着线下销售受阻、现金流紧张、物流延迟等诸多挑战，企业线下的生产经营活动客观上受到较大冲

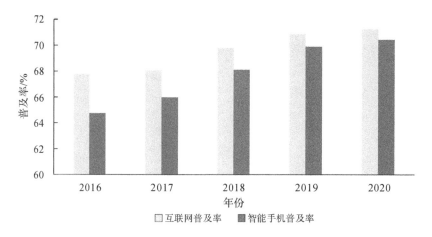

图 1-4　RCEP 区域内数字基础设施发展水平

数据来源：世界银行。

击。但新冠疫情暴发后，RCEP 区域内跨境电商业务也迎来了前所未有的增长。区域内传统出口企业更多地将业务转移至跨境电商平台。大量中小企业也在这一时期主动参与区域内由电商平台主导的跨境贸易协作，主动借鉴并引进数字化经营模式，推动自身的数字化转型。RCEP 区域内各成员也为新冠疫情下本国企业参与跨境电商提供了一系列强有力的帮扶政策。这些内外部因素共同作用，促使 RCEP 区域内企业加快了开展线上业务的步伐。根据亿邦动力研究院针对逾 100 家中国外贸进出口企业的调研，有 84％的企业在新冠疫情暴发后加大了线上业务投入（见图 1-5）。

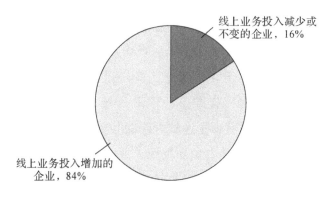

图 1-5　新冠疫情暴发后中小外贸企业线上业务投入变化情况

数据来源：亿邦动力研究院。

第六,RCEP 区域内消费者的数字化消费习惯不断养成,助推跨境电商需求端活跃度上升。在过去的 10 余年间,随着移动互联网的普及和商业模式的不断创新,越来越多的消费者开始尝试线上消费。新冠疫情的暴发则进一步推动了消费习惯的数字化(见图 1-6),为跨境电商的发展带来了更大的机遇。受新冠疫情的影响,消费者更加重视健康安全,倾向于通过电商渠道满足消费需求,而电商所具备的海量选择、高性价比产品、简洁的购物流程等特点则加深了消费者的线上购物偏好。与此同时,由于新冠疫情对跨境旅行的冲击,更高品质的全球购成为新的消费生活方式。虽然新冠疫情导致的消费习惯改变是否具有长期性仍有待观察,但毫无疑问的是,这种变化已经深刻地影响了新冠疫情暴发后 RCEP 区域内跨境电商的发展进程,并有较大可能成为一种长期趋势。

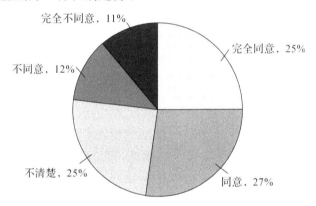

图 1-6　新冠疫情暴发后消费者是否更多地进行网上购物

数据来源:UNCTAD。

第二节　RCEP 跨境电商相关条款简要分析

RCEP 第十二章是亚太区域内第一次达成的范围全面、水平较高的多边电子商务规则,将对区域内跨境电商的发展产生深远的影响。这一章一共包括 17 条具体条款,其中具有实质约束性的条款共有 11 条,相关条款的主要内容详见表 1-1。

表 1-1　RCEP 跨境电商相关条款

条款	简要内容	影响
第十二章第五条	促进无纸化贸易	促进跨境电商的便利化
第十二章第六条	允许电子认证和电子签名	
第十二章第七条	促进线上消费者保护	更好地保障线上消费者的合法权益、个人隐私和消费体验
第十二章第八条	促进线上个人信息保护	
第十二章第九条	杜绝非应邀商业电子信息	
第十二章第十条	建立和完善各成员的国内监管框架	降低企业的监管负担和相关行业的准入门槛
第十二章第十一条	完善针对电子商务的税收政策	降低企业的税收负担和税收风险水平
第十二章第十二条	提升 RCEP 实施过程中的透明度	降低政府与企业间的信息不对称程度
第十二章第十三条	加强网络安全,开展相关国际合作	增强线上交易的安全性
第十二章第十四条	不应当将使用境内的计算设施作为在其境内开展商业活动的先决条件	降低企业的监管负担和相关行业的准入门槛
第十二章第十五条	不得以非正当理由阻止以商业为目的的跨境信息传输	降低企业的监管负担和经营成本

　　除了直接涉及跨境电商的第十二章外,RCEP 倡导的原产地累积规则也将促进成员提升贸易产品的数字化水平,加快产品标识、物流、仓储、结算、通关等相关数据信息的互联互通。此外,在当前新冠疫情严重冲击全球供应链的背景下,RCEP 将进一步整合亚太一体化大市场,释放东盟国家人口红利优势、日本和韩国的技术资本优势、澳大利亚和新西兰的资源禀赋优势,促进亚太区域产业链、价值链和供应链融合发展,倒逼我国顺应数字化发展趋势,加快传统服务向数字化转型,有助于培育物联网、大数据、区块链等跨境电商新业态、新模式。

第二章 RCEP区域跨境电商发展指数分析

第一节 指数简介

本书以企业对企业（B2B）、企业对消费者（B2C）和支付为切入点，分别构建了RCEP区域中小企业跨境电商（B2B）指数、跨境电商进口（B2C）指数与跨境支付服务指数，旨在全面、系统地衡量RCEP区域跨境电商发展情况，研究跨境电商在推动中小微外贸企业数字化转型、促进区域经济一体化进程以及经贸增长中的作用和贡献。本节将从核心特色、指标体系、计算方法三方面对相关指数进行详细介绍。

一、核心特色

作为全球率先提出的RCEP区域贸易相关系列指数，这三大指数可以成为社会各界观察RCEP区域跨境电商（尤其是中小微外贸企业跨境电商）发展的晴雨表、指南针和锦囊计，可多维呈现市场兴衰，直观展示发展趋势，为未来政策制定、企业决策和学术研究提供依托与支撑。指数的特点主要体现在以下三个方面。

（一）主客观权重结合，计算更科学合理

本书采用主客观权重结合的方法构建这三大指数。一方面，考虑到跨境电商理论与实践并重的特点，我们邀请了数十位学术界和业界的专家，组成了相对具有代表性的专家团队，并使用专家打分法确认指标的主观权重。另一方面，根据经济数据常具备的数据分布特征，在广泛参考相关研究的基础上,我们还采用了变异系数法确认指标的客观权重,探索和反映经济数据所呈现的客观信息。变异系数法是一种客观的赋权方法,直接利用各项指标所包含的信息,计算得到指标的权重,被广泛应用于各类框架指数的权重设定。

(二)独特化数据基础,让衡量成为可能

数据是生产要素,亦为研究的基础。依托产学研合作,在数据安全、可控、合规的前提下,本书分别基于阿里巴巴国际站(全球领先的 B2B 跨境电商平台)、天猫国际(中国知名的 B2C 跨境电商进口平台)以及蚂蚁集团的海量数据生成三大指数,让跨境电商发展的衡量成为可能。

(三)季度性计算披露,追踪更及时灵敏

受制于数据可得性等,现有的贸易相关指数多为年度指数。为进一步提高指数的及时性和灵敏度,本书构建的三大指数均每季度进行一次计算和公布,以期更好地反映 RCEP 区域跨境电商的发展趋势及事件影响,并为社会各界了解、研究跨境电商发展奠定良好的数据基础。

二、指标体系

本节将依次对 RCEP 区域中小企业跨境电商(B2B)指数、跨境电商进口(B2C)指数与跨境支付服务指数三大指数的指标体系进行介绍。

(一)RCEP 区域中小企业跨境电商(B2B)指数

RCEP 区域中小企业跨境电商(B2B)指数[RCEP SMEs Cross-Border E-Commerce (B2B) Index,简称 RCEP B2B 指数]从综合结果、供给需求方规模、供给方发展质量、需求方发展质量四个维度出发,包括贸易规模、贸易主体、企业发展、市场关注 4 个一级指标,询盘规模、卖家数量、产品数量等 7 个二级指标,以及 RCEP 区内买家对区内卖家询盘数量、RCEP 区内订单成交数量、RCEP 区内新注册卖家数量等 13 个三级指标,综合衡量 RCEP 区域中小企业跨境电商的发展状况。具体指标体系如表 2-1 所示。

表 2-1　RCEP 区域中小企业跨境电商(B2B)指数指标体系

一级指标	二级指标	三级指标
贸易规模	询盘规模	RCEP 区域内买家对区域内卖家询盘数量
		RCEP 区域内买家对区域外卖家询盘数量
		RCEP 区域外买家对区域内卖家询盘数量
	订单规模	RCEP 区域内订单成交数量
		RCEP 区域内订单成交金额
贸易主体	卖家数量	RCEP 区域内新注册卖家数量
		RCEP 区域内活跃卖家数量
	买家数量	RCEP 区域内新注册买家数量
		RCEP 区域内活跃买家数量
企业发展	产品数量	RCEP 区域内卖家的平均产品数量
	新品数量	RCEP 区域内卖家的平均新品数量
市场关注	中国聚焦	RCEP 区域内买家对中国卖家的订单成交数量
		RCEP 区域内买家对中国卖家的订单成交金额

(二)RCEP 区域跨境电商进口(B2C)指数

RCEP 区域跨境电商进口(B2C)指数[RCEP Cross-Border E-Commerce Purchase (B2C) Index,简称 RCEP B2C 指数]从贸易全局、供给端、需求端、平台中介四个维度出发,包括贸易规模、企业发展、市场需求、平台服务 4 个一级指标,订单规模、品牌发展、订单需求等 9 个二级指标,以及 RCEP 区域内天猫国际订单数量、RCEP 区域内天猫国际订单金额、RCEP 区域内天猫国际新增品牌数量等 11 个三级指标,全方位衡量 RCEP 区域跨境电商进口的发展状况。具体指标体系如表 2-2 所示。

11

表 2-2 RCEP 区域跨境电商进口(B2C)指数指标体系

一级指标	二级指标	三级指标
贸易规模	订单规模	RCEP 区域内天猫国际订单数量
		RCEP 区域内天猫国际订单金额
	品牌数量	RCEP 区域内天猫国际品牌数量
企业发展	品牌发展	RCEP 区域内天猫国际新增品牌数量
	商家孵化	天猫国际新商家孵化成功数量
	产品供应	RCEP 区域内天猫国际品牌的平均产品数量
市场需求	订单需求	RCEP 区域内天猫国际品牌的平均订单数量
	均客单价	RCEP 区域内天猫国际品牌的平均客单价
平台服务	满意程度	RCEP 区域内天猫国际品牌的平均满意度评分
	配送时长	RCEP 区域内天猫国际订单的平均送达时长(只考虑海外发货)
		RCEP 区域内天猫国际订单的平均送达时长(只考虑国内保税仓发货)

(三)RCEP 区域跨境支付服务指数

RCEP 区域跨境支付服务指数(RCEP Cross-Border Payment Service Index,简称 RCEP 跨境支付服务指数)从跨境支付服务的规模和质量两大视角切入,包括跨境支付服务规模、跨境支付服务质量 2 个一级指标,跨境支付广度、跨境支付深度、跨境支付活跃度、跨境支付服务效率、跨境支付服务便利度 5 个二级指标,以及 RCEP 区域内跨境收款的中国卖家数、RCEP 区域内跨境收款的非中国卖家数、RCEP 区域内中国卖家跨境收款的金额等 10 个三级指标。它能帮助研究人员对区域内贸易支付数字化的发展水平进行量化评估,为了解跨境数字支付的发展程度提供事实依据,从而得以更好地发挥跨境数字支付的作用,助力区域内中小外贸企业"走出去",促进 RCEP 区域内经济一体化。具体指标体系如表 2-3 所示。

表 2-3　RCEP 区域跨境支付服务指数指标体系

一级指标	二级指标	三级指标
跨境支付服务规模	跨境支付广度	RCEP 区域内跨境收款的中国卖家数
		RCEP 区域内跨境收款的非中国卖家数
	跨境支付深度	RCEP 区域内中国卖家跨境收款的金额
		RCEP 区域内非中国卖家跨境收款的金额
	跨境支付活跃度	RCEP 区域内中国卖家跨境收款的笔数
		RCEP 区域内非中国卖家跨境收款的笔数
跨境支付服务质量	跨境支付服务效率	RCEP 区域内中国卖家跨境收款平均时长
		RCEP 区域内非中国卖家跨境收款平均时长
	跨境支付服务便利度	RCEP 区域内中国卖家跨境支付支持收款币种
		RCEP 区域内非中国卖家跨境支付支持收款币种

三、计算方法

本书构建的三大指数均是通过逐级、分层、加权的方式计算得到的。计算步骤具体如下。

（一）指标正向化处理

本书构建的指数的数值均为越大越好,但不免存在部分指标本身的原始方向与指数方向相反的情况。例如,RCEP 区域跨境支付服务指数中以 RCEP 区域内中国卖家跨境收款平均时长和 RCEP 区域内非中国卖家跨境收款平均时长来衡量跨境支付服务效率,然而此两项指标本身均属于逆向指标,数值越大代表服务效率越低。因此,本书均对此类指标进行了取倒数的处理,使其保持与指数方向一致。

（二）数据标准化

本书在对采集的所有原始数据进行数据清洗、数据关联、去除量纲后,获得每个相关指标的标准化得分。具体标准化公式如下:

$$X_{k,j}^* = \frac{X_{k,j}}{X_{k,1}}。$$

其中,$X_{k,j}$ 代表指标 k 的第 j 个观测值,$X_{k,j}^*$ 表示第 k 个指数/指标的第 j 个观测值的标准化得分。

（三）指标赋权

如上文"核心特色"所述,本书采用主观的专家打分法与客观的变异系数法相结合的方式确定每级指标的权重。

（四）计算指数

将相关指标的标准化得分与指标权重相乘并加总,即可得本书的每个指数/指标结果,包括指数和一级、二级等指标。具体指数计算公式如下:

$$指数／指标值 = \sum_{j=1}^{N} X_{k,j}^{*} W_{k}。$$

其中,W_{k} 表示第 k 个指数/指标的权重。

（五）指数更新

在分析模型总体不变的基础上,本书将根据实际情况对指标体系、统计方法和权重进行适当的优化调整,确保评价结果的科学性、连续性和一致性。

第二节　RCEP 区域中小企业跨境电商（B2B）指数

本节将分别以 RCEP B2B 指数及其贸易规模、贸易主体、企业发展、市场关注这四大一级指标展示指数分析结果和核心结论。

一、指数:持续稳步上升,新冠疫情下跨境电商凸显强大动力

（一）从总体上看

首先,总趋势稳步上升。如图 2-1 所示,2019 年第一季度至 2021 年第四季度,RCEP B2B 指数呈现出明显且稳健的上升态势,除在 2020 年第一季度和 2021 年第四季度受新冠疫情等影响指数略有下降外,其余季度均保持了增长。

其次,指数高速增长。指数在 3 年内翻了一番,年均增长率为 28.7%,

图 2-1　2019—2021 年的 RCEP B2B 指数

是同期海关总署发布的"中国—东盟贸易指数"(反映了整体贸易情况)增速(19.6%)的1.5倍。此外,从环比增速来看,每年的第二、三季度是中小企业跨境电商增长最快的时期,2020年和2021年第二、三季度两个季度指数的环比增速更是超过了15%。从同比增速来看,2020年与2021年各季度增速维持高位稳定状态,除2020年第一季度的指数同比增速仅为15%外,其余各季度的指数同比增速均保持在25%以上。

(二)从结构上看

外部经济环境及突发事件对 RCEP B2B 指数具有一定的影响。

首先,新冠疫情总体上显著促进了跨境电商的增长,但经济系统间各方相互依存,新冠疫情反复亦会给跨境电商的长远发展带来部分压力。自2020年初起,新冠疫情肆虐全球,传统线下贸易受阻。同年3月,世界卫生组织认定新冠疫情可被称为全球大流行,其对传统贸易的负面作用持续扩大,但跨境电商却逆势快速增长。然而,在全球疫情不断反复之下又出现了变异病毒奥密克戎毒株的扩散,加之世界经济复苏曲折、海运成本高企等原因,2021年第四季度,RCEP B2B 指数出现了继2020年第一季度之后的首次下降(-9.7%),反映出中小企业跨境电商发展亦承受了压力。正因如此,2022 年是提振信心、保持跨境电商健康、可持续发展的重要一年。

其次,RCEP 将为区域内跨境电商发展注入新活力。2020 年 11 月 15 日,RCEP 正式签署,将从消除关税壁垒、建立灵活的原产地规则、促进电子商务、提升贸易便利化水平、重视中小企业和技术合作这五大方面促进区域跨境电商发展。这一重大利好在 RCEP B2B 指数中也迅速得到了体现。2021 年第一至三季度,RCEP B2B 指数的环比增长率分别为 8.1%、17.5%、17.5%,相较于 2020 年 4 个季度的平均增速(8.0%)更上了一层楼。2022 年 1 月 1 日,RCEP 正式生效,协议成果将极大地提振市场信心并实实在在地增强各国疫后的经济恢复能力。

二、一级指标:RCEP 中小企业跨境电商规模与企业发展表现亮眼

将 4 个一级指标的趋势表现与指数放在一个平面上进行对比(见图 2-2),可以清晰看到:一方面,RCEP B2B 贸易规模指标的增幅最大(3 年 3.1 倍);B2B 企业发展指标的增幅次之(3 年 2.8 倍),且在 2021 年第一至三季度出现了较大幅度的攀升;B2B 贸易主体指标的增幅排在第三(3 年 1.4 倍);B2B 市场关注指标的增幅最小(3 年 1.1 倍)。另一方面,各 RCEP B2B 一级指标在 2021 年第四季度均出现了不同程度的下降。正如上文所述,新冠疫情反复、世界经济复苏曲折、海运成本高企等对于中小企业跨境电商的负面影响在各维度上均有体现。

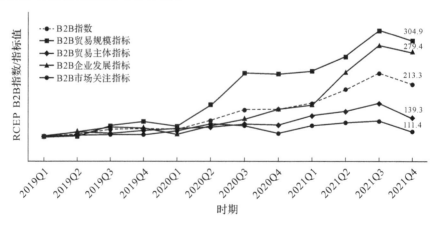

图 2-2　2019—2021 年的 RCEP B2B 指数与四大一级指标

（一）贸易规模：增幅最大，中小企业跨境电商增速超一般贸易5倍以上

如图2-3所示，从总体上看，2019年第一季度至2021年第四季度，RCEP B2B贸易规模指标整体呈现阶梯上升趋势，以年均增长率45.0%位列四大分指标之首，且远高于同期中国对RCEP区域内其他国家（地区）的一般贸易年均增速（7%）。与此同时，每年的第二、三季度B2B贸易规模指标增长相对较快，2020年第二、三季度的B2B贸易规模指标的环比增速分别高达37.4%和39.8%。

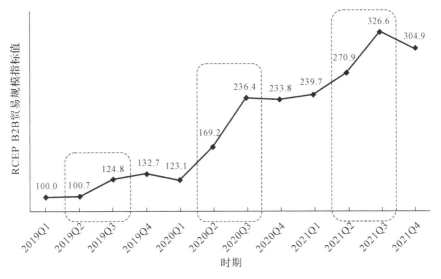

图2-3　2019—2021年的RCEP B2B贸易规模指标

从结构上看：其一，就RCEP区域内外跨境电商询盘（涉及逾215个国家）对比而言，虽然近3年来区域外对区域内的询盘量均是区域内对区域内询盘量的6倍以上，但从国均询盘量看，区域内国均询盘量一直维持在区域外国均询盘量的2倍以上，足见区域内买家对于区域内跨境贸易的重视程度。

其二，就行业对比而言，无论区域内还是区域外，询盘热度前五的行业集聚度越来越高，区域外询盘占比从2018年的39.0%升至2021年第三季度的43.0%，区域内从36.5%升至39.0%。区域外询盘热度前五的行业与区域内略有不同，区域外更侧重消费电子、服装、美容及个人护理、运动及娱乐、家居园艺，机械掉出前五；区域内更侧重消费电子、家居园艺、服装、运动

及娱乐、机械。其中,区域内对中国的偏好主要在机械、电气设备及用品、汽车摩托车及配件、家居园艺、健康医疗、美容及个人护理、建筑、服装、灯具照明、包装印刷、消费电子、运动及娱乐、五金工具行业;近3年来,这些行业的交易占比都在5%及以上。其中,询盘热度前二的行业——机械、家居园艺——的交易额占比分别为12%和8.9%,且交易额仍保持快速上升趋势,2021年第二季度同比增速分别为121.3%和150.6%。另外,安防、环保行业出现负增长。

其三,就国别对比而言,区域内卖家主要分布在中国、泰国、越南、韩国、马来西亚、菲律宾、日本、印度尼西亚、新加坡、澳大利亚、新西兰、缅甸。其中,对中国交易热度前五的国家从2018年的澳大利亚、菲律宾、马来西亚、印度尼西亚、泰国过渡到2021年的菲律宾、澳大利亚、印度尼西亚、马来西亚、新加坡。

其四,聚焦国内,广东、浙江保持在第一梯队,自2018年第一季度起,两省询盘量无论是区域外对中国的询盘还是区域内对中国的询盘,询盘占比都在60%及以上,交易额占比在50%以上。第二梯队为江苏、山东、福建、河北,询盘总体占比在5%以上,尤其是山东、江苏,交易额占比均达10%以上。

(二)贸易主体:稳步增长,2021年第四季度下降幅度大,须重视

如图2-4所示,从总体上看,一方面,RCEP B2B贸易主体指标的3年年均增长率为11.7%,整体增长稳健。且值得关注的是,2020年第四季度RCEP签订后,贸易主体指标加速增长,体现政策巨大利好对贸易主体的积极影响。另一方面,在四大一级指标中,B2B贸易主体指标在2021年第四季度的环比下降幅度相对最大,高达19.0%,为一记警钟,须引起各方重视。

从结构上看,RCEP区域内新注册卖家数量波动较大,曾在2019年第二季度出现246.6%的增幅,也曾于2021年第二季度出现56.2%的收缩。而区域内新注册买家数量则在近3年呈现总体快速增长的良好态势,12个季度中仅有4个季度环比下降,年均增长率达13.2%。这在一定程度上说明,相比买家而言,新入场的卖家对于外部环境的变化更为敏感。除此之外,虽然RCEP区域内活跃买家数量仍远多于卖家,但是活跃卖家和活跃买家数

图 2-4 2019—2021 年的 RCEP B2B 贸易主体指标

量呈现同涨同跌的趋势,且两者都保持了 15% 以上的年均增长率,反映出区域内中小企业对贸易数字化的认可度和参与度逐渐提高。

(三)企业发展:无惧周期,线下贸易加速向线上迁移

如图 2-5 所示,从总体上看,RCEP B2B 企业发展指标的 3 年年均增长率为 40.8%,且其增长趋势受季节影响较小。值得关注的是,在 2020 年第四季度 RCEP 正式签署后,B2B 企业发展指标出现了连续 3 个季度的大幅攀升,第一、二、三季度的同比增速分别达 59.5%、88.5% 和 113.6%,体现了协议签署对 RCEP 区域内企业发展的鼓舞。

从结构上看,一方面,自 2020 年初新冠疫情蔓延后,数字跨境贸易便成为全球关注的重点。而随着海外疫情常态化,2021 年后线下跨境贸易更是加速往线上迁移,越来越多的区域内企业有针对性地加速开拓跨境电商线上市场,不断依据线上贸易的特点将原线下产品推至线上售卖,新产品层出不穷。自此至 2021 年第三季度,RCEP 区域内卖家平均新品数量的季度环比增长均值高达 44.9%,且呈现持续增长态势。另一方面,RCEP 区域内卖家平均产品数量亦稳步增长,但增长速度近期略有放缓。从具体数据来看,在 2020 年第三季度前,区域内卖家平均产品数量季度环比增速均值为 3.8%,但从 2020 年第四季度起,平均产品数量增长逐步进入平台期。

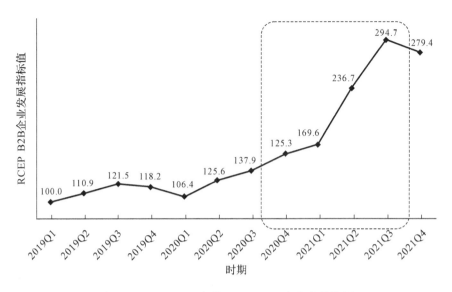

图 2-5　2019—2021 年的 RCEP B2B 企业发展指标

（四）市场关注：波动明显，协议签订推动区内对中国的关注加码

如图 2-6 所示，从总体上来看，RCEP B2B 市场关注指标在每年第一、二季度的增长更为强劲，而在第四季度普遍有下降趋势，季节波动性明显。此外，B2B 市场关注指标在 2021 年第四季度出现了大幅下降，如前文分析，还是主要受海外疫情反扑、物流成本高企等所影响，区域内外买家对中国的订单成交热度出现同步下滑。

从结构上看，一方面，区域内买家对中国卖家的订单成交规模整体呈现逐浪扩大趋势。具体来看，2021 年第四季度的区域内买家对中国卖家的订单成交金额是 2019 年第一季度的 3.5 倍，订单成交数量达 2019 年第一季度的 3.9 倍，再次体现了中国品牌在区域内买家中逐步积累的好口碑和日益扩大的影响力。另一方面，新冠疫情对于中国卖家订单成交金额增长有助推作用。具体来看，2021 年第四季度的区域内买家对中国卖家的订单成交金额是新冠疫情初始时（即 2020 年第一季度）的 3.4 倍，侧面印证了新冠疫情下的居家办公、宅经济等新的生活和工作方式，助推了海外市场对健身器材、居家办公用品、休闲娱乐玩具用品需求量的激增，从而带动了在这些行业方面具有显著优势的中国卖家的订单成交额的增长。

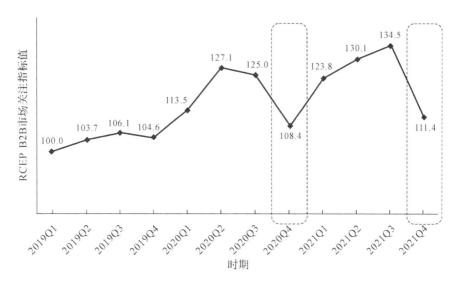

图 2-6 2019—2021 年的 RCEP B2B 市场关注指标

第三节 RCEP 区域跨境电商进口(B2C)指数

本节将分别以 RCEP B2C 指数以及贸易规模、企业发展、市场需求、平台服务这四大一级指标展示指数分析结果和核心结论。

一、指数:高速增长,周期变化

(一)从总体上看

首先,总趋势逐浪上升。如图 2-7 所示,2019 年第一季度至 2021 年第四季度,RCEP B2C 指数值在呈现非常明显的周期性(季度性)变化的同时,也逐浪上升,颇有在复杂经济形势下乘风破浪之意。

其次,指数高速增长。指数 3 年上涨 2.4 倍,年均增长率为 33.2%,2020 年的增速是同期海关总署公布的中国—东盟贸易指数(反映了整体贸易情况)增速(19.6%)的 2.2 倍,从中可以反映出跨境电商进口的巨大活力。

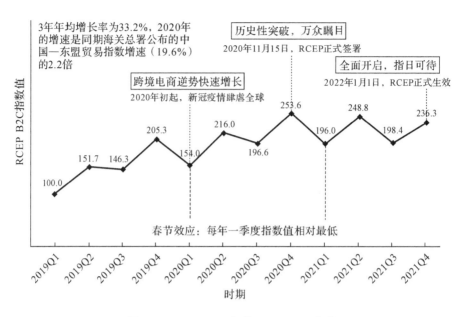

图 2-7　2019—2021 年的 RCEP B2C 指数

（二）从结构上看

RCEP B2C 指数明显受到经济周期和突发事件的影响。

第一,受中国传统春节影响,每年第一季度指数值明显相对最低。

第二,自 2020 年初起,新冠疫情肆虐全球,传统线下贸易受阻,但跨境电商却逆势快速增长,显示出强大韧性。

第三,2020 年 11 月 15 日,RCEP 正式签署,各成员之间"立即降至零关税""10 年内降至零关税"等关税减让承诺万众瞩目,尤其是中国和日本首次达成的双边关税减让安排实现了历史性突破,给了市场巨大的期待和信心。2022 年 1 月 1 日,RCEP 正式生效,虽然从指数趋势来看,RCEP 的效果尚未显现,但协议成果将惠及千千万万消费者和企业,各国"经济距离"有望大幅缩短,RCEP 对进一步增强各国疫后经济恢复能力、促进长期繁荣发展具有极为重要的推动作用,未来可期。

二、一级指标:齐进共升,共促我国跨境电商进口繁荣

将指数的 4 个一级指标的趋势表现与指数放在一个平面上进行对比（见图 2-8）,可以清晰看到:RCEP B2C 贸易规模指标增幅最大（3 年 4.0

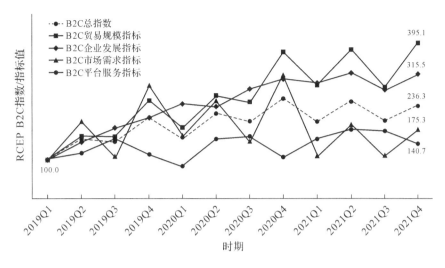

图 2-8　2019—2021 年的 RCEP B2C 指数与四大一级指标

倍),螺旋上升;B2C 企业发展指标增幅次之(3 年 3.2 倍),稳步上升;B2C 市场需求指标增幅第三(3 年 1.8 倍),波动最大;B2C 平台服务指标增幅虽小(3 年 1.4 倍),但总体呈现上升态势。

(一)贸易规模:增速最快,跨境电商活力远超全量贸易

如图 2-9 所示,从总体上看,RECP B2C 贸易规模指标的增速最快,3 年年均增长率为 58.1%,与指数趋势最为接近,且呈明显同样的季节性变化。其中,受"双十一"等影响,每年第四季度贸易规模迅猛增长,相比第三季度的平均增幅为 50%。此外,2021 年第四季度贸易规模指标又创新高,达395.1,充分反映出 RCEP 区域跨境电商进口的繁荣。

从结构上看,RCEP 区域内天猫国际品牌的订单数量、订单金额和品牌数量均实现了两位数以上的高速增长,2020 年第一季度至 2021 年第一季度同比平均增速分别为 31.8%、36.2%和 30.9%,此数据远超 2019—2020 年中国自 RCEP 其他成员进口的商品总额年均增速(2.8%),体现了跨境电商的强大活力。

(二)企业发展:势头强劲,RCEP 区域品牌黏性不断增强

如图 2-10 所示,从总体上看,一方面,RECP B2C 企业发展指标的 3 年年均增长率为 46.7%,凸显 RCEP 区域企业(品牌)发展势头强劲,且是本指

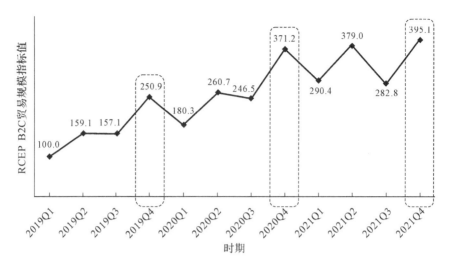

图 2-9　2019—2021 年的 RCEP B2C 贸易规模指标

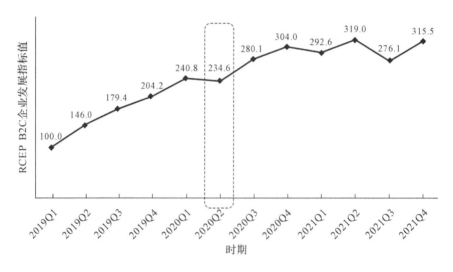

图 2-10　2019—2021 年的 RCEP B2C 企业发展指标

数四大一级指标中唯一不受季节性影响的,反映出 RCEP 区域企业对于中国市场的信心不受到经济周期性波动的影响。另一方面,2020 年第一季度新冠疫情暴发曾对 RCEP 区域内企业发展产生轻微影响,但在第三季度迅速实现大幅反转,又一次印证了跨境电商的强大韧性。

从结构上看,RCEP 区域内新增品牌数量自 2020 年第一季度至 2021 年第二季度的同比平均增速为 31.5%。泰国、马来西亚等是增长最显著的商品来源地,泰国的乳胶枕、马来西亚的燕窝都成了我国消费者购物车里的

"常客",而这种以国家著名产业品牌入驻和发展的模式又进一步带动了当地其他品牌的同步增长,增强了区域影响力和企业合力。此外,RCEP 区域内品牌平均产品数量稳步增长,季度同比平均增速为 8.4%,产品门类持续丰富,品牌黏性不断增强。与此同时,天猫国际新商家孵化成功数量实现了 122.2% 的季度同比迅猛增长,这主要得益于平台通过降低商家参与成本、为商家提供各种横向能力支持、将消费者洞察反向输入到品牌侧进行主动影响,形成正向协同闭环,使得新商家孵化成功率不断攀升。

(三)市场需求:季节波动最大,我国消费者有引领全球价格趋势之态

如图 2-11 所示,从总体上看,RECP B2C 市场需求指标的 3 年年均增长率为 20.6%,其季节性波动居四大一级指标之首。受各类促销活动影响,每年第二、四季度为市场相对需求高峰。此外,新冠疫情之下,2020 年我国对 RCEP 区域产品的市场需求不降反升,2020 年 B2C 市场需求指标值相比 2019 年平均上升了 25.6%。但是也需要意识到,随着新冠疫情常态化,消费回归理性,2021 年全年市场需求表现虽仍好于 2019 年,但相比 2020 年有较大幅度的下降。

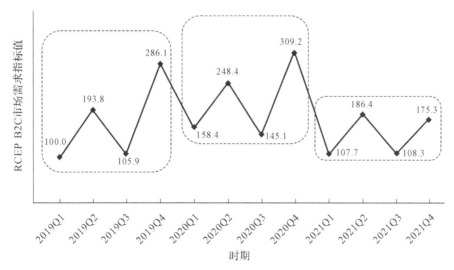

图 2-11 2019—2021 年的 RCEP B2C 市场需求指标

从结构上看,RCEP 区域内品牌平均订单数量及客单价同涨同跌,趋势较为接近。具体而言,RCEP 区域内品牌平均客单价总体上升,2020 年第一

季度至 2021 年第二季度同比平均增速为 3.9%，最高增速为 9.4%，反映出在许多欧美品牌营业额受地缘政治、全球经济形势影响普遍下降背景下，我国消费者对 RCEP 区域内品牌的需求和认可度逆势上升，带动了平均客单价的上升，颇有引领全球市场消费品价格趋势之态。

(四)平台服务：在新冠疫情等外部因素阻碍下仍持续优化，消费者体验不断上台阶

如图 2-12 所示，从总体上看，RECP B2C 平台服务指标 3 年年均增长率虽在四大一级指标中相对较低，仅为 12.1%，但也可明显看到，整体而言消费者体验的不断优化。尤其值得关注的是，以往主要受春节物流停运等影响，每年第一季度均为平台服务指数的相对低点，但从 2021 年春节起，越来越多物流、商家努力优化春节期间的服务，"春节不打烊"逐渐成为新潮流，使得 B2C 平台服务指标在 2021 年第一季度不降反升了 41.9%。2021 年第三、四季度 B2C 平台服务指标的下降主要源于入冬后中国及全球新冠疫情反复，无论是保税仓还是海外发货的平均物流时长均有上升。

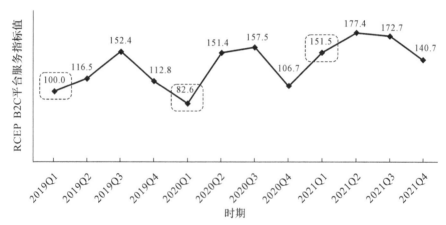

图 2-12 2019—2021 年的 RCEP B2C 平台服务指标

从结构上看，一方面，我国消费者对 RCEP 区域内品牌的平均满意度稳步上升，认可度不断提高。另一方面，海外发货物流时长与保税仓物流时长在全球新冠疫情蔓延、海运成本攀升等因素的"阻碍"之下仍呈现了"总体下降、偶有反复"的良好态势，2021 年第一季度保税仓发货平均物流时长相比2020 年第一季度下降了 42%，海外发货平均物流时长也下降了 21%。这主

要受益于天猫国际与菜鸟合作在海外建立了多个仓储地。通过与多个保税仓达成合作协议优化及与品牌方的多种合作方式,商家开通智能分仓网络,提前将跨境商品放置在离消费者最近的仓库,可将跨境包裹次日达比例最高提升至 90％,进一步优化了消费者体验。

第四节 RCEP 区域跨境支付服务指数

本节将分别以 RCEP 跨境支付服务指数以及跨境支付服务规模、跨境支付服务质量这两大一级指标,由表及里地展示指数分析结果和核心结论。

一、指数:新冠疫情催化贸易数字化,配套支付服务快速增长

(一)从总体上看

首先,总趋势稳步上升。2018 年第一季度至 2021 年第四季度,尽管外部经济形势复杂,RCEP 区域跨境支付服务稳步发展,2021 年 RCEP 跨境支付服务指数持续创新高,2021 年第四季度,指数值更是首次超过 200,达 214.1(见图 2-13)。

其次,指数高速增长。RCEP 跨境支付服务指数 4 年上涨 2.1 倍,年均增长率为 21.0％。其中,2020 年第二季度、2018 年第四季度以及 2020 年第三季度增速最快,环比增长率分别是 15.2％、13.4％和 13.2％,远远高于 4 年来 5.3％的季度平均增长率。2021 年中,第四季度是增长最明显的季度,环比增长率为 13.1％,仅次于 2020 年第三季度的环比增速,为 4 年 16 个季度以来环比增速第四高的季度,同比增长率更是高达 19.1％。

(二)从结构上看

第一,如前文 RCEP B2B 和 B2C 指数所示,自 2020 年初起,虽新冠疫情肆虐全球,但跨境电商却逆势快速增长。数字支付作为跨境电商行业的配套服务,在新冠疫情暴发后依托线上消费和采购的扩张、便捷的支付方式而迅速渗透,由此带来了 2020 年 RCEP 跨境支付服务指数的报告期内最大涨

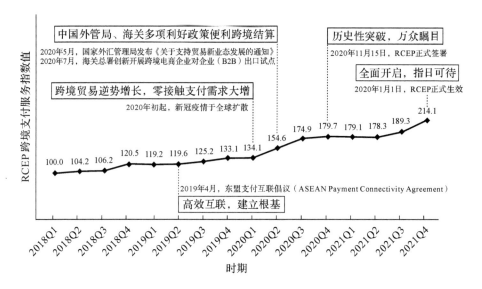

图 2-13　2018—2021 年的 RCEP 跨境支付服务指数

幅以及 2021 年同样的高速增长。

　　第二,2020 年春季,中国经贸有关部门推出多项利好政策便利跨境支付结算,支持跨境贸易新业态创新,简化外汇业务办理流程,优化外汇业务服务,积极支持复工复产,推动涉外贸易经济高质量发展。中国海关方面,创新开展跨境电商 B2B 出口试点,增设"9710""9810"贸易方式,将跨境电商监管创新成果从 B2C 推广到 B2B 领域,并配套便利通关措施。在此背景下,更大的跨境交易量自然也推动了跨境支付的繁荣,使得 RCEP 跨境支付服务指数在 2020 年第三季度大幅攀升,相比 2020 年第二季度上升了 13.2%。

　　第三,2022 年 1 月 1 日,RCEP 正式生效,将会实质上推动区域深化合作,由此必然会进一步带来 RCEP 区内跨境支付服务的持续蓬勃发展。

二、一级指标:规模和质量齐头共进,资金涌向 RCEP 贸易企业

　　对比本指数两大一级指标与指数的表现(见图 2-14),可以清晰看到,一方面,RCEP 跨境支付服务规模指标的增幅更大(4 年增长 2.5 倍),体现出跨境支付服务后期收支需求更强,其中,2020 年规模指标上升最快(同比增长 53.5%),2021 年规模指标上升相对缓慢(同比增长 26.4%);另一方面,RCEP 跨境支付服务质量指标的增幅虽小(4 年增长 1.7 倍),但体现出跨境

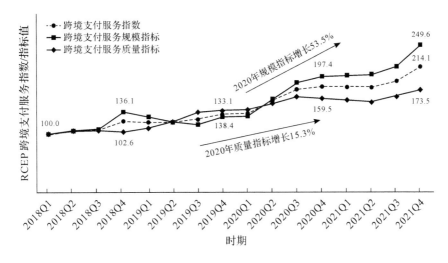

图 2-14　2018—2021 年的 RCEP 跨境支付服务指数与一级指标

支付服务被渐进式优化,其中,2020 年质量指标上升得最快(同比增长
15.3%),2021 年质量指标值也有较大幅度的增长(同比增长 8.8%)。

(一)跨境支付服务规模:海外购买需求保持强劲,支付交易活跃

如图 2-15 所示,从总体上看,首先,RCEP 跨境支付服务活跃度指标的
增速最快,4 年年均增长率为 38.3%,远远领先于其他 2 个二级指标;其中,
2020 年第二季度是支付笔数增长最快的季度,跨境支付服务活跃度指标环
比上升 46.7%。其次,RCEP 跨境支付服务的深度和广度亦保持了两位数
以上的高速增长,4 年年均增长率分别为 23.7% 与 16.3%。跨境支付广度
指标(以收款卖家数目衡量)在 2020 年第二季度经历了微小的下降后,又马
上随着众多新商户(新卖家)加入跨境线上贸易大军而持续上升。与此同
时,RCEP 跨境支付服务深度指标在 2021 年内呈现先降后升趋势。再者,对
比 2021 年 RCEP 跨境支付服务深度与活跃度指标可知,跨境支付收款笔数
虽然变多,但收款金额却变小或增速远低于收款笔数,这表明订单趋向于碎
片化和小单化,在一定程度上体现了微型跨国企业的特征。

从结构上看,就收款地区而言,RCEP 区域内的中国跨境电商(卖家)的
收款规模领先于非中国电商的收款规模。在非中国的地区里,东南亚电商
的卖家数目、收款金额、收款笔数最多,日本商家次之,随后是韩国、澳大利
亚和新加坡。就时间节点而言,2020 年,新冠疫情暴发带动全球电商总体收

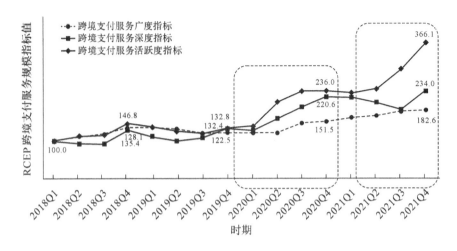

图 2-15　2018—2021 年的 RCEP 跨境支付服务广度、深度、活跃度指标

入上升,而 2021 年受欧洲税改和海外互联网平台整改等政策影响,众多中小商家被迫停止了部分店铺的营业。然而海外购买需求依旧强劲,使得商家逐步转向私域运营、独立站等其他运营渠道以谋求发展。新业态的交易从支付环节中显示出更加高频和小单的特征。

(二)跨境支付服务质量:持续突破效率,保持便利标准

如图 2-16 所示,从总体上看,传统的跨境支付结算方式常存在时间长、费用高、中间环节多、风险难控等共同难题,但从本指标结果中可以看到,一方面,RCEP 跨境支付服务效率 4 年年均增长率为 16.9%,且比支付便利度的增长(年均增长率为 12.4%)更为明显一些。其中,2019 年是到账时长优化的重点时期,2019 年第三季度效率指标环比增长 12.1%,2019 年第四季度效率指标同比增长 33.4%。这主要得益于当时中国跨境支付企业的崛起,支付牌照设置使行业标准逐步建立,跨境支付费率也逐渐下降。同时,2020 年新冠疫情期间,在线上支付需求激增的推动下,跨境支付效率也持续提升,2020 年第二季度效率指标同比增长 39.1%。另一方面,2018 年初至2019 年底,跨境支付平台凭借技术手段和渠道对接增加了多个币种以满足跨国企业更多的收款需求,使得跨境支付服务便利度指标不断上升。此后,便利度指标保持稳定。

从结构上看,跨境支付服务商不断提高资金周转效率,通过增加合作银

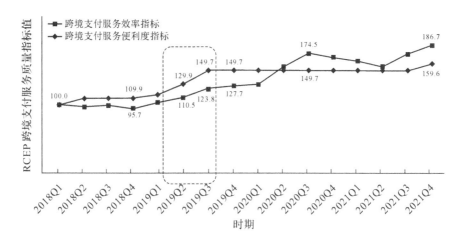

图 2-16 2018—2021 年的 RCEP 跨境支付服务效率、便利度指标

行的结算通道,减小商家的资金压力。现金流对于小型跨国企业来说是至关重要的,即时到账使以往要"T＋7"(T 代表交易发生日期)以上的到账时间缩短成现在的"秒到账",推动了行业发展。除此之外,跨境支付的交易币种已保持相对稳定,顺应贸易链路中的惯用结算币种需求。在跨境电商的各环节中,商家对支付的数字化程度的满意度也较高。

第三章　跨境电商发展相关案例

第一节　连接世界的数字跨境贸易平台

在过去的 20 年里,新技术与全球化进程的深度融合极大地促进了跨境电商的发展,并孕育了一批专业的数字跨境贸易平台。随着时间的推移,相关数字跨境贸易平台所提供的服务也从最初的信息交互,逐渐拓展至交易、支付、物流等跨境贸易过程中的各个环节,为商家和消费者带去了巨大的便利,自由贸易区的建立则进一步降低了跨境贸易的税收成本。在这些因素的共同作用下,如今很多商家已经能够以接近国内贸易的成本和方式从事跨境贸易。

究其根源,数字跨境贸易平台通过信息化的手段对各国市场进行整合,降低买家和卖家之间的信息不对称程度,从而在虚拟空间中拓展贸易的广度和深度。对于平台而言,吸引更多商家参与跨境贸易的边际成本近乎为零;而对于从事跨境贸易的商家而言,数字跨境贸易平台所特有的网络效应则能带来较传统代理式贸易更多的商机。因此,作为跨境电商的重要载体,数字跨境贸易平台能够增进各市场主体的福利,进而实现帕累托改进。以下是关于数字跨境贸易平台的两个典型案例。

一、速卖通

速卖通(AliExpress)成立于 2010 年,是阿里巴巴集团旗下的面向国际市场打造的跨境电商平台。速卖通主要面向国外零售买家,而卖家则主要来自国内,因此也被称为国际版淘宝。平台支持通过支付宝国际账户进行担保交易,并使用自有或第三方国际物流渠道进行商品交付。经过多年发展,速卖通已经开通了 18 个语种的站点,覆盖全球 200 多个国家和地区,成为中国最大的跨境零售电商平台和全球第三大英文在线购物网站。

速卖通不仅为全球跨境电商群体中的中小商家创造了大量机遇,也为各国的消费者带去了崭新的生活方式。对于卖家而言,速卖通提供了一站式的开店服务:中小卖家只需获得平台的资格认证,便可以在平台上开设店铺,把生意做到世界各地。平台同时也为中小卖家提供了代发货、资金结算、跨境物流等诸多服务,显著地降低了参与跨境贸易的门槛。对于世界各地的买家而言,在平台上他们能以更低的价格,买到几乎所有心仪的商品。更为重要的是,速卖通让很多外国消费者体验到了物流行业的"中国速度"。得益于速卖通在世界各地建立的优选仓,目前很多国家和地区的消费者已经能够在 5 个工作日内收到来自中国的商品,而在韩国甚至已经实现了 72 小时送达服务。

速卖通在某种程度上可以被视作 B2C 领域数字跨境贸易平台的中国解决方案。类似于淘宝,平台自身并不直接进行商品销售,而是作为数字跨境贸易的载体,服务广大中小商家,因此具备普惠的属性。随着 RCEP 中关税、跨境电商相关条款的陆续生效,速卖通平台及相关中小卖家将迎来更多的商机,并为 RCEP 区域内的消费者带来更多的便利。

二、亚马逊

亚马逊(Amazon)是一家总部位于美国西雅图的跨国电子商务企业,目前是全球最大的互联网线上零售商之一,在 2021 年《财富》世界 500 强企业里位列第三。亚马逊成立于 1994 年。起初,公司只经营网络图书销售业务,但随着互联网商业模式的创新和信息技术的进步,亚马逊的商业版图不断扩大,已逐渐成长为集自营和第三方销售于一体的综合性数字跨境贸易平台。亚马逊电商部门的主要市场包括北美、欧洲、中东、澳大利亚等,其中北美电商市场的份额在 2021 年超过了 40%,并仍处于高速增长状态。

相较于目前市场上的其他数字跨境贸易平台,亚马逊在两个方面存在较大的区别。第一，亚马逊在过去 10 余年间，投入了大量资源，建立了完善的自有物流体系和仓储设施，用于提高商品配送的效率和优化用户体验。但同时，亚马逊也存在投入大、收益低的问题。其中，亚马逊在世界各地设立了 FBA(fulfillment by Amazon)仓库。海外卖家只需要将货物运输到这些仓库，亚马逊会提供后续的包装、派送、客服等服务，极大地降低了跨境电商的参与门槛。第二，亚马逊还建立了庞大的自营部门，平台本身也参与商品的生产和销售。亚马逊对于自营商品设立了"零假货"和"降价退差价"等政策，在消费者中具有较好的口碑。

第二节 不断革新的物流服务

我国已经成为全世界最大的网购市场和最大的出口国。根据国家统计局数据，2021 年我国社会消费品零售总额超过 44 万亿元，其中全国网上零售额超过 13 万亿元。但与此同时，目前我国年均物流总费用与 GDP 的比率在 15% 左右，高于多数发达国家的水平(8%)。通过新技术、新思路、新架构以及合理的政策，降低境内外的物流成本，对推动物流降本增效、促进产业结构调整和区域协调发展、培育经济发展新动能、提升国民经济整体运行效率具有重要意义。

跨境电商的繁荣离不开快速、便捷、低成本的物流服务。在跨境电商时代，货物在国内和国际的流通规模较先前有了指数级的增长，这也对物流服务提出了更高的要求。近年来，以菜鸟、顺丰、四通一达(申通、圆通、中通、汇通、韵达)为代表的中国物流企业也在通过应用物联网、大数据、海外仓等新技术和新模式，不断提高物流行业的运营效率。以下是关于数字经济时代物流行业发展的两个典型案例。

一、菜鸟物流助力跨境贸易发展

菜鸟物流成立于 2013 年 5 月 28 日，是由阿里巴巴、三通一达(申通、圆通、中通、韵达)等公司成立的新型物流企业。在过去的几年里，为打造安全可靠的国际物流供应链,菜鸟网络持续推进建设全球智能骨干网,已建立包括核心机场枢纽、海外仓在内的海外物流基础设施网络,拥有五大物流枢纽,海外仓容面积超过 200 万平方米。菜鸟联合海运、航空企业,运行 500 多条国际海运航线和 900 多条国际空运航线,并联合海外邮政、快递企业不断改善海外配送服务。2020 年,菜鸟网络组织的跨境包裹日均数量达 400 万个,规模已成为全球之首。

与此同时,一大批新技术陆续投入使用,极大地提升了菜鸟物流的运营效率,并促进绿色物流的快速发展。例如,2020 年"双十一"之前,菜鸟改造完成了面向东南亚 11 个国家的电商物流信息处理系统,使其具备更强大的承载信息和处理信息的能力。如今,该系统承接了东南亚市场上多家电商平台、近百家快递企业、数以万计的中小卖家和海量消费者的对接需求,日均包裹运行保障能力增至亿级,单均成本减少 10%,峰值包裹处理能力提高 10 倍。菜鸟智能装箱算法也能直接让"大材小用、过度包装"的现象大幅减少。通过优化箱型和推荐合理的装箱方案,"双十一"期间仅在菜鸟仓内"瘦身"的包裹就达 2.5 亿个,如今这一技术已经在全行业推广。

菜鸟物流以技术驱动、生态共赢的发展模式,完美地契合了数字经济时代跨境贸易发展的主旋律,也在某种程度上颠覆了人们对传统物流行业的认知。随着 RCEP 的正式实施,菜鸟物流也将迎来更广阔的发展空间,并为区域内数字跨境贸易的发展提供物流保障。

二、顺丰国际

顺丰控股股份有限公司(以下简称顺丰)成立于 1993 年,经过多年发展,已经成长为我国规模最大的民营物流企业。顺丰不仅提供配送端的高质量物流服务,还延伸至价值链前端的产、供、销、配等环节,为客户提供智能仓储管理、销售预测、大数据自助分析等一揽子解决方案,并于 2010 年开始拓展国际业务,成立了顺丰国际事业部(以下简称顺丰国际)。

顺丰国际致力于为国内外制造企业、贸易企业、跨境电商以及消费者提供便捷、可靠的国际快递服务,旨在帮助中国优秀企业和商品"走出去",亦将海外优质企业和商品"引进来"。国际业务方面,顺丰国际标快、特惠业务已经覆盖美国、欧盟国家、俄罗斯等 78 个国家和地区;跨境电商小包系列产品覆盖全球 200 多个国家及地区,为跨境电商出口卖家提供优质、可靠的物流服务。目前,顺丰每年执飞超过 3500 班国际航班,并在欧洲、北美、东南亚建立了 12 个海外仓,利用国内外收派网络、仓储、清关、代理等资源,为客户提供一站式进出口供应链服务。

作为传统物流行业的"优等生",顺丰长期坚持将大部分利润用于物流技术的研发和物流基础设施的布局,并始终坚持以客户为本的经营理念,在消费者群体中建立了良好的口碑。随着 RCEP 框架下跨境电商的持续发展,顺丰也将迎来更多的商业机遇,为各国企业和消费者带去来自中国的高质量物流服务。

第三节　跨境支付平台

支付于贸易而言是必不可少的重要环节,跨境支付平台的多元化、数字化发展相当于为跨境贸易搭建了一条便捷、安全的通道。从此,"天堑变通途",RCEP 区域内企业可以享受到更加安全、顺畅的支付结算服务,对资金的调配也更加灵活并具有保障。正是依靠着数字支付平台的迅速发展,越来越多不同国家的小微企业能够以更加低廉的成本参与到区域内的跨境贸易中来,数字助力普惠真正地"走在了路上"。

一般而言,线上出海的支付方案包括收单、收付款、汇兑三个环节:收单指境外买家和卖家之间信息流和资金流的转移;收付款指跨境银行或第三方支付机构间的资金流和信息流的转移;汇兑指企业收到资金后的结汇环节。当前,跨境支付的各个环节均有第三方支付机构的身影,各类支付平台均以科技手段融入金融服务,为 RECP 区域内的跨境贸易保驾护航。万里汇、空中云汇作为当前在中国与全球具有代表性的跨境支付平台,分别从收付款和汇兑这两个不同环节起家,积极融合现代科技手段,在深耕自身本源业务的同时,逐步拓展其他跨境支付业务,进而为 RECP 区域及全球跨境电商的发展提供更为专业化、系统化的跨境支付服务。

一、万里汇

万里汇（WorldFirst）于 2004 年成立于英国伦敦。自 2019 年加入蚂蚁集团后，万里汇与支付宝携手，成为支付行业内增速最快的跨境金融服务平台，主要为跨国企业提供收款服务。根据德勤公布的 2021 年度《科技赋能下的亚太数字贸易》报告，万里汇在中日韩跨境电商卖家中排名第一，占有率超过四成。

支付宝曾提出"一部手机走天下"的理念，而万里汇则是"一个账户卖全球"。聚焦收付款服务的万里汇更加注重对这一跨境支付环节服务品质的打磨与提升。该平台推出"N10"模式，即"连接 N 种货币、N 个市场，1 分钟内全球收款到账，0 汇率损失"。这一收款模式的创新将外贸企业的整体回款周期从 1—2 个月缩减到了秒级，大大减小了外贸企业的资金周转压力。与此同时，快捷、方便和实惠的跨境收款服务也意味着企业参与跨境贸易的资金门槛大大降低，万里汇也借助自身的收款优势成功地帮助更多跨境电商企业实现了"零门槛卖全球"的目标。该平台的最新数据显示，RCEP 正式生效前，众多该平台上的卖家们都铆足劲地希望从全球"跨年假日经济"里分得一杯羹。从 2021 年 7 月起，因为圣诞和元旦"双旦"长周期备货的资金缺口，中国卖家对网商贷、美元贷等的贷款需求猛增。与此同时，跨年特供的"中国智造"被陆续送到海外消费者手里，跨境收款"流量"也进入了年度高峰值。

二、空中云汇

空中云汇（Airwallex）于 2015 年成立于澳大利亚墨尔本，是一家以外汇避险起家的第三方支付企业。金融机构可以提供的汇兑服务主要包括查汇、锁汇、购汇、结汇、买卖远期外汇等。其中，银行汇兑产品以标准化产品为主。而新型的汇兑科技企业会通过实时锁定汇率、控制汇损等更加友好的方式，帮助用户预判汇率变动和操作汇兑。

空中云汇的建立源于其创始人对小型跨国企业运营困境的切身体会。在跨境贸易活动中，企业，尤其是中小企业，常常需要面临相对自身体量而言较为高昂的外汇费用和银行支付服务费用。空中云汇便致力于设计更精简、更透明、更具成本效益的跨境支付解决方案。该平台自主研发的外汇引擎直连银行间汇率市场,可提供最具竞争力的价格和外汇交易与风险管理技术,这使得其在汇兑业务上具有强大的竞争力。正是基于这一扎实的汇兑聚合能力,空中云汇逐步拓展自身的支付业务范围,持续上线丰富的金融产品。目前,该平台已逐步具备收单、收款、付款、发卡等功能。当前,空中云汇在中国、新加坡、马来西亚等地均设有办公室,为全球 19 个市场的跨境贸易企业提供跨境支付解决方案。其业务范围包括多币种换汇、全球收款账户、全球付款等,所服务的行业涵盖跨境电商、在线旅游、物流、教育与留学、金融机构、数字营销、线上娱乐等领域。

第四节　小而精的微型跨国企业

随着 RECP 的全面建立与不断推进,区域内的跨境贸易必然愈加活跃。与此同时,区域内数字基础设施的发展和互联网技术的普及也推动着跨境电商与各国中小企业的繁荣共生。一方面,跨境电商的发展极大地降低了企业参与跨境贸易的资金与人员门槛。越来越多的中小企业可以愈加便捷地通过线上平台参与到跨境贸易中来,微型跨国企业成为常态,数字普惠梦想照进现实。另一方面,中小企业在发展经济、创造就业、活跃市场、改善民生等方面至关重要。以中国为例,六棱镜的数据显示,截至 2020 年底,中国存续在营的中小企业数量突破 4200 万家,占全国企业总量(4300 余万家)的 98.5%。数量众多的中小企业将成为跨境电商的有生力量,推动 RCEP 区域内跨境电商的持续发展。

对外经济贸易大学北京企业国际化经营研究基地和社会科学文献出版社共同发布的《企业海外发展蓝皮书:中国企业海外发展报告(2020)》显示,2020 年全球跨境电商交易规模突破 10000 亿美元,年均增长速度高达 30%,远远高于货物贸易的增长速度。在此背景下,RCEP 区域内的微型跨国企业们也积极上阵,纷纷利用跨境电商平台实现自身发展。从线下和线上双渠道拓展的普通小微制造企业,到发端于互联网平台注重优势品牌(也常称为 IP)培养的面向消费者(2C)的跨境电商,再到以跨境贸易带动乡村共同富裕的乡镇企业,跨境电商为形形色色的普惠发展需求提出了独到的解决方案。

一、飞马

飞马(Pegasus Official)是泰国的一家小型家族企业,主营箱包类产品。新冠疫情的暴发使飞马的对外销售面临着巨大的不确定性,这一挑战迫使企业 CEO 坎西尼·萨普乔蒂库(Kanseenee Sapchotikul)更加重视该企业对数字服务和渠道的关注与建设,以减轻新冠疫情影响并增强业务弹性。

一方面,该企业积极上线亚马逊等电子商务平台,建立并维护自身的数字销售渠道,拓展并维系企业全球业务。另一方面,该企业及时开展对全球客户在线购物意向的调研,发现国际市场对口罩有极大的需求,便开始向美国和其他国家出口口罩,销售额在短短 6 个月内增长了 300% 以上。此后,飞马将自身既有的箱包产品陆续上线电子商务平台。据估计,仅来自亚马逊平台的收入便将占据其总营业额的 50%。

总而言之,飞马能够成功应对新冠疫情的冲击,除自身积极发掘市场机遇外,跨境电商平台的助力亦不容小觑。通过跨境电商的发展,飞马成功地将线下业务转移至线上,迅速拓展了企业的市场空间,这一做法值得其他小微企业借鉴。

二、东琪团队

众多以电商业务起家的微型跨国企业均面向消费者销售商品。随着时代的迅速更迭,早年"吉祥三宝"(充电宝、数据线、打火机)式的商品已经无法满足消费者的个性化消费需求,越来越多的电商创业者们开始注重小众商品的发掘。来自杭州的东琪团队从负责运营、设计和对接工厂的 3 人起家,对跨境电商有着自己的独到见解。

东琪团队的创始人孙东琪认为,相比于毫无特色的大众商品,个性鲜明、支持定制的小众产品反而更容易受到消费者的欢迎。他的团队曾先后上线为日本宅男定制的榻榻米式游戏椅、为美国奶爸提供的卡通猫头鹰门挡、受日本和欧洲买家青睐的乌龟"高定"彩色毛衣……这些新颖而充满特色的商品往往一抢而光。这在极大鼓舞孙东琪的同时,也让他认识到发掘市场新品、建立独特 IP 的重要性。新冠疫情的到来不仅没有阻挠东琪团队的发展,还为他们的新品设计带来了新的思路。当线上办公成为潮流,欧美日韩的白领们也开始关心如何在 Zoom 视频会上保持良好形象,电脑工作支架、墙面美化装饰等商品便热销起来。对此,东琪团队迅速上线了能让脸部更立体、肤色更漂亮的美颜灯。目前,东琪团队还做起了自有品牌的外贸独立站,不再局限于 B2C,而要向 D2C(直面消费者定制)看齐。

东琪团队的成功源于对消费者个性化需求的精准把握,也得益于广阔的跨境电商平台和大数据分析技术。跨境电商将全球的消费者与生产者更加紧密地联系在了一起,也为众多具有新鲜创意的创业者们打开了一扇致富之门。

第五节　政企合作与政府创新管理

作为全球人口最多、经贸规模最大、最具发展潜力的自由贸易区,RCEP 充分体现了各成员政府共同维护多边主义和自由贸易、促进区域经济一体化的信心与决心,将为区域乃至全球跨境电商发展做出重要贡献。同时,跨境电商的发展也极大地促进了成员间的政企合作、政府间合作、政府创新管理,进而推动了区域经济社会发展。

合作共赢,强国富民——政企合作成为跨境电商时代的主流,政府牵头整合资源,企业助力保障技术,共同促进跨境电商迅速发展。合作共建,利益共享——政府间合作突破国际贸易传统痛点,削减关税,要素流通,促进跨境数据流动,实现关务系统数字化,提效率、降成本、促发展。合作创新,数字政府——政府创新管理是数字时代一大趋势,广泛应用数字技术助力政府科学决策,出台政策法规,落地智慧建设,提升政府管理和服务效能。

一、中国(杭州)跨境电子商务综合试验区

2015年3月7日,国务院同意设立中国(杭州)跨境电子商务综合试验区(以下简称综试区),也是全国首个跨境电商综试区。作为全国电子商务中心,杭州市计划通过3—5年的改革试验,把综试区建设成以"线上集成＋跨境贸易＋综合服务"为主要特征,以"物流通关渠道＋线上综合服务平台信息系统＋金融增值服务"为核心竞争力,以"关""税""汇""检""商""物""融"一体化为特色,线上综合服务平台和线下综合园区平台相结合的全国跨境电子商务创业创新中心、服务中心和大数据中心。

综试区通过线上综合服务平台实现"网上办事",为RCEP区域内电商企业提供免费注册、在线备案、实时申报等各项服务;对接海关、外汇、税务、工商、公安等政府监管部门以及金融、物流等企业,利用政府与企业各部门之间的互联互通和信息共享,实现通关全程无纸化,提高通关效率,降低通关成本;优化跨境电商进出口模式,围绕"数据管住、口岸放开、进出高效、全程可控",创新"数字围网",探索"数据多跑路、人为少干预、货物快通关、退换更便捷"的新型监管模式,促进通关便利和货物贸易自由。

在RCEP框架下,货物贸易实现零关税的产品数量达90％,各成员通过制度政策协调、数字技术应用等手段简化通关流程,提高清关效率,跨境电商进出口迎来新的发展机遇和增长点。综试区率先承接RCEP带来的经贸规则红利,完善跨境电商新基建,打造优质营商环境。2017年,杭州市人民政府、马来西亚数字经济发展局、阿里巴巴集团签署三方合作备忘录。2020年,杭州到吉隆坡的菜鸟国际包机航线正式首航。综试区不断增强同RCEP区域内国家的密切合作,强化中国、亚太供应链在全球的竞争优势。

二、世界电子贸易平台

新技术与全球化的结合创造了全新的贸易形态,新贸易需要新规则。世界电子贸易平台(Electronic World Trade Platform,eWTP)倡议在这个背景下诞生。在2016年3月的博鳌亚洲论坛上,该平台被正式倡议建立,旨在帮助中小企业、发展中国家、年轻人进入全球市场。基于公开、透明和

41

非营利性的特点,世界电子贸易平台致力于帮助 RCEP 区域内的各成员协调跨境贸易各利益攸关方的合作与投入,促进了跨境电子贸易的共同发展。

2017 年 10 月,世界电子贸易平台开始在中国杭州建设试验区,大力支持国内各大电商平台在 RCEP 区域内的国际化发展。试验区通过构建智能物流网络、升级跨境支付体系、拓展第三方服务,拓宽了世界电子贸易进出口的双向通道。试验区利用基础设施互联互通和跨境电子商务的双重便利,推进市场层面和制度层面的创新探索与联动发展,建设自由便捷、开放高效的世界电子贸易大通道,加快打造网上丝绸之路的枢纽。试验区形成了全流程的数据化管理体系,通过交易、支付和物流信息"三单对碰",实现秒级通关。

2017 年 11 月,世界电子贸易项目首个海外数字中枢(e-hub)在马来西亚正式启动。这也标志着 RCEP 成员对世界电子贸易平台的高度认可和广泛采纳。在世界电子贸易落地马来西亚后,该国成为"一带一路"沿线国家中销往中国的商品数量增长最快的国家之一。马来西亚的广大中小卖家切切实实感受到了跨境电商带来的便捷与普惠。例如,在中马两国开通了快速清关系统后,马来西亚的一家经营燕窝的小企业的商品通关时间缩短,在天猫国际的营业额于 1 年内由 2000 万元激增至 1 亿元。

第四章　RCEP 各成员的跨境电商发展状况

第一节　中国跨境电商发展状况

一、中国社会经济与跨境电商发展概况

2020 年,中国 GDP 总量为 14.7 万亿美元,同比增长 2.3%;总人口为 14.1 亿人,其中 0—14 岁人口占比为 17.9%,15—64 岁人口占比为 68.6%,65 岁以上人口占比为 13.5%;人口出生率为 8.52‰,死亡率为 7.07‰,自然增长率为 1.45‰;城镇人均可支配收入为 43834 元,农村人均可支配收入为 17131 元;全体就业人员平均工资为 79854 元。

2020 年我国网民规模达 9.89 亿,互联网普及率达 70%,其中手机网民规模达 9.86 亿,网民使用手机上网的比例达 99.7%,使用电视上网的网民比例为 24.0%,使用台式电脑上网、笔记本电脑上网、平板电脑上网的比例分别为 32.8%、28.2% 和 22.9%。我国农村网民规模达 3.09 亿,占整体网民的 31.3%;城镇网民规模达 6.80 亿,占整体网民的 68.7%。网络购物用户规模达 7.82 亿,占全体网民的 79.1%;手机网络购物用户规模达 7.81 亿,占手机网民的 79.2%(见图 4-1)。

2021 年,跨境电商逆势发展,成为疏通贸易的重要毛细血管。海关统计数据显示,2021 年我国跨境电商进出口总额为 1.98 万亿元,增长 15%,其中出口 1.44 万亿元,增长 25%。在市场采购方面,出口规模突破 9000 亿元。随着全国市场采购试点的增加,2021 年,我国市场采购出口总额为 9303.9

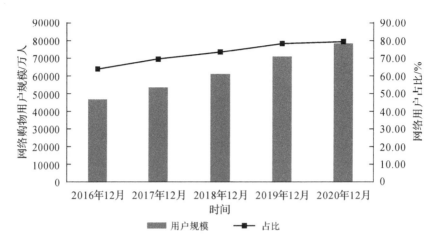

图 4-1　2016—2020 年网络购物用户规模及其占比

数据来源:第 47 次《中国互联网络发展状况统计报告》。

亿元,增长 32.1%,占同期出口总额的 4.3%,拉动出口增长 1.3 个百分点。全国共新增 46 个跨境电商综试区,增设"9710"和"9810"跨境电商 B2B 出口贸易方式,推动通关便利化。2020 年,突如其来的新冠疫情成为冲击全球经济的最大不确定性。新冠疫情于全球蔓延,国际形势中不稳定、不确定因素增多,世界经济形势复杂、严峻。在此背景下,十九届五中全会、"十四五"规划和 2035 年远景目标纲要指出,要推动数字经济和实体经济深度融合,加快构建以国内大循环为主体、国内国际双循环相互促进的新发展格局,加快数字化发展,打造数字经济新优势。"双融合"全面支撑的"双循环"将为构建新发展格局提供强大支撑。

二、中国一般贸易和跨境电商的比较

(一)出口国家(地区)维度

表 4-1 为中国一般贸易与跨境电商前十出口国家(地区)情况。

表 4-1　中国一般贸易与跨境电商前十出口国家(地区)情况

排名	一般贸易(出口前十的国家或地区)			跨境电商(出口需求量前十的国家或地区)		
	2019 年	2020 年	2021 年	2019 年	2020 年	2021 年
1	美国	美国	美国	美国	美国	美国
2	中国香港	中国香港	中国香港	印度	印度	印度
3	日本	日本	日本	加拿大	英国	巴西
4	韩国	韩国	越南	英国	加拿大	英国
5	德国	越南	韩国	俄罗斯	秘鲁	加拿大
6	越南	德国	德国	澳大利亚	澳大利亚	菲律宾
7	印度	印度	荷兰	巴西	菲律宾	巴基斯坦
8	荷兰	荷兰	英国	尼日利亚	墨西哥	秘鲁
9	英国	英国	印度	墨西哥	巴西	墨西哥
10	新加坡	新加坡	新加坡	德国	巴基斯坦	澳大利亚

数据来源:一般贸易为中华人民共和国海关总署;跨境电商为阿里巴巴国际站。

(二)进口国家(地区)维度

表 4.2 为中国一般贸易与跨境电商前十的进口国家(地区)情况。

表 4-2　中国一般贸易与跨境电商前十的进口国家(地区)情况

排名	一般贸易(进口前十的国家或地区)			跨境电商(进口需求量前十的国家或地区)		
	2019 年	2020 年	2021 年	2019 年	2020 年	2021 年
1	韩国	韩国	日本	印度	越南	印度
2	日本	日本	韩国	泰国	马来西亚	越南
3	美国	美国	美国	美国	印度	美国
4	德国	澳大利亚	澳大利亚	越南	泰国	南非
5	中国台湾	德国	德国	巴基斯坦	美国	泰国
6	澳大利亚	巴西	巴西	中国台湾	南非	法国
7	巴西	马来西亚	越南	南非	土耳其	乌克兰
8	俄罗斯	越南	马来西亚	土耳其	巴基斯坦	英国
9	新加坡	俄罗斯	俄罗斯	韩国	韩国	德国
10	越南	沙特	泰国	马来西亚	乌克兰	巴基斯坦

数据来源:一般贸易为中华人民共和国海关总署;跨境电商为阿里巴巴国际站。

（三）出口品类维度

表4-3为中国一般贸易与跨境电商前十的出口品类情况。

表 4-3　中国一般贸易与跨境电商前十的出口品类情况

排名	一般贸易（出口前十的品类）			跨境电商（出口需求量前十的品类）		
	2019 年	2020 年	2021 年	2019 年	2020 年	2021 年
1	广播设备	电机	电气、电子设备	消费电子	安全防护	消费电子
2	计算机	工业机械	机械、核反应堆、锅炉	美容及个人护理	医药保健	服装
3	办公器械零件	家具	家具、照明标志、装配式建筑	服装	美容及个人护理	美容及个人护理
4	集成电路	塑料	塑料	家居用品	消费电子	运动及娱乐
5	电话	汽车及零件	光学、照片、技术、医疗器械	机械	机械	家居园艺
6	车辆零件	精密仪器	铁路、有轨电车以外的车辆	汽车、摩托车	服装	机械
7	精炼石油	针织服装	其他纺织制品、套装、旧衣服	运动及娱乐	运动及娱乐	汽车、摩托车
8	电力变压器	钢铁制品	玩具、游戏、运动用品	包装与印刷	家居用品	包装与印刷
9	半导体器件	非针织服装	钢铁制品	手表、珠宝、眼镜	包装与印刷	家具
10	灯具	玩具及运动器材	非针织或钩编的服装制品	箱包	汽车、摩托车	健康医疗

数据来源：一般贸易为中华人民共和国海关总署；跨境电商为阿里巴巴国际站。

（四）进口品类维度

表 4-4 为中国一般贸易与跨境电商前十的进口品类情况。

表 4-4　中国一般贸易与跨境电商前十的进口品类情况

排名	一般贸易（进口前十的品类）			跨境电商（进口需求量前十的品类）		
	2019 年	2020 年	2021 年	2019 年	2020 年	2021 年
1	原油	电机	电气、电子设备	家居用品	健康医疗	家居园艺
2	集成电路	石油和矿物燃料	矿物燃料、矿物油、蒸馏产品	机械	家居用品	运动及娱乐
3	铁矿石	工业机械	机械、核反应堆、锅炉	消费电子	机械	机械
4	石油气	矿石	矿渣和灰	服装	消费电子	消费电子
5	汽车	精密仪器	光学、照片、技术、医疗器械	矿物和冶金	安全防护	汽车、摩托车
6	黄金	汽车及零件	铁路、有轨电车以外的车辆	食品及饮料	运动及娱乐	服装
7	铜	塑料	塑料	医药保健	包装与印刷	包装与印刷
8	车辆零件	宝石和金属	铜	包装与印刷	建筑	美容及个人护理
9	机械	有机化学品	有机化学品	农业	服装	五金工具
10	精炼石油	铜	油料种子、含油水果、谷物、种子、水果	运动及娱乐	汽车、摩托车	家具

数据来源：一般贸易为中华人民共和国海关总署；跨境电商为阿里巴巴国际站。

第二节　日本跨境电商发展状况

一、日本社会经济与跨境电商发展概况

世界银行数据显示,2020 年,日本 GDP 达 5.06 万亿美元,同比下降 4.59%;人均 GDP 为 4.02 万美元,同比下降 4.26%。与此同时,2020 年,日本总人口达 1.26 亿人,且整体受教育水平较高。经济合作与发展组织(OECD)统计数据显示,截至 2020 年,在日本 25—64 岁人口中,取得学士学位或同等高等教育学位的人口占比为 31.3%,是 OECD 成员平均水平(18.2%)的 1.7 倍。作为发达国家,日本的数字基础设施较为完善。截至 2021 年,该国互联网用户数为 1.17 亿人,互联网普及率高达 93%。DataReportal 的数据显示,截至 2021 年 1 月,日本移动电话用户数达 2.01 亿,移动通信普及率为 159%,社交媒体用户数为 0.94 亿,社交媒体普及率达 74%。与此同时,日本经济产业省统计数据显示,2020 年日本社会零售业总额为 146.46 万亿日元(约 12713.54 亿美元),其中网络零售占据 13.18%。

日本的数字经济发展重点关注数字技术创新、产业数字化、贸易数字化和数字社会建设,政府积极推动数字技术与经济增长、社会治理的深度融合。数字技术创新方面,2020 年 1 月,日本总务省统合创新战略推进会议就"量子技术创新战略"发布最终报告,提出将重点开展四个方面的研究开发:量子通信和加密链路技术、可信节点技术、量子中继技术和广域网构筑与运用技术。在产业数字化方面,2017 年,日本经济产业省发布"互联工业战略",积极推动人工智能、物联网、云计算等科技手段在生产制造领域的应用,突破人口老龄化、劳动力短缺、产业竞争力不足等发展瓶颈。之后,日本相继发布了《日本制造业白皮书》、"综合创新战略"、"集成创新战略"、"第二期战略性创新推进计划"(SIP)等战略和计划,推动产业数字化发展。在贸易数字化方面,2013 年,日本政府通过"日本复兴战略"明确提出利用数字贸易振兴日本经济,并推行税收优惠制度和特定信息通信设备即时折旧制度,极大地激发了企业信息化的发展活力。数字社会建设方面，2016 年，日本政府在"第五期科学技术基本计划(2016—2020)"和"科学技术创新战略 2016"中首次提出超智能"社会 5.0"概念，并在此后相继发布了"下一代人工智能推进战略""科技创新综合战略 2017""集成创新战略"等，从战略规划、制度建设、人才培养等方面为"社会 5.0"和"互联工业"铺平道路。2019 年日本开始全力推进"数字新政"战略，在"后 5G"信息通信基础设施、学校的信息与通信技术(ICT)应用、中小企业信息化等方面加大资金投入力度，推动社会数字化、智能化转型。

在电子商务贸易方面，无论是国内贸易还是跨境贸易，日本的电商规模均呈现出较为明显的扩大趋势。在国内电商贸易上，2020 年，日本 B2C 市场规模达 19.3 万亿日元，B2B 市场规模达 334.9 万亿日元，尽管增速不断放缓，但总体规模在近 5 年基本保持了扩大态势(见图 4-2)。在跨境电商贸易上，2020 年，日本仅对中国消费者的销售金额便达 19499 万亿日元，同比增长 17.8%。

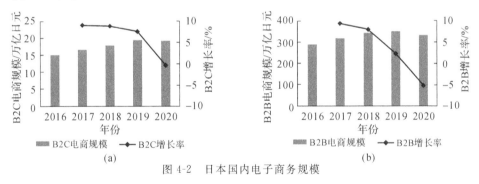

图 4-2　日本国内电子商务规模

数据来源：日本经济产业省。

二、日本一般贸易和跨境电商的比较情况

(一)出口国家(地区)维度

表 4-5 为日本一般贸易与跨境电商前十的出口国家(地区)情况。

表 4-5　日本一般贸易与跨境电商前十的出口国家(地区)情况

排名	一般贸易(出口前十的国家或地区)			跨境电商(出口需求量前十的国家或地区)		
	2019 年	2020 年	2021 年	2019 年	2020 年	2021 年
1	美国	中国	中国	菲律宾	菲律宾	菲律宾
2	中国	美国	美国	中国	印尼	印尼
3	韩国	韩国	中国台湾	印尼	马来西亚	马来西亚
4	中国台湾	中国台湾	韩国	澳大利亚	中国	越南
5	中国香港	中国香港	中国香港	马来西亚	澳大利亚	澳大利亚
6	泰国	泰国	泰国	越南	越南	泰国
7	德国	新加坡	德国	泰国	泰国	中国
8	新加坡	德国	新加坡	韩国	新加坡	柬埔寨
9	越南	越南	越南	新加坡	柬埔寨	新加坡
10	澳大利亚	马来西亚	马来西亚	柬埔寨	韩国	韩国

数据来源:一般贸易为日本海关;跨境电商为阿里巴巴国际站。

(二)进口国家(地区)维度

表 4-6 为日本一般贸易与跨境电商前十的进口国家(地区)情况。

表 4-6　日本一般贸易与跨境电商前十的进口国家(地区)情况

排名	一般贸易(进口前十的国家或地区)			跨境电商(进口需求量前十的国家或地区)		
	2019 年	2020 年	2021 年	2019 年	2020 年	2021 年
1	中国	中国	中国	中国	中国	中国
2	美国	美国	美国	越南	越南	越南
3	澳大利亚	澳大利亚	澳大利亚	泰国	泰国	韩国
4	韩国	中国台湾	中国台湾	韩国	韩国	泰国
5	沙特	韩国	韩国	菲律宾	马来西亚	菲律宾
6	中国台湾	泰国	沙特	马来西亚	菲律宾	马来西亚
7	阿联酋	越南	阿联酋	印尼	印尼	新加坡
8	泰国	德国	泰国	新加坡	新加坡	印尼
9	德国	沙特	德国	澳大利亚	澳大利亚	新西兰
10	越南	阿联酋	越南	新西兰	新西兰	澳大利亚

数据来源:一般贸易为日本海关;跨境电商为阿里巴巴国际站。

（三）出口品类维度

表 4-7 为日本一般贸易与跨境电商前十的出口品类情况。

表 4-7　日本一般贸易与跨境电商前十的出口品类情况

排名	一般贸易（出口前十的品类）			跨境电商（出口需求量前十的品类）		
	2019 年	2020 年	2021 年	2019 年	2020 年	2021 年
1	车辆及其零件、附件（铁道及电车道车辆除外）	车辆及其零件、附件（铁道及电车道车辆除外）	核反应堆、锅炉、机械器具及零件	汽车、摩托车	汽车、摩托车	汽车、摩托车
2	核反应堆、锅炉、机械器具及零件	消费电子	车辆及其零件、附件（铁道及电车道车辆除外）	消费电子	运动及娱乐	家用电器
3	电气、电子设备	电气、电子设备	电气、电子设备	服装	服装	食品及饮料
4	可可及可可制品	核反应堆、锅炉、机械器具及零件	未分类商品	五金工具	食品及饮料	运动及娱乐
5	精密仪器及设备	光学、照相、技术、医疗器械	光学、照相、技术、医疗器械	医药保健	消费电子	消费电子
6	钢铁	船舶及有关运输设备	钢铁	运动及娱乐	五金工具	五金工具
7	塑料及其制品	半导体材料	塑料及其制品	机械	家用电器	服装
8	有机化学品	贵金属	有机化学品	食品及饮料	美容及个人护理	健康医疗
9	矿物燃料、矿物油及其蒸馏产品	家用电器	化工产品	家用电器	医药保健	美容及个人护理
10	船舶及有关运输设备	未分类商品	珍珠、宝石、金属、硬币	家居用品	健康医疗	家居园艺

数据来源：一般贸易为 globalEDGE、Trading Economics、Tracking Docket；跨境电商为阿里巴巴国际站。

（四）进口品类维度

表 4-8 为日本一般贸易与跨境电商前十的进口品类情况。

表 4-8　日本一般贸易与跨境电商前十的进口品类情况

排名	一般贸易（进口前十的品类）			跨境电商（进口需求量前十的品类）		
	2019 年	2020 年	2021 年	2019 年	2020 年	2021 年
1	矿物燃料、矿物油及其蒸馏产品	矿物燃料、矿物油及其蒸馏产品	矿物燃料、矿物油及其蒸馏产品	消费电子	消费电子	服装
2	电气、电子设备	电气、电子设备	电气、电子设备	家居用品	服装	消费电子
3	核反应堆、锅炉、机械器具及零件	核反应堆、锅炉、机械器具及零件	核反应堆、锅炉、机械器具及零件	服装	美容及个人护理	家居园艺
4	精密仪器及设备	光学、照相、技术、医疗器械	医药产品	运动及娱乐	运动及娱乐	运动及娱乐
5	医药产品	医药产品	矿砂、矿渣及矿灰	汽车、摩托车	包装与印刷	包装与印刷
6	车辆及其零件、附件（铁道及电车道车辆除外）	矿砂、矿渣及矿灰	光学、照相、技术、医疗器械	机械	汽车、摩托车	美容及个人护理
7	矿砂、矿渣及矿灰	车辆及其零件、附件（铁道及电车道车辆除外）	珍珠、宝石、金属、硬币	美容及个人护理	机械	机械
8	塑料及其制品	天然或养殖珍珠、宝石或半宝石	车辆及其零件、附件（铁道及电车道车辆除外）	包装与印刷	安全防护	汽车、摩托车
9	有机化学品	有机化学品	塑料及其制品	手表、珠宝、眼镜	家居园艺	健康医疗

排名	一般贸易（进口前十的品类）			跨境电商（进口需求量前十的品类）		
	2019 年	2020 年	2021 年	2019 年	2020 年	2021 年
10	非针织或非钩编的服装及衣着附件	塑料及其制品	有机化学品	箱包	医药保健	家具

数据来源：一般贸易为 globalEDGE、Trading Economics、Tracking Docket；跨境电商为阿里巴巴国际站。

第三节　韩国跨境电商发展状况

一、韩国社会经济与跨境电商发展概况

2020 年，韩国 GDP 为 1.63 万亿美元，人均 GDP 为 31489 美元，同比下降 0.61％。2020 年，韩国人口为 5178 万人，同比增长 0.14％，增长非常缓慢，是世界上出生率最低的国家，并且人口老龄化程度在不断加深。

根据世界经济论坛（WEF）的统计，韩国的 ICT 普及率已连续 3 年位居世界第一。2020 年，韩国互联网用户数约为 4900 万，互联网普及率高达 97％；智能手机用户数约为 3920 万，普及率为 76％。根据一项调查显示，大约 99％的韩国人每周至少上网一次，平均每周上网时长为 14.3 小时。韩国是世界第五大电子商务市场，也是亚太地区第三大电子商务市场，仅次于中国和日本。2020 年韩国社会零售总额为 4134 亿美元，同比增长 0.41％；网上零售总额为 1402 亿美元，同比增长 19.11％，占社会零售总额的 34％（见图 4-3）。韩国拥有完善的数字服务基础设施，这为跨境电商的发展提供了强大的支持。2020 年，韩国跨境电商市场规模为 35 亿美元。

2020 年 7 月，韩国政府推出新政政策（the Korean New Deal）。其中的数字新政（the Digital New Deal）大力支持和推动跨境电商的发展。2020 年，韩国排名前三的电子商务平台是 Coupang Corp、Naver Corp 和 eBay Inc，分别占有 19.2％、13.6％、12.8％的市场份额。其余的电商平台还包括

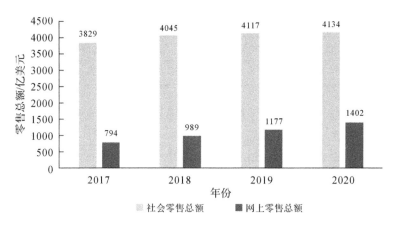

图 4-3　2017—2020 年韩国社会零售总额和网上零售总额

数据来源:韩国统计局。

11ST、Lotteon、SSG 等。信用卡是韩国最常见的支付方式,平均每人拥有 3.9 张信用卡,并且超过 70% 的线上交易是通过信用卡来结算的,其次是借记卡和转账支付。随着快捷支付方式的发展,PayPal、三星支付和支付宝等支付方式也吸引了大量用户。同时,网上零售商和企业也会提供自己的支付系统,如 Coupang 的火箭支付、Shinsegae 的 SSG 支付以及 Lotte Group 的 L 支付等。随着电商平台之间的竞争日益激烈,快速送货服务逐渐成为吸引更多客户的关键。为了满足这方面的需求,Coupang 投资 13 亿美元为其著名的配送服务 Rocket Delivery 建设物流基础设施,以提供当日或次日送达服务。随着 Coupang 的 Rocket Delivery 的成功,其他电商平台也逐渐建立起自己的物流系统。

二、韩国一般贸易和跨境电商的比较情况

(一)出口国家(地区)维度

表 4-9 为韩国一般贸易与跨境电商前十的出口国家(地区)情况。

表 4-9 韩国一般贸易与跨境电商前十的出口国家(地区)情况

排名	一般贸易(出口前十的国家或地区)			跨境电商(出口需求量前十的国家或地区)		
	2019 年	2020 年	2021 年	2019 年	2020 年	2021 年
1	中国	中国	中国	美国	美国	美国
2	美国	美国	美国	印度	印度	印度
3	越南	越南	越南	俄罗斯	菲律宾	菲律宾
4	中国香港	中国香港	中国香港	加拿大	俄罗斯	墨西哥
5	日本	日本	日本	中国	英国	俄罗斯
6	中国台湾	印度	印度	英国	加拿大	秘鲁
7	印度	新加坡	新加坡	巴基斯坦	墨西哥	巴西
8	墨西哥	墨西哥	德国	越南	秘鲁	智利
9	新加坡	马来西亚	马来西亚	印尼	印尼	印尼
10	菲律宾	德国	墨西哥	菲律宾	智利	英国

数据来源:一般贸易为韩国海关;跨境电商为阿里巴巴国际站。

(二)进口国家(地区)维度

表 4-10 为韩国一般贸易与跨境电商前十的进口国家(地区)情况。

表 4-10 韩国一般贸易与跨境电商前十的进口国家(地区)情况

排名	一般贸易(进口前十的国家或地区)			跨境电商(进口需求量前十的国家或地区)		
	2019 年	2020 年	2021 年	2019 年	2020 年	2021 年
1	中国	中国	中国	中国	中国	中国
2	美国	美国	美国	越南	越南	越南
3	日本	日本	日本	印度	印度	印度
4	沙特	沙特	德国	泰国	巴基斯坦	巴基斯坦
5	德国	越南	越南	美国	泰国	美国
6	越南	澳大利亚	澳大利亚	巴基斯坦	美国	泰国
7	俄罗斯	德国	沙特	中国台湾	中国台湾	中国台湾
8	中国台湾	俄罗斯	俄罗斯	菲律宾	英国	南非
9	卡塔尔	卡塔尔	马来西亚	中国香港	马来西亚	英国
10	科威特	科威特	新加坡	印尼	南非	法国

数据来源:一般贸易为韩国海关;跨境电商为阿里巴巴国际站。

（三）出口品类维度。

表 4-11 为韩国一般贸易与跨境电商前十的出口品类情况。

表 4-11　韩国一般贸易与跨境电商前十的出口品类情况

排名	一般贸易（出口前十的品类）			跨境电商（出口需求量前十的品类）		
	2019 年	2020 年	2021 年	2019 年	2020 年	2021 年
1	机电设备	机电设备	机电设备	美容及个人护理	美容及个人护理	美容及个人护理
2	工业机械	工业机械	工业机械	汽车、摩托车	汽车、摩托车	消费电子
3	车辆及零部件	车辆及零部件	车辆及零部件	医药保健	机械	食品及饮料
4	石油和矿物燃料	石油和矿物燃料	塑料	机械	健康医疗	健康医疗
5	塑料	塑料	石油和矿物燃料	消费电子	医药保健	汽车、摩托车
6	精密仪器	钢铁	医疗器械	家用电器	消费电子	服装
7	有机化学品	精密仪器	钢铁	食品及饮料	家用电器	机械
8	钢铁	有机化学品	船舶	五金工具	服装	家用电器
9	船舶	船舶	有机化学品	运动及娱乐	安全防护	包装与印刷
10	钢铁制品	钢铁制品	钢铁制品	纺织及皮革制品	家居用品	运动及娱乐

数据来源：一般贸易为韩国海关；跨境电商为阿里巴巴国际站。

（四）进口品类维度

表 4-12 为韩国一般贸易与跨境电商前十的进口品类情况。

表 4-12　韩国一般贸易与跨境电商前十的进口品类情况

排名	一般贸易（进口前十的品类）			跨境电商（进口需求量前十的品类）		
	2019 年	2020 年	2021 年	2019 年	2020 年	2021 年
1	石油和矿物燃料	石油和矿物燃料	机电设备	家居用品	消费电子	家居园艺
2	机电设备	机电设备	石油和矿物燃料	消费电子	机械	消费电子

排名	一般贸易(进口前十的品类)			跨境电商(进口需求量前十的品类)		
	2019 年	2020 年	2021 年	2019 年	2020 年	2021 年
3	工业机械	工业机械	工业机械	机械	运动及娱乐	机械
4	精密仪器	精密仪器	医疗器械	运动及娱乐	家居园艺	运动及娱乐
5	车辆及零部件	车辆及零部件	车辆及零部件	医药保健	五金工具	包装与印刷
6	钢铁	钢铁	矿石	汽车、摩托车	包装与印刷	汽车、摩托车
7	有机化学品	矿石	有机化学品	包装与印刷	安全防护	服装
8	塑料	有机化学品	塑料	五金工具	汽车、摩托车	五金工具
9	无机化学品	塑料	钢铁	美容及个人护理	家居用品	健康医疗
10	非针织服装	化学产品	药品	电气设备和产品	美容及个人护理	建筑

数据来源:一般贸易为韩国海关;跨境电商为阿里巴巴国际站。

第四节　澳大利亚跨境电商发展状况

一、澳大利亚社会经济与跨境电商发展概况

2020 年,澳大利亚的 GDP 为 13309 亿美元,同比增长－0.28%,比 2019 年减少了 657 亿美元,比 2010 年增长了 1848 亿美元。受到新冠疫情影响,澳大利亚在 2020 年经历了约 30 年来首次经济衰退。2020 年,澳大利亚人均 GDP 为 51812 美元,同比增长－1.53%,比 2019 年减少了 3245 美元,与 2010 年相比,减少了 210 美元;国民总收入(GNI)为 13802 亿美元,人均国民总收入为 53730 美元,比 2019 年减少了 1370 美元,与 2010 年相比,增长了 7100 美元。

澳大利亚总人口约为 2500 万人,国土面积排名世界第六,平均每平方

千米只有 2 个人,城镇化率约为 90%。澳大利亚拥有 2100 万名互联网用户,网络渗透率约为 81%,互联网普及率约为 88%,其中智能手机用户占48%。预计到 2025 年,澳大利亚的互联网用户数量将超过 2150 万。

澳大利亚是世界第十大电子商务市场,约 80% 的澳大利亚人民会通过网络购买商品,平均每人每年的电商支出为 1527 美元。目前澳大利亚的电子商务市场由 eBay、亚马逊主导。有调查显示,消费者们更重视商品的品牌价值和产品质量。目前澳大利亚人的在线支付方式以卡为主,占 42%,其次是网银转账、电子钱包等。POLi 是澳大利亚本土的支付机构,也是澳大利亚邮政公司的实时银行转账工具,目前已经成为除了信用卡、PayPal 以外的主要在线支付选择。

二、澳大利亚一般贸易和跨境电商的比较情况

(一)出口国家(地区)维度

表 4-13 为澳大利亚一般贸易与跨境电商前十的出口国家(地区)情况。

表 4-13　澳大利亚一般贸易与跨境电商前十的出口国家(地区)情况

排名	一般贸易(出口前十的国家或地区)			跨境电商(出口需求量前十的国家或地区)		
	2019 年	2020 年	2021 年	2019 年	2020 年	2021 年
1	中国	中国	中国	美国	美国	美国
2	日本	日本	日本	印度	印度	印度
3	韩国	韩国	韩国	英国	英国	巴西
4	印度	英国	美国	中国	加拿大	英国
5	美国	美国	英国	尼日利亚	澳大利亚	加拿大
6	中国台湾	印度	新加坡	加拿大	菲律宾	菲律宾
7	中国香港	新加坡	新西兰	澳大利亚	巴西	法国
8	马来西亚	新西兰	印度	俄罗斯	尼日利亚	沙特
9	新西兰	马来西亚	中国香港	巴西	沙特	巴基斯坦
10	新加坡	中国香港	马来西亚	法国	法国	西班牙

数据来源:一般贸易为 globalEDGE、OEC、Trading Economics;跨境电商为阿里巴巴国际站。

（二）进口国家（地区）维度

表 4-14 为澳大利亚一般贸易与跨境电商前十的进口国家（地区）情况。

表 4-14　澳大利亚一般贸易与跨境电商前十的进口国家（地区）情况

排名	一般贸易（进口前十的国家或地区）			跨境电商（进口需求量前十的国家或地区）		
	2019 年	2020 年	2021 年	2019 年	2020 年	2021 年
1	中国	中国	中国	中国	中国	中国
2	美国	美国	美国	印度	印度	印度
3	日本	日本	日本	巴基斯坦	巴基斯坦	巴基斯坦
4	德国	泰国	泰国	越南	越南	越南
5	泰国	德国	德国	美国	美国	美国
6	韩国	韩国	马来西亚	中国台湾	中国台湾	英国
7	新加坡	马来西亚	韩国	中国香港	土耳其	南非
8	马来西亚	新加坡	新加坡	泰国	南非	法国
9	新西兰	新西兰	英国	韩国	韩国	中国台湾
10	英国	英国	新西兰	土耳其	英国	西班牙

数据来源：一般贸易为 globalEDGE、OEC、Trading Economics；跨境电商为阿里巴巴国际站。

（三）出口品类维度

表 4-15 为澳大利亚一般贸易与跨境电商前十的出口品类情况。

表 4-15　澳大利亚一般贸易与跨境电商前十的出口品类情况

排名	一般贸易（出口前十的品类）			跨境电商（出口需求量前十的品类）		
	2019 年	2020 年	2021 年	2019 年	2020 年	2021 年
1	煤球	矿石	矿渣和灰	食品及饮料	服装	食品及饮料
2	铁矿石	石油和矿物燃料	未按种类指定的商品	服装	食品及饮料	家居园艺
3	液化石油气	其他商品	矿物燃料、油类、蒸馏产品	农业	运动及娱乐	运动及娱乐

续表

排名	一般贸易（出口前十的品类）			跨境电商（出口需求量前十的品类）		
	2019 年	2020 年	2021 年	2019 年	2020 年	2021 年
4	黄金	宝石和金属	珍珠、宝石、金属、硬币	运动及娱乐	家居用品	农业
5	氧化铝	肉类	肉类及食用肉类内脏	美容及个人护理	美容及个人护理	消费电子
6	铜	工业机械	机械、核反应堆、锅炉	医药保健	农业	商务服务
7	冷冻牛肉	药品	谷物	家居用品	消费电子	美容及个人护理
8	小麦	电机	医药产品	汽车、摩托车	矿物和冶金	包装与印刷
9	铝	精密仪器	电气、电子设备	包装与印刷	健康医疗	汽车、摩托车
10	羊毛	谷物	铝	矿物和冶金	包装与印刷	服装

数据来源：一般贸易为 globalEDGE、OEC、Trading Economics；跨境电商为阿里巴巴国际站。

（四）进口品类维度

表 4-16 为澳大利亚一般贸易与跨境电商前十的进口品类情况。

表 4-16　澳大利亚一般贸易与跨境电商前十的进口品类情况

排名	一般贸易（进口前十的品类）			跨境电商（进口需求量前十的品类）		
	2019 年	2020 年	2021 年	2019 年	2020 年	2021 年
1	精炼石油	工业机械	机械、核反应堆、锅炉	家居用品	家居园艺	家居园艺
2	汽车	石油和矿物燃料	铁路、有轨电车以外的车辆	服装	包装与印刷	服装
3	原油	汽车及零件	电气、电子设备	包装与印刷	服装	包装与印刷

排名	一般贸易（进口前十的品类）			跨境电商（进口需求量前十的品类）		
	2019 年	2020 年	2021 年	2019 年	2020 年	2021 年
4	送货卡车	电机	矿物燃料、矿物油、蒸馏产品	美容及个人护理	美容及个人护理	美容及个人护理
5	广播设备	药品	医药产品	运动及娱乐	运动及娱乐	运动及娱乐
6	电脑	精密仪器	珍珠、宝石、金属、硬币	消费电子	礼品与工艺品	汽车、摩托车
7	包装药品	宝石和金属	光学、照相、技术、医疗器械	汽车、摩托车	汽车、摩托车	礼品与工艺品
8	黄金	其他商品	塑料	机械	消费电子	消费电子
9	医疗器械	塑料	家具、照明标志、装配式建筑	礼品工艺品	机械	机械
10	车辆零件	家具	钢铁制品	箱包	健康医疗	家具

数据来源：一般贸易为 globalEDGE、OEC、Trading Economics；跨境电商为阿里巴巴国际站。

第五节　新西兰跨境电商发展状况

一、新西兰社会经济与跨境电商发展概况

世界银行数据显示，2020 年，新西兰的 GDP 达 210.70 亿美元，同比上涨 1.86%，人均 GDP 为 4.14 万美元，同比下降 0.24%。与此同时，2020 年，新西兰总人口达 508.43 万人，且受教育水平整体较高。OECD 统计数据显示，截至 2020 年，在新西兰 25—64 岁人口中，取得学士学位或同等高等教育学位的人口占比为 29.1%。

新西兰的数字基础设施较为完善。截至 2021 年,该国互联网普及率高达 94%。DataReportal 的数据显示,截至 2021 年 1 月,新西兰移动电话用户数达 656 万,相当于其总人口的 135.6%,且数据显示该国人均每日网络使用时长为 6 小时 39 分钟。根据 eCommerceDB 的统计数据,2020 年,新西兰网络零售市场总额位列全球第 39 名,同比增速达 31%,为全球网络零售市场增长贡献了 29% 的份额。2020 年,新西兰人均网络消费为 1529 美元,72% 的民众曾经访问网上零售商店,61% 的民众在网上下单了至少 1 件产品。

新西兰邮政报告称,自 2019 年至今,新西兰的电子商务发展稳中向好、逐年递增,2021 年前 10 个月,线上消费相比 2020 年同期增长 18%,较 2019 年增长近 50%。电子商务的发展也推动了电子支付平台和电子商务平台的成长。2020 年,新西兰当地前五的支付平台分别为 Flo2Cash、Paystation、Windcave、Bambora、Stripe,销售额排名前三的电商平台依次为 Countdown、Apple、Mitre10。此外,得益于电商的迅猛发展,新西兰的物流运输业近几年扩张迅速,但市场仍有巨大发展空间,尚未出现明显的行业龙头。

新西兰政府积极支持数字经济的发展,并看好其所带来的商业利益和社会利益。2020 年 6 月,新西兰与智利、新加坡共同提出数字经济伙伴关系协议(DEPA),是全球第一个"纯数字"贸易协定,旨在帮助中小国家通过合作打造服务其利益的跨境数字贸易框架。此外,新西兰政府还积极研究增强现实(AR)、虚拟现实(UR)、物联网(IoT)、人工智能(AI)等新技术对新西兰社会和经济的潜在影响,推动数字政府建设,鼓励企业最大限度地利用数字技术提高生产率。

二、新西兰一般贸易和跨境电商的比较情况

(一)出口国家(地区)维度

表 4-17 为新西兰一般贸易与跨境电商前十的出口国家(地区)情况。

表 4-17　新西兰一般贸易与跨境电商前十的出口国家(地区)情况

排名	一般贸易(出口前十的国家或地区)			跨境电商(出口需求量前十的国家或地区)		
	2018 年	2019 年	2020 年	2019 年	2020 年	2021 年
1	中国	中国	中国	中国	中国	澳大利亚
2	澳大利亚	澳大利亚	澳大利亚	澳大利亚	澳大利亚	菲律宾
3	美国	美国	美国	马来西亚	菲律宾	马来西亚
4	日本	日本	日本	韩国	马来西亚	日本
5	英国	英国	英国	印尼	泰国	泰国
6	韩国	韩国	韩国	越南	印尼	越南
7	印度	德国	新加坡	泰国	越南	新加坡
8	新加坡	中国香港	中国台湾	菲律宾	新加坡	韩国
9	德国	印度	中国香港	新加坡	韩国	中国
10	中国香港	新加坡	德国	日本	日本	印尼

数据来源:一般贸易为新西兰统计局;跨境电商为阿里巴巴国际站。

(二)进口国家(地区)维度

表 4-18 为新西兰一般贸易与跨境电商前十的进口国家(地区)情况。

表 4-18　新西兰一般贸易与跨境电商前十的进口国家(地区)情况

排名	一般贸易(进口前十的国家或地区)			跨境电商(进口需求量前十的国家或地区)		
	2018 年	2019 年	2020 年	2019 年	2020 年	2021 年
1	澳大利亚	澳大利亚	中国	中国	中国	中国
2	中国	中国	澳大利亚	越南	越南	越南
3	美国	美国	美国	泰国	泰国	泰国
4	日本	新加坡	新加坡	菲律宾	马来西亚	韩国
5	德国	德国	德国	韩国	韩国	印尼
6	新加坡	日本	日本	印尼	印尼	马来西亚
7	泰国	英国	韩国	日本	日本	日本
8	韩国	泰国	泰国	马来西亚	菲律宾	菲律宾
9	阿联酋	阿联酋	英国	新加坡	新加坡	新加坡
10	英国	韩国	马来西亚	澳大利亚	澳大利亚	澳大利亚

数据来源:一般贸易为新西兰统计局;跨境电商为阿里巴巴国际站。

（三）出口品类维度

表4-19为新西兰一般贸易与跨境电商前十的出口品类情况。

表4-19　新西兰一般贸易与跨境电商前十的出口品类情况

排名	一般贸易（出口前十的品类）			跨境电商（出口需求量前十的品类）		
	2018年	2019年	2020年	2019年	2020年	2021年
1	旅游业	乳制品	乳制品	食品及饮料	食品及饮料	美容及个人护理
2	乳制品	旅游业	旅游业	消费电子	安全防护	健康医疗
3	肉类	肉类	肉类	医药保健	汽车、摩托车	包装与印刷
4	木材	木材	木材	汽车、摩托车	运动及娱乐	灯具照明
5	交通	交通	水果和坚果	农业	农业	食品及饮料
6	水果和坚果	水果和坚果	谷物制品	办公文教用品	消费电子	运动及娱乐
7	饮料	谷物制品	饮料	包装与印刷	家居用品	农业
8	商业服务	饮料	商业服务	家居用品	办公文教用品	建筑
9	谷物制品	商业服务	交通	美容及个人护理	包装与印刷	家居园艺
10	机械	机械	机械	运动及娱乐	医药保健	机械

数据来源：一般贸易为新西兰统计局；跨境电商为阿里巴巴国际站。

（四）进口品类维度

表4-20为新西兰一般贸易与跨境电商前十的进口品类情况。

表4-20　新西兰一般贸易与跨境电商前十的进口品类情况

排名	一般贸易（进口前十的品类）			跨境电商（进口需求量前十的品类）		
	2018年	2019年	2020年	2019年	2020年	2021年
1	交通工具	机械	机械	家居用品	运动及娱乐	服装
2	机械	交通工具	交通工具	运动及娱乐	服装	家居园艺
3	燃料和原油	燃料和原油	电子机械	包装与印刷	包装与印刷	运动及娱乐

排名	一般贸易（进口前十的品类）			跨境电商（进口需求量前十的品类）		
	2018 年	2019 年	2020 年	2019 年	2020 年	2021 年
4	旅游	旅游	燃料和原油	服装	汽车、摩托车	汽车、摩托车
5	电子机械	电子机械	其他商业服务	机械	机械	包装与印刷
6	交通	交通	交通	汽车、摩托车	美容及个人护理	机械
7	其他商业服务	其他商业服务	信息技术	消费电子	消费电子	消费电子
8	塑料及其制品	塑料及其制品	旅游	美容及个人护理	家居园艺	美容及个人护理
9	信息技术	保险与养老	塑料及其制品	建筑	家居用品	家具
10	光学、医疗、测量仪器	信息技术	保险与养老	五金工具	五金工具	礼品与工艺品

数据来源：一般贸易为新西兰统计局；跨境电商为阿里巴巴国际站。

第六节　印度尼西亚跨境电商发展状况

一、印度尼西亚社会经济与跨境电商发展概况

世界银行数据显示，2020 年，印度尼西亚（以下简称印尼）的 GDP 为 1.06 万亿美元，同比下降 2.07％；人均 GDP 为 0.39 万美元，同比下降 3.11％。与此同时，2020 年，印尼总人口达 2.74 亿人。OECD 统计数据显示，截至 2020 年，在印尼 25—64 岁人口中，取得学士学位或同等高等教育学位的人口占比为 4.9％，与 OECD 成员的平均水平（18.2％）相比偏低。印尼的数字基础设施建设已经有所发展。截至 2021 年，该国互联网用户数为 2.04 亿，互联网普及率达 74％。DataReportal 的数据显示，截至 2021 年 1 月，印尼移动电话用户数达 3.47 亿，移动通信普及率为 126％；社交媒体用户数为 1.71 亿，社交媒体普

及率达 62%。

与此同时,印尼的电子商务贸易呈现增长态势。2020 年,印尼的电子商务市场总市值达 440 亿美元,占商品零售总额的 2.82%。美国国际贸易管理局预计,印尼电子商务市场规模至 2025 年将达到 830 亿美元。在跨境电商贸易上,摩根大通的研究显示,2017—2019 年,印尼的电商进口产品数增长了814%,从 2017 年的 610 万件增加到 2019 年的 4970 万件。其中,中国是印尼跨境电子商务贸易的重要伙伴。根据英国著名跨境支付公司 PPRO 发布的报告,截至 2020 年 1 月,印尼 41% 的跨境电商贸易来自中国。

印尼高度重视数字技术和数字经济对国家经济的带动性与倍增性,曾提出 2020 年前将印尼打造成为东南亚地区最大数字经济体的目标。当前,印尼数字经济的发展主要呈现出三个趋势。第一,金融技术蓬勃发展。2016 年,金融领域初创公司增速高达 78%,电子支付交易总额达 14.5 亿美元,涌现出一批具有代表性的金融科技公司,如 Dompetku、Doku、Kartuk 等。第二,共享经济领域独角兽公司迅猛发展,如估值高达 1.53 亿美元的 Go-Jek 平均每秒处理8 个订单。其他具有代表性的公司还有 Grab、Ruangguru、Sejasa.com 等。第三,电子商务发展动力强劲,大型的平台公司包括 Tokopedia、Bukalapak、Bhinneka 等。印尼政府也将其发展数字经济的着力点集中在电子商务领域,曾设定发展目标:2020 年前,印尼电子商务交易额超过 1300 亿美元,年增长率达到 50%,并培育 1000 家市值达到 100 亿美元的科技企业。为推动印尼电子商务的发展,印尼政府制定了电子商务发展路线图,计划将在资金支持、税收、消费者保护、教育和人力资源、电信基础设施、物流、网络安全和管理实施等八个方面为印尼电子商务提供支持。此外,2018 年 4 月,印尼政府发布"印尼制造 4.0"路线图,以期在第四次工业革命中进一步挖掘潜力和提升经济竞争力。

二、印度尼西亚一般贸易和跨境电商的比较情况

(一)出口国家(地区)维度

表 4-21 为印度尼西亚一般贸易与跨境电商前十的出口国家(地区)情况。

表 4-21　印度尼西亚一般贸易与跨境电商前十的出口国家(地区)情况

排名	一般贸易(出口前十的国家或地区)			跨境电商(出口需求量前十的国家或地区)		
	2019 年	2020 年	2021 年	2019 年	2020 年	2021 年
1	中国	中国	中国	中国	菲律宾	澳大利亚
2	美国	美国	美国	澳大利亚	马来西亚	菲律宾
3	日本	日本	日本	马来西亚	新加坡	马来西亚
4	新加坡	新加坡	印度	菲律宾	中国	中国
5	印度	印度	马来西亚	韩国	澳大利亚	越南
6	马来西亚	马来西亚	新加坡	越南	泰国	泰国
7	韩国	韩国	韩国	新加坡	越南	新加坡
8	菲律宾	菲律宾	菲律宾	泰国	韩国	新西兰
9	泰国	泰国	泰国	新西兰	柬埔寨	韩国
10	越南	越南	越南	日本	新西兰	柬埔寨

数据来源:一般贸易为印尼统计局;跨境电商为阿里巴巴国际站。

(二)进口国家(地区)维度

表 4-22 为印度尼西亚一般贸易与跨境电商前十的进口国家(地区)情况。

表 4-22　印度尼西亚一般贸易与跨境电商前十的进口国家(地区)情况

排名	一般贸易(进口前十的国家或地区)			跨境电商(进口需求量前十的国家或地区)		
	2019 年	2020 年	2021 年	2019 年	2020 年	2021 年
1	中国	中国	中国	中国	中国	中国
2	新加坡	新加坡	新加坡	泰国	泰国	越南
3	日本	日本	日本	韩国	越南	泰国
4	泰国	美国	美国	越南	韩国	韩国
5	美国	马来西亚	马来西亚	马来西亚	日本	日本
6	韩国	韩国	韩国	菲律宾	马来西亚	马来西亚
7	马来西亚	泰国	澳大利亚	日本	新加坡	菲律宾
8	澳大利亚	澳大利亚	泰国	新加坡	菲律宾	新加坡
9	印度	印度	印度	澳大利亚	澳大利亚	柬埔寨
10	越南	越南	越南	新西兰	新西兰	缅甸

数据来源:一般贸易为印尼统计局,跨境电商为阿里巴巴国际站。

（三）出口品类维度

表 4-23 为印度尼西亚一般贸易与跨境电商前十的出口品类情况。

表 4-23　印度尼西亚一般贸易与跨境电商前十的出口品类情况

排名	一般贸易（出口前十的品类）			跨境电商（出口需求量前十的品类）		
	2018 年	2019 年	2020 年	2019 年	2020 年	2021 年
1	电气、电子设备	矿物燃料、矿物油及其蒸馏产品	矿物燃料、矿物油及其蒸馏产品	家具和室内装饰品	家具	家具
2	车辆及其零件、附件,但铁道及电车道车辆除外	树胶、树脂及其他植物液、汁	树脂及其他植物液、汁	食品及饮料	医药保健	食品及饮料
3	核反应堆、锅炉、机械器具及零件	电气、电子设备	钢铁	农业	食品及饮料	农业
4	钢铁	车辆及其零件、附件,但铁道及电车道车辆除外	电气、电子设备	服装	美容及个人护理	美容及个人护理
5	天然或养殖珍珠、宝石或半宝石、贵金属、包贵金属及其制品	钢铁	天然或养殖珍珠、宝石或半宝石、贵金属、包贵金属及其制品	美容及个人护理	农业	家居园艺
6	鞋、帽、伞、杖、鞭及其零件	天然或养殖珍珠、宝石或半宝石、贵金属、包贵金属及其制品	车辆及其零件、附件,但铁道及电车道车辆除外	家居用品	消费电子	能源
7	杂项化学产品	橡胶及其制品	橡胶及其制品	能源	能源	服装

排名	一般贸易（出口前十的品类）			跨境电商（出口需求量前十的品类）		
	2018 年	2019 年	2020 年	2019 年	2020 年	2021 年
8	非针织或非钩编的服装及衣着附件	核反应堆、锅炉、机械器具及零件	核反应堆、锅炉、机械器具及零件	建筑	汽车、摩托车	建筑
9	纸、纸板及其制品	非针织或非钩编的服装及衣着附件	鞋、帽、伞、杖、鞭及其零件	医药保健	家居用品	礼品与工艺品
10	针织或钩编的服装及衣着附件	鞋、帽、伞、杖、鞭及其零件	纸、纸板及其制品	运动及娱乐	家居园艺	化工

数据来源：一般贸易为 globalEDGE、World's Top Exports、Connect2India；跨境电商为阿里巴巴国际站。

（四）进口品类维度

表 4-24 为印度尼西亚一般贸易与跨境电商前十的进口品类情况。

表 4-24　印度尼西亚一般贸易与跨境电商前十的进口品类情况

排名	一般贸易（进口前十的品类）			跨境电商（进口需求量前十的品类）		
	2018 年	2019 年	2020 年	2019 年	2020 年	2021 年
1	核反应堆、锅炉、机械器具及零件	核反应堆、锅炉、机械器具及零件	核反应堆、锅炉、机械器具及零件	消费电子	消费电子	消费电子
2	电气、电子设备	矿物燃料、矿物油及其蒸馏产品	电气、电子设备	机械	运动及娱乐	服装
3	钢铁	电气、电子设备	矿物燃料、矿物油及其蒸馏产品	家居用品	机械	运动及娱乐
4	塑料及其制品	钢铁	塑料及其制品	汽车、摩托车	汽车、摩托车	汽车、摩托车
5	车辆及其零件、附件，但铁道及电车道车辆除外	塑料及其制品	钢铁	运动及娱乐	服装	机械

续表

排名	一般贸易(进口前十的品类)			跨境电商(进口需求量前十的品类)		
	2018 年	2019 年	2020 年	2019 年	2020 年	2021 年
6	有机化学品	车辆及其零件、附件,但铁道及电车道车辆除外	有机化学品	服装	五金工具	家居园艺
7	矿物燃料、矿物油及其蒸馏产品	有机化学品	车辆及其零件、附件,但铁道及电车道车辆除外	五金工具	医药保健	五金工具
8	钢铁制品	钢铁制品	谷物	医药保健	安全防护	礼品与工艺品
9	食品工业的残渣及废料;配制的动物饲料	谷物	其他化学产品	美容及个人护理	包装与印刷	鞋靴及配件
10	光学、照相、技术、医疗器械	精密仪器及设备	稻草、秸秆及饲料	电气设备和产品	家居园艺	健康医疗

数据来源:一般贸易为 globalEDGE、World's Top Exports、Connect2India;跨境电商为阿里巴巴国际站。

第七节 泰国跨境电商发展状况

一、泰国社会经济与跨境电商发展概况

2020 年,泰国的 GDP 为 5018 亿美元,人均 GDP 为 7189 美元,同比下降 7.8%。2020 年泰国人口为 6980 万,同比增长 0.25%。其中,有 52% 的人口居住在城市地区,48% 的人口居住在农村地区。

2021 年,泰国互联网用户数为 4859 万,同比增长 7.4%,互联网普及率为 70%;智能手机用户数约为 5357 万,普及率为 77%。根据谷歌、淡马锡和贝恩公司联合发布的《2020 年东南亚电子商务报告》,新冠疫情暴发前,泰国居民每

天平均上网时长约为 3.7 小时,而 2020 年新冠疫情期间,泰国居民每天平均上网时长上升到 4.3 小时。

　　根据泰国电子交易发展署(ETDA)的数据,泰国的电子商务平台分为三类——B2B、B2C 和 B2G,分别占有 55％、29％和 16％的市场份额。2020 年,泰国电子商务市场规模为 1136 亿美元,同比下降 6.6％,而跨境电商规模约为 341 亿美元,占据泰国电子商务市场近 30％的市场份额(见图 4-4)。

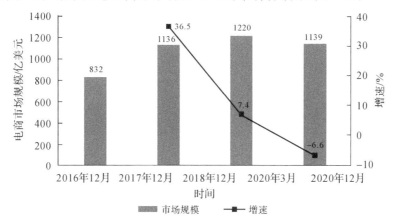

图 4-4　2017—2020 年泰国电子商务市场规模及其增速

数据来源:泰国统计局。

　　泰国流量排名前三的电子商务平台分别是 Shopee、Lazada、Facebook Fanpage。除了电子商务平台,泰国消费者还喜欢在 Line、Instagram、Twitter 等社交媒体平台购买产品。泰国消费者的线上支付方式比较多,信用卡和银行转账是最常使用的方式,市场份额分别为 26％和 27％。据统计,泰国人均拥有 0.93 张借记卡和 0.34 张信用卡,而现金支付和数字钱包的市场份额分别为 20％和 19％。在政府鼓励电子支付和智能手机高普及率的背景下,数字钱包的使用人数在逐渐增加。国内市场占有率较高的电子支付平台包括 TrueMoney 和 PayPal 等。泰国消费者喜欢在社交媒体平台购物,但是与电商平台相比,这些渠道没有综合物流支持,企业必须自行管理物流系统或者外包给其他第三方物流供应商(3PL)。泰国几个主要的物流企业包括 Thailand Post、Kerry Express、DHL 以及 Honestbee GoodShip 等。

二、泰国一般贸易和跨境电商的比较情况

(一)出口国家(地区)维度

表 4-25 为泰国一般贸易与跨境电商前十的出口国家(地区)情况。

表 4-25　泰国一般贸易与跨境电商前十的出口国家(地区)情况

排名	一般贸易(出口前十的国家或地区)			跨境电商(出口需求量前十的国家或地区)		
	2019 年	2020 年	2021 年	2019 年	2020 年	2021 年
1	中国	美国	美国	印度	印度	印度
2	美国	中国	中国	美国	美国	美国
3	日本	日本	日本	巴基斯坦	巴基斯坦	巴基斯坦
4	越南	越南	中国香港	中国	菲律宾	巴西
5	中国香港	中国香港	越南	俄罗斯	马来西亚	孟加拉国
6	马来西亚	马来西亚	澳大利亚	英国	英国	菲律宾
7	印尼	澳大利亚	新加坡	埃及	孟加拉国	沙特
8	新加坡	印尼	马来西亚	加拿大	巴西	印尼
9	菲律宾	新加坡	印尼	土耳其	印尼	埃及
10	印度	印度	瑞士	孟加拉国	沙特	土耳其

数据来源:一般贸易为泰国海关、globalEDGE;跨境电商为阿里巴巴国际站。

(二)进口国家(地区)维度

表 4-26 为泰国一般贸易与跨境电商的前十的进口国家(地区)情况。

表 4-26　泰国一般贸易与跨境电商前十的进口国家(地区)情况

排名	一般贸易(进口前十的国家或地区)			跨境电商(进口需求量前十的国家或地区)		
	2019 年	2020 年	2021 年	2019 年	2020 年	2021 年
1	中国	中国	中国	中国	中国	中国
2	日本	日本	日本	印度	印度	越南
3	马来西亚	美国	美国	越南	越南	印度
4	美国	马来西亚	马来西亚	美国	巴基斯坦	美国
5	新加坡	韩国	韩国	韩国	美国	巴基斯坦
6	阿联酋	阿联酋	新加坡	巴基斯坦	英国	南非

排名	一般贸易（进口前十的国家或地区）			跨境电商（进口需求量前十的国家或地区）		
	2019 年	2020 年	2021 年	2019 年	2020 年	2021 年
7	韩国	新加坡	印尼	中国台湾	韩国	中国香港
8	印尼	印尼	阿联酋	中国香港	南非	英国
9	中国台湾	德国	越南	菲律宾	中国台湾	法国
10	沙特	沙特	德国	英国	日本	中国台湾

数据来源：一般贸易为泰国海关、globalEDGE；跨境电商为阿里巴巴国际站。

（三）出口品类维度

表 4-27 为泰国一般贸易与跨境电商前十的出口品类情况。

表 4-27 泰国一般贸易与跨境电商前十的出口品类情况

排名	一般贸易（出口前十的品类）			跨境电商（出口需求量前十的品类）		
	2019 年	2020 年	2021 年	2019 年	2020 年	2021 年
1	工业机械	工业机械	工业机械	农业	消费电子	农业
2	机电设备	机电设备	机电设备	办公文教用品	农业	食品及饮料
3	车辆及其零件	车辆及其零件	车辆及其零件	消费电子	食品及饮料	消费电子
4	橡胶及其制品	橡胶及其制品	贵金属	食品及饮料	汽车、摩托车	办公文教用品
5	塑料	贵金属	橡胶及其制品	汽车、摩托车	办公文教用品	汽车、摩托车
6	贵金属	塑料	塑料	矿物和冶金	美容及个人护理	美容及个人护理
7	石油和矿物燃料	石油和矿物燃料	肉、鱼	美容及个人护理	安全防护	矿物和冶金
8	肉、鱼	肉、鱼	石油和矿物燃料	橡塑原料及制品	矿物和冶金	鞋靴及配件
9	有机化学品	精密仪器	医疗器械	医药保健	健康医疗	机械
10	木及木制品	有机化学品	水果	家居用品	医药保健	整车及交通

数据来源：一般贸易为泰国海关、globalEDGE；跨境电商为阿里巴巴国际站。

（四）进口品类维度

表 4-28 为泰国一般贸易与跨境电商前十的进口品类情况。

表 4-28 泰国一般贸易与跨境电商前十的进口品类情况

排名	一般贸易（进口前十的品类）			跨境电商（进口需求量前十的品类）		
	2019 年	2020 年	2021 年	2019 年	2020 年	2021 年
1	石油和矿物燃料	机电设备	机电设备	消费电子	机械	消费电子
2	机电设备	石油和矿物燃料	石油和矿物燃料	机械	安全防护	机械
3	工业机械	工业机械	工业机械	家居用品	消费电子	运动及娱乐
4	贵金属	贵金属	车辆及其零件	汽车、摩托车	医药保健	家居园艺
5	钢铁	钢铁	钢铁	服装	汽车、摩托车	汽车、摩托车
6	车辆及其零件	车辆及其零件	塑料	运动及娱乐	五金工具	服装
7	塑料	塑料	贵金属	包装与印刷	包装与印刷	包装与印刷
8	精密仪器	钢铁制品	钢铁制品	五金工具	运动及娱乐	健康医疗
9	有机化学品	精密仪器	医疗器械	美容及个人护理	家居用品	五金工具
10	鱼、甲壳动物	有机化学品	杂项化学产品	电气设备和产品	健康医疗	美容及个人护理

数据来源：一般贸易为泰国海关、globalEDGE；跨境电商为阿里巴巴国际站。

第八节　菲律宾跨境电商发展状况

一、菲律宾社会经济与跨境电商发展概况

2020 年，菲律宾的 GDP 为 3614.89 亿美元，同比增长 −9.57％，比 2019 年减少了 153.34 亿美元；人均 GDP 为 3298.83 美元，同比增长 −10.78％，

比 2019 年减少了 186.51 美元。2020 年,菲律宾国民总收入为 3759.98 亿美元,人均国民总收入为 3430 美元,增速为 -12.58%,比 2019 年减少了 420 美元。

菲律宾银行设施较健全,但包容性不强,导致该国电子支付使用率低。菲律宾有 10700 万人口,其中移动用户数有 7300 万,24 小时在线的有 6700 万。金融普惠程度低的现实也阻碍了该国电子支付方式的普及。新冠疫情期间,由于对接触感染的担忧和政府"强化社区隔离"的要求,菲律宾的数字支付交易量激增。零售电商、外卖送餐和数字商品成为数字支付全新的增长点。菲律宾的数字支付正在逐渐改变这个国家的企业与消费者。菲律宾的数字支付金额从 2016 年的 37.11 亿美元增长到 2020 年的 78.61 亿美元,2020 年菲律宾数字商务规模达到 3.1 亿美元,移动销售终端支付规模达到 49.8 亿美元。

数字化转型一直是菲律宾的一大主题。全国各地的企业都在寻求利用第四次工业革命技术的进步以进入新的发展阶段。5G 服务在菲律宾的推出将加速数字化转型,并为企业带来可观的利益。与此同时,消费者也热切期待 5G 服务的推出,以优化个人设备上的消费体验。菲律宾消费者在流媒体和电商方面的支出已有数十亿美元之多,5G 服务不仅将为他们提供更好的体验,而且还将在全国范围内增强数字连接性。这些趋势将为未来菲律宾的经济增长发挥关键作用。

二、菲律宾一般贸易和跨境电商的比较情况

(一)出口国家(地区)维度

表 4-29 为菲律宾一般贸易与跨境电商前十的出口国家(地区)情况。

表 4-29 菲律宾一般贸易与跨境电商前十的出口国家(地区)情况

排名	一般贸易(出口前十的国家或地区)			跨境电商(出口需求量前十的国家或地区)		
	2019 年	2020 年	2021 年	2019 年	2020 年	2021 年
1	中国香港	美国	日本	印度	美国	美国
2	美国	日本	美国	美国	印度	印度
3	中国	中国	中国	巴基斯坦	英国	巴西
4	日本	中国香港	中国香港	中国	法国	意大利
5	新加坡	新加坡	新加坡	英国	沙特	巴基斯坦
6	德国	韩国	泰国	加拿大	加拿大	印尼
7	韩国	泰国	韩国	沙特	南非	法国
8	泰国	德国	德国	土耳其	巴西	秘鲁
9	中国台湾	荷兰	荷兰	俄罗斯	阿联酋	俄罗斯
10	荷兰	马来西亚	马来西亚	尼日利亚	巴基斯坦	西班牙

数据来源:一般贸易为 globalEDGE、OEC、Trading Economics;跨境电商为阿里巴巴国际站。

(二)进口国家(地区)维度

表 4-30 为菲律宾一般贸易与跨境电商前十的进口国家(地区)情况。

表 4-30 菲律宾一般贸易与跨境电商前十的进口国家(地区)情况

排名	一般贸易(进口前十的国家或地区)			跨境电商(进口需求量前十的国家或地区)		
	2019 年	2020 年	2021 年	2019 年	2020 年	2021 年
1	中国	中国	中国	中国	中国	中国
2	韩国	日本	日本	泰国	日本	巴基斯坦
3	日本	韩国	美国	巴基斯坦	巴基斯坦	印度
4	中国台湾	美国	韩国	印度	印度	美国
5	美国	印尼	印尼	韩国	越南	越南
6	泰国	泰国	新加坡	中国台湾	美国	南非
7	新加坡	新加坡	泰国	美国	韩国	英国
8	印尼	马来西亚	马来西亚	越南	南非	德国
9	马来西亚	越南	越南	中国香港	泰国	中国台湾
10	越南	中国香港	中国香港	日本	中国香港	法国

数据来源:一般贸易为 globalEDGE、OEC、Trading Economics;跨境电商为阿里巴巴国际站。

（三）出口品类维度

表 4-31 为菲律宾一般贸易与跨境电商前十的出口品类情况。

表 4-31　菲律宾一般贸易与跨境电商前十的出口品类情况

排名	一般贸易（出口前十的品类）			跨境电商（出口需求量前十的品类）		
	2019 年	2020 年	2021 年	2019 年	2020 年	2021 年
1	机电设备	电机	电气、电子设备	农业	食品及饮料	汽车、摩托车
2	工业机械	工业机械	机械、核反应堆、锅炉	食品及饮料	美容及个人护理	消费电子
3	精密仪器	水果和坚果	食用水果、坚果、柑橘类水果皮、瓜类	汽车、摩托车	农业	农业
4	食用水果	精密仪器	光学、照相、技术、医疗器械	矿物和冶金	消费电子	机械
5	贵金属	宝石和金属	矿渣和灰	办公文教用品	汽车、摩托车	食品及饮料
6	石油和矿物燃料	铜	铜	美容及个人护理	五金工具	美容及个人护理
7	铜及其制品	矿石	珍珠、宝石、金属、硬币	消费电子	机械	矿物和冶金
8	动植物油脂	石油和矿物燃料	铁路、有轨电车以外的车辆	医药保健	办公文教用品	五金工具
9	矿砂	塑料	动植物油脂、裂解产品	橡塑原料及制品	矿物和冶金	运动及娱乐
10	船舶	汽车及零件	塑料	家居用品	家居园艺	健康医疗

数据来源：一般贸易为 globalEDGE、OEC、Trading Economics；跨境电商为阿里巴巴国际站。

（四）进口品类维度

表 4-32 为菲律宾一般贸易与跨境电商前十的进口品类情况。

表 4-32　菲律宾一般贸易与跨境电商前十的进口品类情况

排名	一般贸易（进口前十的品类）			跨境电商（进口需求量前十的品类）		
	2019 年	2020 年	2021 年	2019 年	2020 年	2021 年
1	机电设备	电机	电气、电子设备	消费电子	消费电子	消费电子
2	石油和矿物燃料	石油和矿物燃料	机械、核反应堆、锅炉	机械	运动及娱乐	家居园艺
3	工业机械	工业机械	矿物燃料、矿物油、蒸馏产品	汽车、摩托车	家居用品	服装
4	车辆及零部件	汽车及零件	铁路、有轨电车以外的车辆	家居用品	服装	汽车、摩托车
5	钢铁	钢铁	钢铁	服装	包装与印刷	运动及娱乐
6	塑料	塑料	塑料	运动及娱乐	汽车、摩托车	家具
7	精密仪器	谷物	谷物	美容及个人护理	健康医疗	机械
8	谷物	飞机	光学、照片、技术、医疗器械	包装与印刷	机械	包装与印刷
9	纸	精密仪器	钢铁制品	医药保健	美容及个人护理	鞋靴及配件
10	杂项食品	钢铁制品	医药产品	箱包	家用电器	玩具

数据来源：一般贸易为 globalEDGE、OEC、Trading Economics；跨境电商为阿里巴巴国际站。

第九节　新加坡跨境电商发展状况

一、新加坡社会经济与跨境电商发展概况

新加坡是一个快速发展的国际商业中心,人均GDP排名亚洲第一。2020年,新加坡的GDP为3400亿美元,人均GDP为59758美元,同比下降9.2%。新加坡是一个完全城市化的国家,新加坡2020年的人口为568万人,同比下降0.31%。

2021年,新加坡互联网用户数为529万,同比增长2.8%,互联网普及率为90%;智能手机用户数约为517万,普及率为88%。根据谷歌、淡马锡和贝恩公司联合发布的《2020年东南亚电子商务报告》,新冠疫情暴发前,新加坡居民每天平均上网时长约为3.6小时,而2020年新冠疫情期间,居民每天平均上网时长上升到4.1小时。

新加坡是亚太地区许多跨境电子商务平台的枢纽。得益于新加坡优惠的税收政策和友好开放的商业环境,Shopee、Lazada、亚马逊和Zalora等许多电子商务公司都在此设立总部。2020年,新加坡社会零售总额为381亿美元,同比下降15%;网上零售总额为48亿美元,同比增长86%,占社会零售总额的12.7%(见图4-5)。跨国网络购物是新加坡电子商务市场的一个重要特征,约78%的网络购物者会选择从国外购买商品。2020年,新加坡跨境电商规模达24亿美元,在电子商务市场上占据55%的市场份额,超过了国内的电子商务市场。

数字经济协议(digital economy agreements,DEA)是在两个或多个经济体之间建立数字贸易规则和数字经济合作的条约,旨在促进本国企业参与国际跨境电商和电子商务活动。截至2021年,新加坡已经完成了四项数字经济协议的谈判。新加坡流量排名前三的电子商务公司分别是Shopee、Lazada、亚马逊,每月的网络访问量分别为1200万、730万和646万。其余的电商平台还包括Qoo10、EZBuy等。新加坡银行卡的整体普及率很高,人

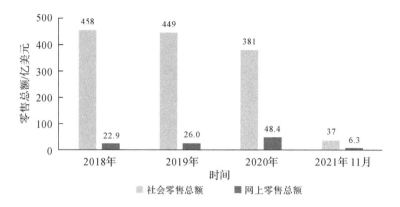

图 4-5　2018—2021 年 11 月新加坡社会零售和网上零售总额

数据来源：新加坡统计局

均大约拥有 1.6 张借记卡和 1.5 张信用卡。目前，信用卡仍然是新加坡最受欢迎的线上支付方式，大约占有 63％的市场份额，而数字钱包和银行转账分别占有 21％、10％的市场份额。与此同时，全国实时电子支付计划 PayNow 正在快速发展，大约有 18.2％的新加坡公民将其作为首选支付方式。新加坡地处国际航运航线的十字路口，是东南亚地区的交通和物流中心。发达的物流基础设施吸引了联邦快递、UPS 和 DHL 等国际物流公司在此设立主要货运枢纽。

二、新加坡一般贸易和跨境电商的比较情况

（一）出口国家（地区）维度

表 4-33 为新加坡一般贸易与跨境电商前十的出口国家（地区）情况。

表 4-33　新加坡一般贸易与跨境电商前十的出口国家（地区）情况

排名	一般贸易（出口前十的国家或地区）			跨境电商（出口需求量前十的国家或地区）		
	2019 年	2020 年	2021 年	2019 年	2020 年	2021 年
1	中国	中国	中国	美国	美国	美国
2	中国香港	中国香港	中国香港	印度	印度	印度
3	马来西亚	马来西亚	美国	中国	英国	巴西
4	美国	美国	马来西亚	俄罗斯	菲律宾	越南
5	印尼	印尼	印尼	英国	加拿大	巴基斯坦

排名	一般贸易（出口前十的国家或地区）			跨境电商（出口需求量前十的国家或地区）		
	2019 年	2020 年	2021 年	2019 年	2020 年	2021 年
6	印度	日本	日本	加拿大	巴基斯坦	孟加拉国
7	日本	泰国	韩国	印尼	印尼	秘鲁
8	中国台湾	韩国	泰国	巴西	沙特	埃及
9	泰国	越南	越南	巴基斯坦	巴西	菲律宾
10	澳大利亚	印度	荷兰	马来西亚	马来西亚	哥伦比亚

数据来源：一般贸易为新加坡海关、globalEDGE；跨境电商为阿里巴巴国际站。

（二）进口国家（地区）维度

表 4-34 为新加坡一般贸易与跨境电商前十的进口国家（地区）情况。

表 4-34　新加坡一般贸易与跨境电商前十的进口国家（地区）情况

排名	一般贸易（进口前十的国家或地区）			跨境电商（进口需求量前十的国家或地区）		
	2019 年	2020 年	2021 年	2019 年	2020 年	2021 年
1	中国	中国	中国	中国	中国	中国
2	马来西亚	美国	马来西亚	印度	印度	印度
3	美国	马来西亚	美国	泰国	越南	越南
4	中国台湾	日本	日本	韩国	泰国	巴基斯坦
5	日本	印尼	韩国	越南	马来西亚	泰国
6	印尼	韩国	印尼	马来西亚	巴基斯坦	中国台湾
7	韩国	法国	法国	中国台湾	韩国	韩国
8	沙特	阿联酋	泰国	巴基斯坦	印尼	美国
9	法国	德国	德国	美国	中国台湾	南非
10	印度	英国	英国	中国香港	美国	中国香港

数据来源：一般贸易为新加坡海关、globalEDGE；跨境电商为阿里巴巴国际站。

（三）出口品类维度

表 4-35 为新加坡一般贸易与跨境电商前十的出口品类情况。

表 4-35　新加坡一般贸易与跨境电商前十的出口品类情况

排名	一般电商（出口前十的品类）			跨境电商（出口需求量前十的品类）		
	2019 年	2020 年	2021 年	2019 年	2020 年	2021 年
1	机电设备	机电设备	机电设备	农业	农业	农业
2	石油和矿物燃料	工业机械	工业机械	食品及饮料	食品及饮料	食品及饮料
3	工业机械	石油和矿物燃料	石油和矿物燃料	汽车、摩托车	机械	机械
4	有机化学品	其他杂环化合物	医疗器械	家居用品	消费电子	消费电子
5	精密仪器	精密仪器	贵金属	机械	汽车、摩托车	汽车、摩托车
6	贵金属	贵金属	未分类	消费电子	安全防护	家居园艺
7	塑料	塑料	塑料	医疗保健	五金工具	商用服务设备
8	药品	有机化学品	有机化学品	能源	家居用品	橡胶原料及制品
9	船舶	化妆品	化妆品	电气设备和产品	健康医疗	健康医疗
10	杂项食品	药品	药品	礼品与工艺品	医药保健	能源

数据来源：一般贸易为新加坡海关、globalEDGE；跨境电商为阿里巴巴国际站。

（四）进口品类维度

表 4-36 为新加坡一般贸易与跨境电商前十的进口品类情况。

表 4-36　新加坡一般贸易与跨境电商前十的进口品类情况

排名	一般贸易（进口前十的品类）			跨境电商（进口需求量前十的品类）		
	2019 年	2020 年	2021 年	2019 年	2020 年	2021 年
1	石油和矿物燃料	机电设备	机电设备	家居用品	包装与印刷	包装与印刷
2	机电设备	石油和矿物燃料	工业机械	包装与印刷	消费电子	家居园艺

排名	一般贸易(进口前十的品类)			跨境电商(进口需求量前十的品类)		
	2019 年	2020 年	2021 年	2019 年	2020 年	2021 年
3	工业机械	工业机械	石油和矿物燃料	消费电子	美容及个人护理	消费电子
4	贵金属	贵金属	贵金属	服装	安全防护	机械
5	精密仪器	精密仪器	医疗器械	美容及个人护理	服装	服装
6	船舶	航空器	塑料	机械	医药保健	家具
7	塑料	塑料	有机化学品	箱包	家居园艺	运动及娱乐
8	航空器	有机化学品	航空器	礼品与工艺品	机械	美容及个人护理
9	有机化学品	车辆及其零件	化妆品	运动及娱乐	运动及娱乐	健康医疗
10	杂项化学产品	化妆品	杂项化学产品	建筑	家居用品	礼品与工艺品

数据来源:一般贸易为新加坡海关、globalEDGE;跨境电商为阿里巴巴国际站。

第十节　马来西亚跨境电商发展状况

一、马来西亚社会经济与跨境电商发展概况

2020 年,马来西亚的 GDP 为 3367 亿美元,人均 GDP 为 10402 美元,同比下降 8.2%。2020 年马来西亚人口为 3237 万人,同比增长 1.3%。其中,有 77% 的人口居住在城市地区,23% 的人口居住在农村地区。

2021 年,马来西亚互联网用户数为 2743 万人,同比增长 2.8%,互联网普及率为 84%;智能手机用户数约为 2836 万,普及率达到 87%。根据谷歌、淡马锡和贝恩公司联合发布的《2020 年东南亚电子商务报告》,新冠疫情暴发前,马来西亚居民每天平均上网时长约为 3.7 小时,而 2020 年新冠疫情期间,马来西亚居民每天平均上网时长上升到 4.2 小时。2020 年,马来西亚

电子商务市场规模为 72 亿美元,同比上升 24.8%(见图 4-6),而跨境电商规模达到 33 亿美元,在电子商务市场占有 45% 的市场份额。

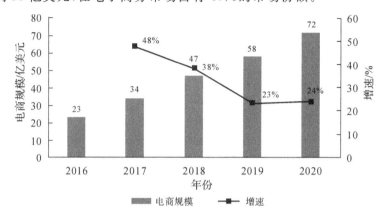

图 4-6   2016—2020 年马来西亚电子商务市场规模及其增速

数据来源:马来西亚统计局。

为了促进电子商务的发展,马来西亚政府于 2021 年批准了国家电子商务战略蓝图(National eCommerce Strategic Roadmap 2.0,NESR 2.0),旨在通过数字化提高经济竞争力和构建数字型社会。马来西亚流量排名前三的电子商务公司分别是 Shopee、Lazada、PG Mall,每月的网络访问量分别为5400 万、1375 万和 706 万。其余的电商平台还包括 LeLong、Qoo10 等。

银行转账是马来西亚最重要的支付方式,占有 45% 的市场份额。第二大支付方式是卡支付,大约占 36% 的市场份额。据统计,马来西亚人均拥有1.33 张借记卡和 0.32 张信用卡。现金支付方式的比例虽然正在逐渐降低,但仍然占 10% 的市场份额。而数字钱包仅占 6% 的市场份额,PayPal、Visa Checkout 和 Masterpass 都是比较受欢迎的电子支付方式。在马来西亚运营数字钱包需要拥有政府颁发的数字货币许可证,其他获得许可的国际支付品牌还包括支付宝、微信和谷歌支付等。马来西亚的供应链和物流部门非常分散,有大量的中小企业参与,而大型的物流企业包括 NEC、Fujitsu、DHL 和 Pos Malaysia 等。

二、马来西亚一般贸易和跨境电商的比较情况

（一）出口国家（地区）维度

表 4-37 为马来西亚一般贸易与跨境电商前十的出口国家（地区）情况。

表 4-37　马来西亚一般贸易与跨境电商前十的出口国家（地区）情况

排名	一般贸易（出口前十的国家或地区）			跨境电商（出口需求量前十的国家或地区）		
	2019 年	2020 年	2021 年	2019 年	2020 年	2021 年
1	新加坡	中国	中国	美国	美国	美国
2	中国	新加坡	新加坡	印度	印度	印度
3	美国	美国	美国	中国	中国	法国
4	中国香港	中国香港	中国香港	加拿大	法国	巴西
5	日本	日本	日本	英国	英国	菲律宾
6	泰国	泰国	泰国	沙特	菲律宾	巴基斯坦
7	印度	印度	韩国	印尼	土耳其	印尼
8	韩国	越南	越南	法国	巴基斯坦	埃及
9	墨西哥	韩国	印度	俄罗斯	意大利	加拿大
10	中国台湾	印尼	印尼	巴基斯坦	加拿大	英国

数据来源：一般贸易为马来西亚海关、globalEDGE；跨境电商为阿里巴巴国际站。

（二）进口国家（地区）维度

表 4-38 为马来西亚一般贸易与跨境电商的前十的进口国家（地区）情况。

表 4-38　马来西亚一般贸易与跨境电商前十的进口国家（地区）情况

排名	一般贸易（进口前十的国家或地区）			跨境电商（进口需求量前十的国家或地区）		
	2019 年	2020 年	2021 年	2019 年	2020 年	2021 年
1	中国	中国	中国	中国	中国	中国
2	新加坡	新加坡	新加坡	印度	印度	印度
3	日本	美国	美国	泰国	泰国	越南
4	美国	日本	日本	巴基斯坦	越南	南非

续表

排名	一般贸易（进口前十的国家或地区）			跨境电商（进口需求量前十的国家或地区）		
	2019 年	2020 年	2021 年	2019 年	2020 年	2021 年
5	泰国	泰国	韩国	越南	巴基斯坦	巴基斯坦
6	中国台湾	印尼	印尼	韩国	美国	泰国
7	印尼	韩国	泰国	美国	英国	美国
8	韩国	德国	印度	中国台湾	南非	英国
9	印度	印度	德国	菲律宾	韩国	法国
10	德国	澳大利亚	澳大利亚	英国	日本	德国

数据来源：一般贸易为马来西亚海关、globalEDGE；跨境电商为阿里巴巴国际站。

（三）出口品类维度

表 4-39 为马来西亚一般贸易与跨境电商前十的出口品类情况。

表 4-39　马来西亚一般贸易与跨境电商前十的出口品类情况

排名	一般贸易（出口前十的品类）			跨境电商（出口需求量前十的品类）		
	2019 年	2020 年	2021 年	2019 年	2020 年	2021 年
1	机电设备	机电设备	机电设备	食品及饮料	健康医疗	食品及饮料
2	石油和矿物燃料	石油和矿物燃料	石油和矿物燃料	汽车、摩托车	食品及饮料	机械
3	工业机械	工业机械	工业机械	医药保健	安全防护	农业
4	动植物油脂	动植物油脂	动植物油脂	机械	机械	汽车、摩托车
5	精密仪器	精密仪器	橡胶及其制品	农业	医药保健	健康医疗
6	塑料	塑料	医疗器械	消费电子	汽车、摩托车	家居园艺
7	橡胶及其制品	橡胶及其制品	塑料	家居用品	农业	家具
8	有机化学品	钢铁	钢铁	美容及个人护理	美容及个人护理	建筑
9	木及木制品	杂项化学产品	杂项化学产品	建筑	家居用品	消费电子

排名	一般贸易（出口前十的品类）			跨境电商（出口需求量前十的品类）		
	2019 年	2020 年	2021 年	2019 年	2020 年	2021 年
10	铝及其制品	有机化学品	铝及其制品	家具和室内装饰品	消费电子	美容及个人护理

数据来源：一般贸易为马来西亚海关、globalEDGE；跨境电商为阿里巴巴国际站。

（四）进口品类维度

表 4-40 为马来西亚一般贸易与跨境电商前十的进口品类情况。

表 4-40　马来西亚一般贸易与跨境电商前十的进口品类情况

排名	一般贸易（进口前十的品类）			跨境电商（进口需求量前十的品类）		
	2019 年	2020 年	2021 年	2019 年	2020 年	2021 年
1	机电设备	机电设备	机电设备	消费电子	机械	消费电子
2	石油和矿物燃料	石油和矿物燃料	石油和矿物燃料	机械	消费电子	机械
3	工业机械	工业机械	工业机械	家居用品	包装与印刷	家居园艺
4	塑料	塑料	塑料	服装	安全防护	汽车、摩托车
5	车辆及其零件	钢铁	医疗器械	包装与印刷	汽车、摩托车	运动及娱乐
6	钢铁	车辆及其零件	钢铁	汽车、摩托车	医药保健	服装
7	精密仪器	精密仪器	铝及其制品	美容及个人护理	服装	包装与印刷
8	贵金属	贵金属	车辆及其零件	运动及娱乐	美容及个人护理	家具
9	有机化学品	有机化学品	贵金属	医药保健	运动及娱乐	美容及个人护理
10	橡胶及其制品	杂项化学产品	橡胶及其制品	五金工具	家居用品	健康医疗

数据来源：一般贸易为马来西亚海关、globalEDGE；跨境电商为阿里巴巴国际站。

第十一节　越南跨境电商发展状况

一、越南社会经济与跨境电商发展概况

2020 年,越南的 GDP 达到 2712 亿美元,增速达 2.91%,GDP 比 2015 年增长约 1.4 倍(根据国际货币基金组织的数据,2020 年,越南可能成为东盟排名第四的经济体)。由此,越南跻身世界 GDP 增长最高国家行列。2020 年,越南人均 GDP 约为 2750 美元。同时,越南进出口总额增长 2.3 倍,从 2010 年的 1571 亿美元增加到 2019 年的 5170 亿美元。2020 年,由于新冠疫情的严重影响,进出口总额约为 5270 亿美元,相当于 GDP 的 190% 以上。出口总额迅速增长,从 2010 年的 722 亿美元增长到 2020 年的约 2670 亿美元,平均每年增长 14%,因此商品贸易顺差达到创纪录的 191 亿美元。2020 年,越南人口为 9733.86 万人,比 2019 年增长了 87.65 万人,人口增长率为 0.9%。2020 年,越南 65 岁及以上人口占比为 8%,已步入老龄化社会;性别上看,女性人口也相对多于男性。2020 年,越南城镇化率为 37.3%,城镇化率在逐年稳步提高。

越南的互联网发展走在发展中国家前列,目前超过 70% 的老百姓都在使用智能手机,互联网渗透率约为 66%。其电商渗透率(在互联网用户中)约为 77%,电商用户总数高达 5000 万,超过全球的平均水平(46.5%)。根据谷歌、淡马锡和贝恩公司联合发布的《2021 年东南亚互联网经济报道》,越南的互联网经济 2021 年预计将增长 31%,达到 210 亿美元,其中电商营收为 130 亿美元,与马来西亚持平。

Visa 的一项研究显示,2020 年,越南的电子钱包用户和支付应用程序显著增加,超过 85% 的消费者至少拥有 1 种无现金支付方式,其中 71% 的消费者每周至少使用 1 次。虽然目前最受欢迎的付款方式仍然是货到付款;Statista 的一项调查显示,78% 的网购者仍然更喜欢用现金支付网购费用;但随着 Momo、Zalopay 等电子钱包的强势发展,数字支付的繁荣指日可

待。展望未来,预计2025年,越南电商总营收将达390亿美元,超越泰国的350亿美元,排名东南亚第二。根据iPrice的报告,目前越南最常用的电子商务平台分别是Shopee、Lazada、Tiki和Sendo。该报告表明,越南的电子商务市场正逐渐成熟,平台获取流量的渠道和方法更加多样化了,不再拘泥于折扣形式。

二、越南一般贸易和跨境电商的比较情况

(一)出口国家(地区)维度

表4-41为越南一般贸易与跨境电商前十的出口国家(地区)情况。

表 4-41　越南一般贸易与跨境电商前十的出口国家(地区)情况

排名	一般贸易(出口前十的国家或地区)			跨境电商(出口需求量前十的国家或地区)		
	2019 年	2020 年	2021 年	2019 年	2020 年	2021 年
1	美国	美国	美国	美国	美国	美国
2	中国	中国	中国	印度	印度	印度
3	日本	日本	日本	英国	英国	巴西
4	韩国	韩国	韩国	中国	加拿大	英国
5	德国	中国香港	中国香港	尼日利亚	澳大利亚	加拿大
6	中国香港	荷兰	荷兰	加拿大	菲律宾	菲律宾
7	印度	印度	德国	澳大利亚	巴西	法国
8	荷兰	德国	印度	俄罗斯	尼日利亚	沙特
9	阿联酋	英国	英国	巴西	沙特	巴基斯坦
10	泰国	泰国	泰国	法国	法国	西班牙

数据来源:一般贸易为globalEDGE、OEC、Trading Economics;跨境电商为阿里巴巴国际站。

(二)进口国家(地区)维度

表4-42为越南一般贸易与跨境电商前十的进口国家(地区)情况。

表 4-42　越南一般贸易与跨境电商前十的进口国家(地区)情况

排名	一般贸易(进口前十的国家或地区)			跨境电商(进口需求量前十的国家或地区)		
	2019 年	2020 年	2021 年	2019 年	2020 年	2021 年
1	中国	中国	中国	中国	中国	中国
2	韩国	韩国	韩国	泰国	泰国	美国
3	日本	日本	日本	印度	美国	法国
4	泰国	美国	美国	美国	南非	印度
5	中国台湾	泰国	泰国	韩国	印度	巴基斯坦
6	美国	马来西亚	马来西亚	中国台湾	韩国	南非
7	马来西亚	印尼	印尼	德国	巴基斯坦	泰国
8	新加坡	印度	澳大利亚	中国香港	马来西亚	英国
9	印度	澳大利亚	印度	马来西亚	英国	德国
10	德国	新加坡	爱尔兰	巴基斯坦	中国台湾	日本

数据来源:一般贸易为 globalEDGE、OEC、Trading Economics;跨境电商为阿里巴巴国际站。

(三)出口品类维度

表 4-43 为越南一般贸易与跨境电商前十的出口品类情况。

表 4-43　越南一般贸易与跨境电商前十的出口品类情况

排名	一般贸易(出口前十的品类)			跨境电商(出口需求量前十的品类)		
	2019 年	2020 年	2021 年	2019 年	2020 年	2021 年
1	机电设备	电机	电气、电子设备	美容及个人护理	美容及个人护理	美容及个人护理
2	鞋靴	鞋类	机械、核反应堆、锅炉	消费电子	消费电子	家居园艺
3	非针织服装	非针织服装	鞋类、紧身裤等	食品及饮料	家居用品	食品及饮料
4	工业机械	针织服装	针织或钩编服装	家居用品	食品及饮料	农业
5	针织服装	工业机械	非针织或钩编服装	农业	农业	家具

排名	一般贸易（出口前十的品类）			跨境电商（出口需求量前十的品类）		
	2019年	2020年	2021年	2019年	2020年	2021年
6	家具	家具	家具、照明标志、装配式建筑	服装	服装	服装
7	鱼	海鲜	鱼类、甲壳类动物、软体动物、水生无脊椎动物	建筑	家具	机械
8	水果	水果和坚果	铁和钢	箱包	安全防护	消费电子
9	精密仪器	精密仪器	塑料	家具和室内装饰品	健康医疗	建筑
10	塑料	塑料	食用水果、坚果、柑橘类水果皮、瓜类	机械	机械	运动及娱乐

数据来源：一般贸易为globalEDGE、OEC、Trading Economics；跨境电商为阿里巴巴国际站。

（四）进口品类维度

表4-44为越南一般贸易与跨境电商前十的进口品类情况。

表4-44　越南一般贸易与跨境电商前十的进口品类情况

排名	一般贸易（进口前十的品类）			跨境电商（进口需求量前十的品类）		
	2019年	2020年	2021年	2019年	2020年	2021年
1	机电设备	电机	矿渣和灰	消费电子	医药保健	消费电子
2	工业机械	工业机械	未按种类指定的商品	机械	机械	机械
3	石油和矿物燃料	塑料	矿物燃料、矿物油、蒸馏产品	电气设备和产品	消费电子	汽车、摩托车
4	塑料	石油和矿物燃料	珍珠、宝石、金属、硬币	汽车、摩托车	安全防护	运动及娱乐

续表

排名	一般贸易(进口前十的品类)			跨境电商(进口需求量前十的品类)		
	2019 年	2020 年	2021 年	2019 年	2020 年	2021 年
5	钢铁	钢铁	肉类及食用内脏	家居用品	五金工具	五金工具
6	精密仪器	精密仪器	机械、核反应堆、锅炉	五金工具	汽车、摩托车	家居园艺
7	车辆及零部件	汽车及零件	谷物	医药保健	家居用品	美容及个人护理
8	水果	针织面料	医药产品	运动及娱乐	运动及娱乐	健康医疗
9	鱼	棉花	电气、电子设备	美容及个人护理	电气设备及用品	电气设备及用品
10	有机化学品	钢铁制品	铝	包装与印刷	包装与印刷	服装

数据来源:一般贸易为 globalEDGE、OEC、Trading Economics;跨境电商为阿里巴巴国际站。

第十二节　缅甸跨境电商发展状况

一、缅甸社会经济与跨境电商发展概况

世界银行数据显示,2020 年,缅甸的 GDP 达 798.52 亿美元,同比上涨 3.17%;人均 GDP 为 1467.60 美元,同比上涨 2.48%。与此同时,2020 年,缅甸人口达 5440.98 万人。

缅甸的数字基础设施尚不完善。截至 2021 年 1 月,缅甸互联网用户总数为 2365 万,同比增长 12%,互联网普及率为 43%。移动手机用户数量为 6943 万,同比下跌 0.9%,移动手机普及率达 127%。缅甸的网络零售发展较为滞后。截至 2019 年,缅甸网络零售规模仅为 600 万美元,不足零售市场总规模的 1%,但 Statista 的分析师认为其网络零售发展潜力巨大。2015 年,2C2P 和 MPU 推出了缅甸第一个线上支付平台。2020 年,缅甸中央银行首度推出线上银行服务。目前,缅甸排名前三的电商平台为 Shop MM、

Spree、365Myanmar。

缅甸政府逐渐认识到跨境电商的重要性，并开始鼓励电子商务的发展。2020 年，政府成立了数字贸易和电子商务发展小组委员会（DTECD）。委员会积极联通私营部门和公共部门，根据私营部门的反馈调整相关监管措施，以鼓励企业实现数字化转型。此外，该委员会的主要目标还包括通过电子商务增加农村人口收入。

二、缅甸一般贸易和跨境电商的比较情况

（一）出口国家（地区）维度

表 4-45 为缅甸一般贸易与跨境电商前十的出口国家（地区）情况。

表 4-45　缅甸一般贸易与跨境电商前十的出口国家（地区）情况

排名	一般贸易（出口前十的国家或地区）			跨境电商（出口需求量前十的国家或地区）		
	2018 年	2019 年	2020 年	2019 年	2020 年	2021 年
1	中国	中国	中国	中国	中国	菲律宾
2	泰国	泰国	泰国	越南	泰国	印尼
3	日本	日本	日本	泰国	菲律宾	马来西亚
4	印度	美国	美国	印尼	马来西亚	澳大利亚
5	香港	德国	印度	马来西亚	越南	越南
6	德国	印度	英国	韩国	澳大利亚	柬埔寨
7	新加坡	西班牙	西班牙	新加坡	韩国	中国
8	美国	英国	德国	菲律宾	印尼	泰国
9	韩国	韩国	荷兰	澳大利亚	新加坡	新加坡
10	英国	荷兰	韩国	柬埔寨	日本	日本

数据来源：一般贸易为缅甸中央统计局；跨境电商为阿里巴巴国际站。

（二）进口国家（地区）维度

表 4-46 为缅甸一般贸易与跨境电商前十的进口国家（地区）情况。

表 4-46　缅甸一般贸易与跨境电商前十的进口国家(地区)情况

排名	一般贸易(进口前十的国家或地区)			跨境电商(进口需求量前十的国家或地区)		
	2018 年	2019 年	2020 年	2019 年	2020 年	2021 年
1	中国	中国	中国	中国	中国	中国
2	新加坡	新加坡	新加坡	泰国	泰国	泰国
3	泰国	泰国	泰国	越南	越南	越南
4	印度	马来西亚	印尼	韩国	日本	日本
5	印尼	印尼	马来西亚	日本	韩国	韩国
6	马来西亚	印度	印度	马来西亚	马来西亚	马来西亚
7	日本	越南	韩国	菲律宾	菲律宾	新加坡
8	越南	日本	越南	新加坡	新加坡	印尼
9	韩国	韩国	日本	印尼	印尼	菲律宾
10	美国	美国	美国	澳大利亚	澳大利亚	澳大利亚

数据来源:一般贸易为缅甸中央统计局;跨境电商为阿里巴巴国际站。

(三)出口品类维度

表 4-47 为缅甸一般贸易与跨境电商前十的出口品类情况。

表 4-47　缅甸一般贸易与跨境电商前十的出口品类情况

排名	一般贸易(出口前十的品类)			跨境电商(出口需求量前十的品类)		
	2018 年	2019 年	2020 年	2019 年	2020 年	2021 年
1	服装	服装	服装	农业	服装	服装
2	气体燃料	气体燃料	气体燃料	美容及个人护理	农业	消费电子
3	基础金属	基础金属	基础金属	食品及饮料	箱包	农业
4	大米	大米	大米	汽车、摩托车	食品及饮料	汽车、摩托车
5	翡翠	翡翠	鱼与鱼肉制品	矿物和冶金	美容及个人护理	家具
6	鱼与鱼肉制品	鱼与鱼肉制品	黑吉豆	消费电子	汽车、摩托车	整车及交通

排名	一般贸易（出口前十的品类）			跨境电商（出口需求量前十的品类）		
	2018 年	2019 年	2020 年	2019 年	2020 年	2021 年
7	黑吉豆	绿豆	绿豆	商务服务	安全防护	家用电器
8	绿豆	黑吉豆	玉米	箱包	商务服务	面料及纺织原材料
9	玉米	生橡胶	生橡胶	建筑	面料及纺织原材料	五金工具
10	生橡胶	花生种子	花生种子	手表、珠宝、眼镜	家具	食品及饮料

数据来源：一般贸易为缅甸中央统计局；跨境电商为阿里巴巴国际站。

（四）进口品类维度

表 4-48 为缅甸一般贸易与跨境电商前十的进口品类情况。

表 4-48　缅甸一般贸易与跨境电商前十的进口品类情况

排名	一般贸易（进口前十的品类）			跨境电商（进口需求量前十的品类）		
	2018 年	2019 年	2020 年	2019 年	2020 年	2021 年
1	矿物燃料	矿物燃料	非电动机械和运输设备	消费电子	消费电子	消费电子
2	核反应堆、锅炉、机械器具及零件	非电动机械和运输设备	精制矿物油	机械	机械	玩具
3	非电动机械和运输设备	基础金属及制品	电气、电子设备	汽车、摩托车	汽车、摩托车	服装
4	电气、电子设备	电气、电子设备	基础金属及制品	服装	服装	健康医疗
5	人造纤维	人造纤维	人造纤维	家居用品	包装与印刷	机械
6	塑料及其制品	塑料及其制品	塑料及其制品	医药保健	运动及娱乐	运动及娱乐
7	食用植物油	食用植物油	食用植物油	五金工具	运动及娱乐	汽车、摩托车
8	药品	药品	药品	电气设备和产品	健康医疗	家居园艺

续表

排名	一般贸易(进口前十的品类)			跨境电商(进口需求量前十的品类)		
	2018 年	2019 年	2020 年	2019 年	2020 年	2021 年
9	肥料	肥料	肥料	包装与印刷	医药保健	美容及个人护理
10	纸、纸板及其制品	纸、纸板及其制品	煤和焦炭	美容及个人护理	家居园艺	包装与印刷

数据来源:一般贸易为缅甸中央统计局;跨境电商为阿里巴巴国际站。

第十三节　柬埔寨跨境电商发展状况

一、柬埔寨社会经济与跨境电商发展概况

2020 年,柬埔寨的 GDP 为 252.9 亿美元,人均 GDP 为 1512.73 美元,同比下降 6.6%。2020 年,柬埔寨人口为 1672 万人,同比增长 1.4%。其中,有 24.5% 的人口居住在城市地区,75.5% 的人口居住在农村地区。

2021 年,柬埔寨互联网用户数为 886 万,同比增长 14%,互联网普及率为 53%。另外,柬埔寨约有 1000 多万部智能手机连接到互联网,移动互联网接入价格实惠,处于全球最低水平,大约 0.13 美元/GB。和东南亚其他国家相比,由于互联网基础设施不完善、物流业发展落后、消费者受众不足和信用卡等电子支付体系落后等限制,柬埔寨的电子商务市场相对欠发达。2021 年,柬埔寨年电子商务市场的规模为 9.71 亿美元,同比增长 19%(见图 4-7)。

2020 年,柬埔寨推出电子商务发展战略(E-Commerce Strategy),旨在发展数字经济,促进贸易发展。柬埔寨最受欢迎的电子商务平台是 Glad Market、Mall855 和 MAIO Mall。其余的电商平台还包括 RoseRb、Aliexpress、淘宝等。同时,人们还喜欢在 Facebook 等社交媒体上进行线上购物。在柬埔寨,绝大部分的交易都是通过现金结算的。但近几年随着金融科技的快速发展,越来越多的柬埔寨人开始使用智能手机进行各种电子

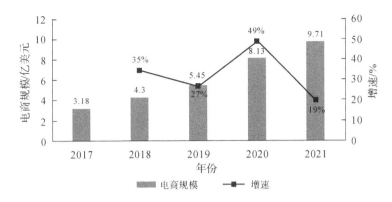

图 4-7　2017—2021 年柬埔寨电子商务市场规模及增速

数据来源:柬埔寨统计局。

支付,包括二维码支付、电子钱包和银行转账、手机充值、账单支付、叫车和购物等。许多第三方支付平台应运而生,例如 ABA PAY、Dura Pay、Mpay 等。

柬埔寨的交通基础设施相对落后,物流成本较高,这极大影响了电子商务的发展。公路运输是柬埔寨的主要运输方式,在客运和货运中所占比重约为 90%,而水路运输和铁路运输所占比重则较小。虽然水路运输在柬埔寨货运部门中所占比重很小,但两个国际港口——金边自治港(PPAP)和西哈努克自治港(SAP)——对柬埔寨的出口贸易和经济发展起着重要作用。

二、柬埔寨一般贸易和跨境电商的比较情况

(一)出口国家(地区)维度

表 4-49 为柬埔寨一般贸易与跨境电商前十的出口国家(地区)情况。

表 4-49　柬埔寨一般贸易与跨境电商前十的出口国家(地区)情况

排名	一般贸易(出口前十的国家或地区)			跨境电商(出口需求量前十的国家或地区)		
	2019 年	2020 年	2021 年	2019 年	2020 年	2021 年
1	美国	美国	美国	美国	美国	美国
2	德国	日本	新加坡	印度	秘鲁	秘鲁
3	日本	德国	中国	中国	印度	埃及

续表

排名	一般贸易（出口前十的国家或地区）			跨境电商（出口需求量前十的国家或地区）		
	2019 年	2020 年	2021 年	2019 年	2020 年	2021 年
4	英国	中国	日本	沙特	沙特	智利
5	中国	英国	德国	俄罗斯	英国	巴西
6	法国	加拿大	英国	埃及	加拿大	印尼
7	加拿大	比利时	加拿大	秘鲁	俄罗斯	加拿大
8	越南	西班牙	中国香港	澳大利亚	尼日利亚	哥伦比亚
9	西班牙	泰国	泰国	加拿大	埃及	沙特
10	泰国	荷兰	比利时	英国	中国	菲律宾

数据来源：一般贸易为柬埔寨海关总署、globalEDGE；跨境电商为阿里巴巴国际站。

（二）进口国家（地区）维度

表 4-50 为柬埔寨一般贸易与跨境电商的前十的进口国家（地区）情况。

表 4-50　柬埔寨一般贸易与跨境电商前十的进口国家（地区）情况

排名	一般贸易（进口前十的国家或地区）			跨境电商（进口需求量前十的国家或地区）		
	2019 年	2020 年	2021 年	2019 年	2020 年	2021 年
1	泰国	中国	中国	中国	中国	中国
2	中国	泰国	泰国	泰国	泰国	越南
3	新加坡	越南	越南	韩国	越南	巴基斯坦
4	越南	日本	新加坡	越南	韩国	美国
5	中国台湾	印尼	印尼	美国	印度	泰国
6	韩国	韩国	日本	印度	美国	印度
7	中国香港	新加坡	韩国	中国香港	巴基斯坦	韩国
8	印尼	马来西亚	中国香港	日本	英国	英国
9	美国	中国香港	瑞士	巴基斯坦	日本	日本
10	马来西亚	美国	马来西亚	中国台湾	南非	法国

数据来源：一般贸易为柬埔寨海关总署、globalEDGE；跨境电商为阿里巴巴国际站。

（三）出口品类维度

表 4-51 为柬埔寨一般贸易与跨境电商前十的出口品类情况。

表 4-51　柬埔寨一般贸易与跨境电商前十的出口品类情况

排名	一般贸易(出口前十的品类)			跨境电商(出口需求量前十的品类)		
	2019 年	2020 年	2021 年	2019 年	2020 年	2021 年
1	针织服装	针织服装	针织服装	机械	机械	机械
2	非针织服装	非针织服装	贵金属	电子元器件、模组、附件及通信	电子元器件、模组、附件及通信	电子元器件、模组、附件及通信
3	鞋类	鞋类	非针织服装	通信	美容及个人护理	美容及个人护理
4	皮革制品	皮革制品	鞋类	美容及个人护理	农业	物料搬运
5	机电设备	机电设备	皮革制品	农业	食品及饮料	食品及饮料
6	车辆及其零件	车辆及其零件	机电设备	食品及饮料	消费电子	健康医疗
7	谷物	贵金属	家具	消费电子	健康医疗	家纺
8	蔬菜	谷物	车辆及其零件	机械设备	医药保健	消费电子
9	水果	家具	谷物	建筑	汽车、摩托车	服装
10	塑料	皮毛	印刷书籍	医药保健	家纺	农业

数据来源:一般贸易为柬埔寨海关总署、globalEDGE;跨境电商为阿里巴巴国际站。

(四)进口品类维度

表 4-52 为柬埔寨一般贸易与跨境电商前十的进口品类情况。

表 4-52　柬埔寨一般贸易与跨境电商前十的进口品类情况

排名	一般贸易(进口前十的品类)			跨境贸易(进口需求量前十的品类)		
	2019 年	2020 年	2021 年	2019 年	2020 年	2021 年
1	贵金属	针织织物	针织面料	消费电子	消费电子	消费电子
2	石油和矿物燃料	车辆及其零件	石油和矿物燃料	美容及个人护理	服装	玩具
3	针织织物	石油和矿物燃料	车辆及其零件	服装	美容及个人护理	服装

续表

排名	一般贸易(进口前十的品类)			跨境贸易(进口需求量前十的品类)		
	2019 年	2020 年	2021 年	2019 年	2020 年	2021 年
4	车辆及其零件	工业机械	工业机械	汽车、摩托车	汽车、摩托车	运动及娱乐
5	工业机械	机电设备	机电设备	家居用品	运动及娱乐	汽车、摩托车
6	机电设备	人造纤维	贵金属	箱包	机械	家居园艺
7	钢铁	塑料	人造纤维	机械	安全防护	美容及个人护理
8	棉	棉	塑料	手表、珠宝、眼镜	医药保健	机械
9	塑料	钢铁	纸	医药保健	玩具	健康医疗
10	酒	纸	棉	家用电器	家居用品	手表、珠宝、眼镜

数据来源:一般贸易为柬埔寨海关总署、globalEDGE;跨境电商为阿里巴巴国际站。

第十四节　老挝跨境电商发展状况

一、老挝社会经济与跨境电商发展概况

2020 年,老挝的 GDP 总量为 191.36 亿美元,人均 GDP 为 2546 美元。2020 年,老挝人口总数为 727.56 万人,比 2019 年增长了 10.61 万人,人口增长率为 1.5%。2020 年,老挝 65 岁及以上人口占比为 4%,尚未步入老龄化社会。从性别上看,男性人口也相对多于女性。2020 年,老挝城镇化率为 36.3%,城镇化率在逐年稳步提高。

老挝互联网基础设施连接性较弱,在东盟国家中连接比例最低,老挝的人均移动宽带用户数量在东盟地区排名倒数第二。2020 年,老挝互联网用户数为 310 万,比 2019 年增长 6.5%,互联网的普及率达到 43%。老挝政府将每年接收贷款和援助的 60% 以上,即 4800 万—6000 万美元用于公路和

桥梁建设,以进一步降低运输成本,促进老挝与邻国之间高效的跨境贸易和运输。在老挝的社交媒体中,Facebook、YouTube 和 Twitter 的用户渗透率最高,分别占 58.97%、24.94% 和 11.26%,它们是老挝民众获取信息最重要的新媒体平台。老挝网购达人们也更习惯在社交平台上进行购物。

国际上通常用联合国贸易和发展会议(UNCTAD)B2C 电子商务指数和国际电信联盟 ICT 发展指数(IDI)两个通用指数来衡量一个国家的电子商务发展概况。2020 年,老挝的 UNCTAD B2C 电子商务指数在接受调查的 151 个国家中排名第 98 位。在该指数中,尽管在其他指标中得分较低,老挝在邮政可靠性方面的表现非常出色。老挝在邮政可靠性方面获得了 85 分(满分 100 分),超过了中国(61 分)、印度(54 分)和马来西亚(80 分),在前 10 名发展中经济体名单中排名第五。这有力地促使老挝加强其邮政系统,同时提高其他 3 个指标的表现,以便更好地为发展电子商务做准备。

国际电信联盟的 ICT 发展指数(IDI)包含 11 个衡量 ICT 接入、使用和技能等关键方面的指标。2019 年,国际电信联盟的 ICT 发展指数(IDI)中,老挝在 176 个国家中排名第 139 位,整体呈现出良好的发展态势,从 2018 年的第 144 位攀升至第 139 位,但落后于分别排名 134 位、135 位的印度和缅甸。应中国工业和信息化部国际经济技术合作中心邀请,老挝邮政通信部国家互联网中心、规划与合作司、信息通信技术司代表出席了中国—东盟数字经济发展与合作研讨会,介绍了"2016—2025 年 ICT 战略发展计划及 2030 年前发展愿景",其为老挝正在实施的 ICT 以及数字领域的国家战略。

二、老挝一般贸易和跨境电商的比较情况

(一)出口国家(地区)维度

表 4-53 为老挝一般贸易与跨境电商前十的出口国家(地区)情况。

表 4-53　老挝一般贸易与跨境电商前十的出口国家(地区)情况

排名	一般贸易(出口前十的国家或地区)			跨境电商(出口需求量前十的国家或地区)		
	2019 年	2020 年	2021 年	2019 年	2020 年	2021 年
1	泰国	泰国	泰国	美国	巴拿马	美国
2	中国	中国	中国	西班牙	美国	印度
3	越南	越南	越南	英国	阿尔及利亚	巴西
4	日本	日本	印度	俄罗斯	泰国	英国
5	印度	印度	澳大利亚	哈萨克斯坦	韩国	菲律宾
6	美国	德国	日本	法国	乌克兰	意大利
7	德国	中国香港	德国	越南	意大利	墨西哥
8	瑞士	瑞士	中国香港	葡萄牙	中国	加拿大
9	加拿大	美国	印尼	巴基斯坦	阿富汗	俄罗斯
10	阿联酋	意大利	柬埔寨	加拿大	哈萨克斯坦	沙特

数据来源:一般贸易为 globalEDGE、OEC、Trading Economics;跨境电商为阿里巴巴国际站。

(二)进口国家(地区)维度

表 4-54 为老挝一般贸易与跨境电商前十的进口国家(地区)情况。

表 4-54　老挝一般贸易与跨境电商前十的进口国家(地区)情况

排名	一般贸易(进口前十的国家或地区)			跨境电商(进口需求量前十的国家或地区)		
	2019 年	2020 年	2021 年	2019 年	2020 年	2021 年
1	泰国	泰国	泰国	中国	中国	中国
2	中国	中国	中国	泰国	泰国	孟加拉国
3	越南	越南	越南	越南	美国	越南
4	日本	日本	日本	中国香港	丹麦	韩国
5	韩国	新加坡	美国	菲律宾	南非	巴基斯坦
6	新加坡	美国	澳大利亚	印度	中国香港	英国
7	俄罗斯	韩国	新加坡	中国台湾	韩国	印度
8	奥地利	澳大利亚	韩国	美国	马来西亚	南非
9	印度	英国	阿联酋	韩国	巴基斯坦	美国
10	印尼	印度	印度	英国	越南	中国香港

数据来源:一般贸易为 globalEDGE、OEC、Trading Economics;跨境电商为阿里巴巴国际站。

（三）出口品类维度

表 4-55 为老挝一般贸易与跨境电商前十的出口品类情况。

表 4-55　老挝一般贸易与跨境电商前十的出口品类情况

排名	一般贸易（出口前十的品类）			跨境电商（出口需求量前十的品类）		
	2019 年	2020 年	2021 年	2019 年	2020 年	2021 年
1	石油和矿物燃料	石油和矿物燃料	矿物燃料、矿物油、蒸馏产品	消费电子	汽车、摩托车	消费电子
2	矿石	矿石	矿渣和灰	家具和室内装饰品	农业	商用服务设备
3	机电设备	铜	珍珠、宝石、金属、硬币	汽车、摩托车	服装	包装与印刷
4	铜及其制品	电机	食用水果、坚果、柑橘类水果皮、瓜类	食品及饮料	包装与印刷	家纺
5	饮料、酒	木浆	活体动物	美容及个人护理	食品及饮料	农业
6	木浆	水果和坚果	木浆、纤维状纤维素材料、废料	运动及娱乐	建筑	食品及饮料
7	贵金属	饮料	电气、电子设备	家居用品	钟表、珠宝、眼镜	家居园艺
8	木及木制品	活体动物	食用蔬菜、某些块根和块茎	医药保健	橡胶原料及制品	健康医疗
9	橡胶	宝石和金属	饮料、烈酒和醋	矿物和冶金	矿物和冶金	家具
10	肥料	橡胶	橡胶	手表、珠宝、眼镜	家具	鞋靴及配件

数据来源：一般贸易为 globalEDGE、OEC、Trading Economics；跨境电商为阿里巴巴国际站。

（四）进口品类维度

表 4-56 为老挝一般贸易与跨境电商前十的进口品类情况。

表 4-56　老挝一般贸易与跨境电商前十的进口品类情况

排名	一般贸易(进口前十的品类)			跨境电商(进口需求量前十的品类)		
	2019 年	2020 年	2021 年	2019 年	2020 年	2021 年
1	石油和矿物燃料	石油和矿物燃料	矿物燃料、矿物油、蒸馏产品	汽车、摩托车	医药保健	消费电子
2	机电设备	电机	电气、电子设备	消费电子	安全防护	汽车、摩托车
3	车辆及零部件	汽车及零件	机械、核反应堆、锅炉	机械	机械	机械
4	钢铁	工业机械	铁路、有轨电车以外的车辆	医药保健	消费电子	玩具
5	钢铁制品	钢铁制品	活体动物	运动及娱乐	五金工具	服装
6	塑料	钢铁	饮料、烈酒和醋	手表、珠宝、眼镜	汽车、摩托车	运动及娱乐
7	动物	饮料	钢铁制品	家居用品	家居用品	健康医疗
8	贵金属	活体动物	铁和钢	食品及饮料	服装	五金工具
9	饮料、酒	塑料	塑料	包装与印刷	运动及娱乐	手表、珠宝、眼镜
10	纸	糖和糖果	纸和纸板、纸浆制品	电气设备和产品	电气设备及用品	家居园艺

数据来源:一般贸易为 globalEDGE、OEC、Trading Economics;跨境电商为阿里巴巴国际站。

第十五节　文莱跨境电商发展状况

一、文莱社会经济与跨境电商发展概况

世界银行数据显示,2020 年,文莱的 GDP 达 120.06 亿美元,同比上涨 1.13%。人均 GDP 为 2.74 万美元,同比上涨 0.17%。与此同时,2020 年,文莱总人口达43.75万人。截至2018年,文莱的识字率达到97.21%,且2020年,初中辍学率仅为0.256%。文莱的数字经济基础相对较好。截至2021年1月,文莱的互联网用户数为41.8万,同比增长1.1%,互联网普及率达95%,是东南亚网络渗透率最高的国家。移动手机数量为56.8万,同比增长0.2%,移动手机普及率达129%。Janio的数据显示,2020年,文莱电子商务市场价值达7.5千万美元。Statista的分析师预估,2022年,文莱网络零售市场收入将达到1.7亿美元,2022—2025年,该收入将以10.14%的年均增长率持续增长,发展潜力巨大。目前,文莱主要的电商平台均来自国外,eBay、Zalora、亚马逊分列前三。

文莱数字经济和电子商务发展起步较晚,但数字经济硬件设施基础较好,这在一定程度上得益于其较强的政策支持。2019年,文莱政府成立了数字经济委员会,以探索数字经济行业的潜力。随后,文莱交通和信息通信部发布了该国第一份2025年数字经济总体规划,概述了建设智慧国家的战略计划和关键项目。

二、文莱一般贸易和跨境电商的比较情况

(一)出口国家(地区)维度

表4-57为文莱一般贸易与跨境电商前十的出口国家(地区)情况。

表 4-57　文莱一般贸易与跨境电商前十的出口国家(地区)情况

排名	一般贸易(出口前十的国家或地区)			跨境电商(出口需求量前十的国家或地区)		
	2018 年	2019 年	2020 年	2019 年	2020 年	2021 年
1	日本	日本	日本	澳大利亚	马来西亚	—
2	泰国	新加坡	新加坡	日本	菲律宾	—
3	韩国	澳大利亚	中国	菲律宾	澳大利亚	—
4	澳大利亚	马来西亚	马来西亚	马来西亚	日本	—
5	新加坡	印度	印度	越南	新加坡	—
6	马来西亚	泰国	澳大利亚	韩国	越南	—
7	印度	中国	泰国	印尼	印尼	—

续表

排名	一般贸易(出口前十的国家或地区)			跨境电商(出口需求量前十的国家或地区)		
	2018 年	2019 年	2020 年	2019 年	2020 年	2021 年
8	亚洲其他地区	韩国	越南	新加坡	新加坡	—
9	中国	越南	菲律宾	泰国	柬埔寨	—
10	美国	菲律宾	韩国	缅甸	韩国	—

数据来源:一般贸易为文莱统计局;跨境电商为阿里巴巴国际站。

(二)进口国家(地区)维度

表 4-58 为文莱一般贸易与跨境电商前十的进口国家(地区)情况。

表 4-58　文莱一般贸易与跨境电商前十的进口国家(地区)情况

排名	一般贸易(进口前十的国家或地区)			跨境电商(进口需求量前十的国家或地区)		
	2018 年	2019 年	2020 年	2019 年	2020 年	2021 年
1	中国	中国	马来西亚	中国	中国	中国
2	新加坡	新加坡	新加坡	马来西亚	泰国	越南
3	马来西亚	马来西亚	中国	泰国	马来西亚	泰国
4	美国	美国	英国	韩国	越南	马来西亚
5	日本	德国	澳大利亚	越南	韩国	日本
6	英国	尼日利亚	美国	印尼	印尼	韩国
7	泰国	阿联酋	阿联酋	菲律宾	菲律宾	印尼
8	韩国	日本	俄罗斯	日本	日本	新加坡
9	德国	哈萨克斯坦	日本	新加坡	新加坡	菲律宾
10	印尼	印尼	沙特	澳大利亚	澳大利亚	缅甸

数据来源:一般贸易为文莱统计局;跨境电商为阿里巴巴国际站。

(三)出口品类维度

表 4-59 为文莱一般贸易与跨境电商前十的出口品类情况。

表 4-59　文莱一般贸易与跨境电商前十的出口品类情况

排名	一般贸易（出口前十的品类）			跨境电商（出口需求量前十的品类）		
	2019 年	2020 年	2021 年	2019 年	2020 年	2021 年
1	矿物燃料	矿物燃料	矿物燃料	食品及饮料	食品及饮料	—
2	化学物品	化学物品	化学物品	运动及娱乐	运动及娱乐	—
3	机械与交通设备	机械与交通设备	机械与交通设备	美容及个人护理	农业	—
4	机器制品	机器制品	机器制品	农业	美容及个人护理	—
5	工业品	工业品	食品	医药保健	消费电子	—
6	不可食用原料	食品	工业品	能源	安全防护	—
7	食品	不可食用原料	不可食用原料	商务服务	健康医疗	—
8	动植物油脂	动植物油脂	动植物油脂	消费电子	能源	—
9	饮料与烟草	饮料与烟草	饮料与烟草	汽车、摩托车	商务服务	—
10	织品	织品	织品	体育娱乐	家用电器	—

数据来源：一般贸易为文莱统计局；跨境电商为阿里巴巴国际站。

（四）进口品类维度

表 4-60 为文莱一般贸易与跨境电商前十的进口品类情况。

表 4-60　文莱一般贸易与跨境电商前十的进口品类情况

排名	一般贸易（进口前十的品类）			跨境电商（进口需求量前十的品类）		
	2019 年	2020 年	2021 年	2019 年	2020 年	2021 年
1	燃料	燃料	燃料	汽车、摩托车	汽车、摩托车	园艺
2	机械与交通设备	机械与交通设备	机械与交通设备	家居用品	消费电子	家居用品
3	工业品	工业品	食品	消费电子	服装	汽车、摩托车
4	食品	食品	化学物品	服装	包装与印刷	消费电子
5	化学物品	化学物品	工业品	机械	园艺	服装
6	机器制品	机器制品	机器制品	包装与印刷	机械	运动及娱乐

续表

排名	一般贸易（进口前十的品类）			跨境电商（进口需求量前十的品类）		
	2019 年	2020 年	2021 年	2019 年	2020 年	2021 年
7	饮料与烟草	饮料与烟草	饮料与烟草	运动及娱乐	家具和室内装饰品	玩具
8	不可食用原料	不可食用原料	动植物油脂	箱包	家居用品	家具和室内装饰品
9	动植物油脂	动植物油脂	不可食用原料	家具和室内装饰品	建筑	包装与印刷
10	织品	织品	织品	礼品、工艺品	安全防护	机械

数据来源：一般贸易为文莱统计局；跨境电商为阿里巴巴国际站。

第五章　总　结

RCEP 就有关跨境电商的一系列具体问题进行了顶层设计,例如跨境数据流动、消费者保护、计算设施的位置等。这有助于减少跨境电商的发展壁垒,促进区内数字要素的互联互通,进一步释放 RCEP 区域市场的巨大潜力。因此,我们预计,随着 RCEP 的正式实施,区域内跨境电商的规模将在未来数年内继续保持高速增长,数字基础设施将进一步完善,相应的制度规范也将逐渐成形,跨境电商将成为一股推动区域经济发展的重要力量。具体而言,RCEP 将在以下四个方面为区域内跨境电商行业带来深远的影响。

第一,RCEP 将为从事跨境电商相关产业的企业提供更加广阔的市场和发展空间。RCEP 区域既涵盖了像日本、韩国、澳大利亚等成熟市场,也涵盖了中国、东盟等仍在快速扩张的新兴市场,用户体量巨大,跨境电商增长动力及潜力俱佳。从前文指数分析中可以看到,2019 年第一季度至 2021 年第四季度,RCEP B2B 指数、RCEP B2C 指数和 RCEP 跨境支付服务指数均呈现出明显的上升态势,3 年内年均增长率分别为 28.7%、33.2% 和 21.0%,其中前两者增速分别是同期海关总署发布的中国—东盟贸易指数(反映了整体贸易情况)增速(19.6%)的 1.5 倍和 2.2 倍,RCEP 区域内的跨境电商正呈现巨大活力和韧性。与此同时,有别于传统的一般性贸易,跨境电商具有高度的普惠性。随着零关税政策的逐步落地和物流服务的逐步完善,我们预计未来 RCEP 区域内将有大量的中小微商家以微型跨国公司的身份参与到市场中来,而这一趋势也在我们的指数中有所体现。一方面,RCEP B2B 贸易主体指标的 3 年年均增长率为 11.7%,且在 2020 年第四季度,RCEP 签订后,加速增长,反映出政策巨大利好对贸易主体的积极影响。另一方面,RECP 企业发展 B2C 指标 3 年年均增长率为 46.7%,且是 RCEP

B2C 指数四大一级指标中唯一不受季节影响的指标,增长迅猛且稳定。

第二,随着 RCEP 框架下跨境贸易的深入发展,区域内消费者将能够享受到更加质优价廉的商品和更加快速便捷的物流服务。本书数据显示,RCEP 区域内天猫国际新增品牌数量 2020 年第一季度至 2021 年第二季度的同比平均增速为 31.5%。泰国、马来西亚是增长最显著的热门商品来源地,而泰国的乳胶枕、马来西亚的燕窝都是我国消费者购物车里的"常客"。我国消费者对 RCEP 区域内品牌的平均满意度也稳步上升,认可度不断提高。从物流服务来看,海外发货物流时长与保税仓物流时长在全球新冠疫情蔓延、海运成本攀升等因素的阻碍之下仍呈现了"总体下降、偶有反复"的良好态势。2021 年第一季度,保税仓发货平均物流时长相比 2020 年第一季度下降了 42%,海外发货平均物流时长也下降了 21%。与此同时,随着 RCEP 具体条款的落实,各成员也将为线上消费者提供更为安心、可靠的消费者保护承诺,减少其线上消费的后顾之忧。

第三,RCEP 区域内跨境电商的繁荣将促进各成员政府间的监管合作和服务创新。2020 年成立的 ICC TradeFlow 联盟、2021 年发布的《东盟数据管理框架》(DMF)以及《东盟跨境数据流动示范合同条款》(MCCs)等,均是 RCEP 各成员在政府层面推动合作共赢、强国富民的集中体现。RCEP 的签署和生效更是充分体现了成员共同维护多边主义和自由贸易、促进区域经济一体化的信心和决心,而跨境电商的发展也极大地促进了成员的政企合作、政府间合作、政府创新管理,推动各成员顺应数字时代趋势,突破国际贸易传统痛点,广泛应用数字技术助力政府科学决策,出台政策法规,落地智慧建设,提升政府管理和服务效能,进而推动区域经济社会发展。

第四,RCEP 区域内跨境电商的蓬勃发展将进一步推动区域经济贸易融合和普惠共同发展。一方面,RCEP 已经成为区域内各成员经济合作与贸易往来的行动框架和准则,各成员正以实际行动推动数字经济和实体经济深度融合,以"双融合"全面支撑"双循环"。例如,2017 年建设的 eWTP 杭州试验区已成为连接世界的数字跨境贸易平台,并在 RCEP 区域内建设多个 e-hub,利用基础设施互联互通和跨境电子商务的双重便利,促进区域跨境电商和实体经济融合发展。另一方面,基于跨境电商的普惠性与重要性,RCEP在强调跨境数字传统规则的同时,就消费者权益保护、网络安全与数据隐私、数字贸易对话与争端解决机制等制定了相应条款,进一步规范了跨境电商的组织形式与流程体系,以此弥合区域内各成员之间客观存在的数字鸿沟,推动跨境电商的普惠共同发展,数字助力普惠真正地"走在路上"。与此同时,跨境电商还将有望通过应用更多的新技术与新理念,促进绿色贸易的蓬勃发展,为人类可持续发展事业做出更大的贡献。

然而,我们也需要清醒地认识到,受限于RCEP中跨境贸易相关条款不够详细、约束性弱等客观因素,协定也将在跨境电商方面对我国企业和政府提出更大的挑战。首先,RCEP实施后,我国跨境贸易相关企业在获得更多市场机遇的同时,也将面临来自境外企业更加激烈的竞争,以及不同市场的监管风险。其次,在发生跨境纠纷时,RCEP仅能承担争端调节的功能,这将使得我国企业权益的保障存在一定的不确定性。并且,由于RCEP并未就线上消费者保护提供强制性约束,因而我国线上消费者的权益能否在协议实施后得到切实有效的保障,仍有待观察。再次,RCEP对我国的数字监管提出了更高的要求。因为随着跨境电商的深入发展,跨境信息传输、消费者隐私、数字税收等方面的问题将会对我国的信息安全、消费者保护等方面造成风险。最后,外部经济环境及突发事件均会对RCEP跨境电商的发展有所影响。例如,近年来新冠疫情总体上显著促进了跨境电商的增长,但经济系统间各方相互依存、疫情反复、世界经济复苏曲折、海运成本高企等亦会给跨境电商的长远发展带来部分压力,RCEP B2B贸易主体指标在2021年第四季度的环比下降幅度相对最大,达19.0%,为一记警钟,需引起各方重视。针对以上所列的潜在问题,本书提出以下建议,以期促进我国跨境电商的健康发展。

第一,强化企业引导,借力RCEP增强我国企业核心竞争力。鼓励我国企业充分发挥主观能动性,吃透、用好原产地累积规则,深度参与区域产业链、供应链,积极主动适应协定实施后更加开放的环境、竞争更加充分的新形势,对标国际提高管理水平,提高产品质量,加强参与国际合作与竞争的本领。例如:鼓励技术密集型企业积极创新发展,增加产品研发、管理咨询、专业设计等附加值高、利润空间大的产业布局;引导劳动密集型企业向高端化、精细化方向发展,不断提高出口产品质量和品牌影响力。与此同时,增强我国企业对 RCEP 可能带来区域产业链、供应链调整变化的认识,谋划适应区域经济一体化的企业的发展战略和经营策略,投资优质资源、能源和先进技术产业,增强重要产品、资源、技术和供给渠道的掌控力。

第二,积极优化地方政府营商环境,助力企业适应并对标 RCEP 的高水平规则。一是鼓励各地政府组织团队深入分析与 RCEP 成员的贸易情况发展现状,研究重点产品、重点企业和重点国家(地区)市场清单,为当地企业开拓市场提供参考。二是通过不定期座谈会、问卷调研等形式,及时收集企业在与 RCEP 成员开展贸易、投资过程中遇到的困难,解答相关疑问,帮助企业更好地"吃透外情、通晓内情",良好应对与 RCEP 区域内企业合作的风险和挑战。三是引导各地政府以 RCEP 实施为契机,对照协定实行更高标准的规则,提升地方治理能力,积极优化营商环境,为企业用好投资兴业的新机遇保驾护航。

第三,积极实践更高水平的跨境电商规则,在国内完善 RCEP 的部分重要条款以保障企业和消费者权益。具体措施包括但不限于:在自由贸易试验区、海南自由贸易港等对外开放高地先行先试 CPTPP、USMCA 等高水平自贸协定中的跨境电商规则,为我国在更高水平、更大范围、更宽领域的跨境电商规则探索上进行压力测试,并以此总结经验;积极开展跨境合作,共同探索制定针对跨境贸易的消费者保护措施,切实保障我国线上消费者的合法权益;针对 RCEP 纠纷解决机制较为薄弱的现实,加快完善相关法律法规,为我国从事跨境贸易的相关企业提供更好的法律保障。

第四,优化企业经营生态,支持跨境电商平台建设与专项人才培养。一方面,针对亚太地区 85% 以上的跨境电商是小型企业这一特征,充分肯定数字外贸平台在为微型跨国公司提供销售、支付、物流、管理等服务上的优势和作用,创新制度环境,通过政策支持、税收优惠等形式进一步支持我国数字外贸平台创新发展,鼓励其为我国企业拓展 RCEP 市场以及 RCEP 成员企业进入中国市场搭建更好的合作平台,带动企业充分挖掘与 RCEP 成员的合作潜力。另一方面,围绕国内超过 70% 的跨境电商认为"专业人才缺乏是经营与发展最大瓶颈"这一情况,鼓励各级政府、高校、跨境电商头部企业通过共建跨境电商人才在线学习平台、共建跨境电商国际人才库和共建跨境电商人才创新创业生态等形式，开展跨境电商相关人才的培养和培训。

第五，完善我国数字监管立法，制定更为健全的跨境数据流动机制。具体措施包括但不限于：进一步完善现有法律框架，例如《阻断外国法律与措施不当域外适用办法》；在借鉴国际优秀经验的基础上，有针对性地出台保障数据网络安全的相关法律，例如《电子商务法》《跨境数据传输法》《个人信息保护法》等；加快制定与跨境数据传输相关的法律法规与监管条例，对跨境数据进行分类管理，如对机密数据禁止流动，对重要数据实行有限制流动，对非敏感数据则在境外接收方符合我国法律要求的情况下允许数据自由流动。

第六，综合强化跨境电商发展韧性，提升抗逆性的同时促进可持续发展。一方面，积极应对海外新冠疫情反扑、物流成本高企等外部经济环境变化及突发事件冲击，助力跨境电商企业提升抗逆性，精准把握疫情下居家办公、宅经济等新的生活和工作方式对跨境贸易需求的改变，协助疫情下承压的跨境电商中小企业化压力为机遇。另一方面，积极寻找 RCEP 跨境贸易情境下可持续发展的新路径，例如加强多方低碳合作，加快发展绿色经贸，在充分认识碳达峰、碳中和全球性经济社会变革的基础上，进一步加强我国与欧美发达国家的"双碳"对话，积极参加双边、多边绿色贸易协定谈判，重视对碳排放标准以及碳关税的研究，防止绿色贸易壁垒的出现。此外，可以努力挖掘我国与 RCEP 其他成员在绿色低碳产业方面的合作潜力，学习日本、韩国、新加坡等先进的绿色低碳技术和发展经验，通过设立海外低碳研发中心、创新中心，投资并购先进低碳技术项目等多样化方式，助力我国新能源、新材料、高端装备、清洁技术等相关绿色产业高质量发展。

后　记

本书的作者按贡献排序为周闻宇、吕佳敏、陆嘉骏。其中,周闻宇负责15万字,吕佳敏负责15万字,陆嘉骏负责2万字。

本书的写作和出版离不开全体课题组成员以及各位专家的鼎力支持,在此,我们对他们表示最诚挚的感谢。具体名单如下:

课题组专家:

贲圣林　浙江大学国际联合商学院院长、浙江大学金融科技研究院院长

欧阳澄　阿里研究院全球化研究中心主任

李振华　蚂蚁集团研究院院长

阿里研究院:

任　洁　阿里研究院研究合作项目负责人

李　鹏　阿里研究院数据分析专家

范秋辞　阿里研究院产业研究中心高级研究专家

蚂蚁研究院:

王　芳　蚂蚁集团研究院研究总监

倪丹成　蚂蚁集团研究院研究总监

李韵菁　蚂蚁集团研究院专家

程志云　蚂蚁集团研究院研究总监

研究助理:

陈胜男、贾玥、龚教伟、汪思涵、程琦喻、邵逸宁、陈楚天、赵芸曦、张环宇

RCEP 指数权重打分专家:

俞洁芳　浙江大学经济学院副教授

张洪胜　浙江大学经济学院副教授

诸竹君　浙江工商大学国际经济与贸易系主任

马　啸　北京大学汇丰商学院助理教授

罗　丹　杭州师范大学阿里巴巴商学院讲师

顾　月　浙大城市学院数字金融研究院副研究员

梁　婕　虾酱传媒首席执行官

1 Overview

The Regional Comprehensive Economic Partnership (RCEP) entered into force on January 1, 2022. At the moment, the RCEP brings together 15 members, including 10 ASEAN countries as well as China, Japan, R. O. Korea, Australia, and New Zealand. It covers about a population of 2. 27 billion and generates over $26 trillion of GDP and $10 trillion of foreign trade, respectively accounting for about 33% and 30% of the world total. Compared to the US-Mexico-Canada Agreement (USMCA), the Comprehensive and Progressive Agreement for Trans-Pacific Partnership (CPTPP), and the European Union (EU) of the same period, RCEP covers the largest involved population, the most diverse membership, and the largest economic and trade scale. The entry into force of the RCEP is expected to create new opportunities to deepen regional cooperation, inject robust momentum into the connectivity and openness of global economy, and provide a strong engine for the sustained prosperity of China's economy.

To better understand the agreement's far-reaching impact on the development of the regional cross-border e-commerce, the International School of Business of Zhejiang University launched a study together with AliResearch and Ant Group Research Institute on a host of issues related to this field by rigorous and detailed data analysis. Based on comprehensive big data related to cross-border e-commerce, this book mainly answers the following three questions: (1) How to scientifically measure the development of cross-border e-commerce in the RCEP region? (2) What's the development situation of this sector of the RCEP members respectively? (3) What's its future development trend in this region?

In order to measure the development of cross-border e-commerce in the RCEP region, we have compiled the RCEP SMEs Cross-Border E-Commerce (B2B) Index, the RCEP Cross-Border E-Commerce Purchase (B2C) Index, and the RCEP Cross-Border Payment Service Index to measure its activity in terms of B2B, B2C, and the development level of payment services related to this sector. Base on the comprehensive cross-border e-commerce big data and scientific computing methods, these three indexes illustrate the status quo and future trend of cross-border e-commerce development in the RCEP region from three different dimensions. Together, they serve as a monitor to measure the overall development of cross-border e-commerce in this region.

When it comes to its status quo, we collected related information on the socio-economic situations and the development of cross-border e-commerce of 15 member states, and made comparisons between the cross-border e-commerce and the general trade in terms of nationality and product category. In terms of its future development trend, we compiled a series of relevant cases to reveal its development process and evolution trends in different countries and regions. Specifically, these cases cover five different aspects, including digital cross-border trade platforms, logistics services, cross-border payments, micro-multinational enterprises, and innovative governance. In addition, this book also puts forward relevant policy suggestions on the issues and challenges that China may encounter in the development of cross-border e-commerce.

RCEP is going to inject strong momentum into the regional development of cross-border e-commerce. As the outcome of the deep integration of new technologies such as the Internet, big data, cloud computing, and socio-economic development, cross-border e-commerce can enable more countries and people to share the dividends of human economic development by expanding the scope of trade and increasing the trade bodies? For the development of regional cross-border e-commerce, RCEP has made a series of targeted institutional arrangements. While emphasizing the traditional rules of cross-border e-commerce, it has also formulated corresponding provisions in terms of protection of customers' rights and interests, network security and data privacy, dialogue and dispute resolution mechanisms, etc. By doing so, the parties can further regulate the organizational form and process system of cross-border e-commerce, so as to promote the integration of online consume markets and the development and prosperity of this sector.

In recent years, with the rapid evolution of information technology and logistics models, the business model of cross-border e-commerce has also been continuously innovated and popularized worldwide at a rapid pace. For small-and medium-sized businesses, cross-border e-commerce enables them to integrate into the global market without leaving their homes and fulfills their aspiration to do business everywhere easily; for consumers, it allows them to enjoy high-quality goods and services from all over the world, thus greatly improving the well-being of consumers. More importantly, cross-border e-commerce itself is highly inclusive. Countries or regions with different natural endowments can integrate into the global value chain through cross-border e-commerce and share the achievements of human economic development. It is this inclusiveness that has prompted a large number of businesses and consumers to shift from offline to online over the past two decades, and this process has been fueled by the outbreak of the COVID-19 pandemic. With the entry into force of RCEP, industries related to cross-border e-commerce in the region are bound to have broader space for development. Therefore, it is particularly important for each and every country (or region) and individual to seize the opportunities of the times.

The structure of this book as follows: later in this chapter, we will briefly describe the current development of cross-border e-commerce in the RCEP region and analyze the relevant provisions of cross-border e-commerce in RCEP. In Chapter 2, we will share methods for establishing the three indexes and analyse them. In Chapter 3, we will provide a series of classic cases related to the development of cross-border e-commerce; in Chapter 4, we will describe and analyze the development of cross-border e-commerce of each RCEP member. In Chapter 5, we will look forward to the future development trend of cross-border e-commerce in the RCEP region and offer corresponding policy suggestions for the challenges that Chinese enterprises may face.

1. 1   Current Situation of Cross-Border E-Commerce Development in the RCEP Region

Cross-border e-commerce in the RCEP region boasts a large scale and a high rate of growth. According to the data from Statista and bureaus of statistics from different countries, the RCEP region has a comparatively large scale of cross-border e-commerce globally. Specifically, the total scale of this sector in its members is worth about 1. 8 trillion RMB yuan, equivalent to approximately $285 billion, accounting for 47. 9% of the world total (around $595 billion). Among them, China has contributed 1. 69 trillion RMB yuan, 93. 8% of the region's total. This figure reached 1. 98 trillion RMB yuan in 2021 at a growth rate of 17. 2%. Figure 1-1 shows the overall scale of cross-border e-commerce in different regions of the world in 2020.

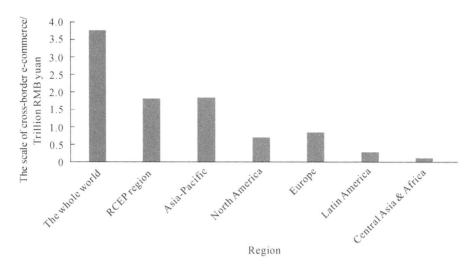

Figure 1-1   The Scale of Cross-Border E-Commerce in Different Regions of the World in 2020

Data Source: Statista and bureaus of statistics from different countries.

Cross-border e-commerce in the RCEP region is growing faster than general trade. According to the latest data released by the Statista and bureaus of statistics from participant countries, the scale of cross-border e-commerce in the RCEP region has increased from about $86.2 billion in 2016 to about $285 billion in 2020, with an average annual growth rate of 34.8% (see Figure 1-2). This growth rate far exceeds the growth rate of general trade in the same period, as well as the growth rate of domestic trade of member countries, and maintains a steady growth trend. It is noteworthy that the rapid growth of cross-border e-commerce in the RCEP region is mainly due to the rapid growth of Chinese consumers' demand for overseas goods. According to the calculation of the research group, the annual growth rates of the overall scale of cross-border e-commerce in China were higher than 30% from 2018 to 2021, which account for more than 85% of the region's total.

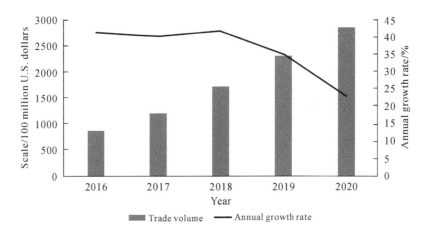

Figure 1-2   The Scale and Annual Growth Rate of Cross-Border E-Commerce in the RCEP Region

Data Source: Statista and bureaus of statistics from different countries.

The development of cross-border e-commerce varies greatly among RCEP members. At the moment, the 15 RCEP members are at obviously different stages of economic development. Australia, New Zealand, Japan, Singapore and R. O. Korea are in the first echelon, with a GDP per capita of more than \$30,000 in 2021. China and Brunei fall into the second echelon with a GDP per capita of around \$10,000 in 2021, while countires of the third echelon including Malaysia, Thailand, Indonesia, Vietnam, the Philippines, Laos, Myanmar and Cambodia have a GDP per capita of less than \$10, 000 in 2021. The huge difference in the level of economic development of members can also be seen in their development level of cross-border e-commerce. According to the latest data released by United Nations Conference on Trade and Development(UNCTAD) and bureaus of statistics of relevant countries, the total scale of digital trade (including cross-border e-commerce) in the five first-echelon developed countries accounted for more than 4% of GDP in 2020, while the global average is 3. 8% (see Figure 1-3).

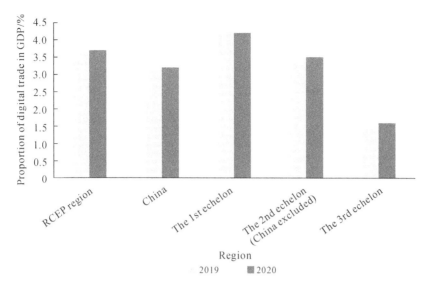

Figure 1-3   Proportion of Digital Trade in GDP in the RCEP Region

Data source: UNCTAD and bureaus of statistics from different countries.

As digital infrastructure development level in RCEP members varies greatly, it's inevitable that there is a digital gap, but the overall situation is gradually improving. The prosperity and development of cross-border e-commerce hinge on the support of digital infrastructure. However, the development of digital infrastructure in the RCEP region is still uneven. According to the latest data from the World Bank, the average Internet penetration rate in the five developed countries is over 85%, while the average Internet penetration of the rest developing countries is merely 66%, and average Internet penetration rate of China is 71%. It is worth mentioning that this indicator also varies greatly within these developing countries. Among them, the Internet penetration rate in Malaysia is as high as 80%, while it is only 25% in Laos. A similar digital divide is reflected in smartphone penetration. In the RCEP region, the average smartphone penetration rate in developed countries is 80%, which is still significantly higher than the 64% in developing countries. However, this difference is smaller than the penetration rate of the Internet, which also reflects the mobile Internet has the relative universality? It is worth noting that the digital infrastructure in the RCEP region is also being improved (see Figure 1-4), which will contribute to the long-term healthy development of cross-border e-commerce in the region.

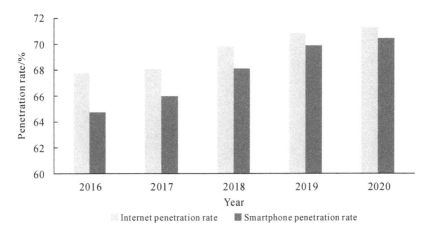

Figure 1-4   Digital Infrastructure Development Level in the RCEP Region

Data Source: World Bank.

Enterprises in the RCEP region have expedited their online businesses, thus improving the supply end of cross-border e-commerce. Over the past decade or so, with the rapid development of cross-border e-commerce around the world, enterprises in the region have continued to expand their online businesses, and this process has been accelerated after the outbreak of the COVID-19 pandemic. The impact of the virus has posed many challenges to enterprises in the region, such as blocked offline sales, tight cash flow, and logistic postponement, dealing a heavy blow to their offline business activities. After the virus outbreak, however, cross-border e-commerce business in the region has grown at an unprecedented rate as evidenced by the fact that export enterprises have shifted their businesses to cross-border e-commerce platforms. During this period, a large number of SMEs also have taken the initiative to participate in the cross-border trade cooperation led by e-commerce platforms in the region, learned from and introduced digital business models to promote their own digital transformation. RCEP members have also provided a series of strong support policies to help domestic enterprises participate in cross-border e-commerce in the context of the pandemic. The synergy of these internal and external factors has accelerated the development of online business by companies in this region. According to a survey of more than 100 Chinese import and export companies conducted by Ebrun Research, 84% of enterprises have increased their investment in online business after the pandemic outbreak(see Figure 1-5).

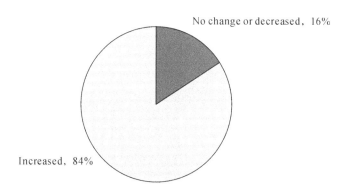

No change or decreased, 16%

Increased, 84%

Figure 1-5   Online Business Investment of Small- and Medium-Sized Foreign Trade Companies after the COVID-19 Pandemic Outbreak

Data Source: Ebrun Research.

The deepening of consumers' digital habits in the RCEP region has boosted the demand-end activity of cross-border e-commerce. In the past ten years or so, with the popularization of mobile Internet and the continuous innovation of business models, more and more consumers have begun to dabble in online consumption. The outbreak of the COVID-19 pandemic has further digitized their consumption habits (see Figure 1-6), bringing greater opportunities for the development of cross-border e-commerce. Moreover, the pandemic has made consumers more focused on health and safety.

Therefore, they tend to meet their consumption needs through e-commerce, which can offer them a wide range of choices, cost-effective goods, and simple shopping process. All these have made consumers more willing to go shopping online. In addition, as it takes time to resume international travel, higher-quality overseas online shopping has become a new way of life and consumption. Although it remains to be seen whether the changes in consumption habits caused by the pandemic are long-term, there is no doubt that such changes have profoundly affected the development process of cross-border e-commerce in the RCEP region after the outbreak, and are likely to become a long-term trend.

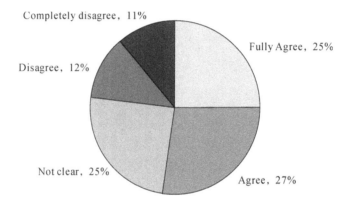

Figure 1-6   Whether Consumers Shop More Online after the Outbreak of the COVID-19 Pandemic

Data source: UNCTAD.

1. 2   Brief Analysis of Relevant Provisions of RCEP Cross-Border E-Commerce

Chapter 12 of RCEP is the first comprehensive and high-level multilateral e-commerce rules in the Asia-Pacific region, which will have a profound impact on the development of cross-border e-commerce in the region. This chapter includes a total of 17 specific provisions, 11 of which are mandatory. The main contents of these provisions are detailed in Table 1-1.

Table 1-1   RCEP Cross-Border E-Commerce Provisions

Provision	Brief Content	Impact
Article 12. 5	Promote paperless trading	Promoting the facilitation of cross-border e-commerce
Article 12. 6	Allow for electronic authentication and electronic signature	
Article 12. 7	Improve online consumer protection	Better protecting the legitimate rights and interests, personal privacy, and customer experience for online consumers
Article 12. 8	Improve online personal information protection	
Article 12. 9	Forbid unsolicited commercial electronic messages	
Article 12. 10	Estabish and improve domestic regulatory framework	Reducing the regulatory burden on enterprises and the entry barriers for related industries
Article 12. 11	Improve tax policies for e-commerce	Reducing tax burdens and tax risks for businesses
Article 12. 12	Improve transparency in the implementation of RCEP	Reducing the information gap between governments and businesses
Article 12. 13	Strengthen cyber security & international cooperation	Enhancing the security of online transactions
Article 12. 14	Do not make the location of computing facilities a prerequisite for conducting business without justification	Reducing the regulatory burden on enterprises and the entry barriers for related industries
Article 12. 15	Cross-border transfer of information for commercial purposes must not be blocked for unjustified reasons	Reducing the regulatory burden and business costs for enterprises

In addition to Chapter 12, which directly involves cross-border e-commerce, the RCEP cumulative rules of origin will also promote members to enhance the digital level of trade products and accelerate the connectivity of data information, including product labeling, logistics, warehousing, settlement, and customs clearance. Besides, given the fact that the pandemic has taken a heavy toll on global supply chains, the agreement will further integrate the Asia-Pacific market after it entries into force. More importantly, it will unleash the advantages of demographic dividend in the ASEAN member states, of technological and capital advantages in R. O. Korea and Japan, and of resource endowment in Australia and New Zealand, thus promoting the integration of industrial chains, value chains, and supply chains in the region. All these could enable China to follow the trend of digitalization and shift services from offline to online, so as to help foster new forms of business and new models in cross-border e-commerce, such as the Internet of Things, big data, and blockchains.

2　Analysis of Cross-Border E-Commerce Development Indexes in the RCEP Region

2. 1　Introduction to Indexes

This book, taking business-to-business (B2B), business-to-costumer (B2C), and payment as the starting points, compiles three indexes: the RCEP SMEs Cross-Border E-Commerce (B2B) Index, the RCEP Cross-Border E-Commerce Purchase (B2C) Index, and the RCEP Cross-Border Payment Service Index. It aims to comprehensively and systematically measure the development of cross-border e-commerce in the RCEP region, and study the contribution of cross-border e-commerce in promoting the digital transformation of micro-, small- and medium- sized foreign trade enterprises, and advancing the regional economic integration and trade growth. This section will introduce in detail the indexes involved from the aspects of **core features, indication system, and calculation method.**

2. 1. 1　Core Features

The three indexes above, which are part of the first set of RCEP-related indexes for cross-border trade, can serve as barometers, compasses, and kits for all walks of life to observe the development of cross-border e-commerce in the RCEP region (especially for micro-, small- and medium-sized foreign trade enterprises). They demonstrate the market changes from a multi-dimensional perspective and present the development trend intuitively, providing support for future policy formulation, enterprise decision-making, and academic research. The three features of the indexes are as follows.

2. 1. 1. 1　Combination of Subjective and Objective Weights for Scientific Calculation

The indexes in this book combine both subjective and objective weights. On the one hand, as theory and practice share equal parts in cross-border e-commerce, both experts in the academic and industrial worlds are invited to form the research team which uses the expert scoring method to weight the subjective factors. On the other hand, given the distribution features of economic data, we also employs the coefficient of variation method to weight the objective factors based on relevant research, exploring and reflecting the information behind the economic data. The coefficient of variation method is an objective weighting method, which directly uses the information contained in each index to weight the objective factors by calculation. This method is also widely applied to the weight setting of various framework indexes.

2. 1. 1. 2　Unique Data Base for Measurement

Data is a factor of production and the basis of research. Relying on industry-university-research cooperation and under the precondition of data security, controllability and compliance, this book is based on data from Alibaba. com (the world's leading B2B cross-border e-commerce platform), Tmall Global (the well-known B2C cross-border e-commerce import platform in China), and Ant Group to compile the three indexes, making it possible to measure the development of cross-border e-commerce.

2. 1. 1. 3   Quarterly Calculation Disclosure for In-Time and Sensitive Data
             Tracking

Due to data availability and other factors, the available trade-related indexes are mostly annual indexes. In order to further improve their timeliness and sensitivity, the three indexes are calculated and released once a quarter to better reflect the development trend and events' influence on cross-border e-commerce in the RCEP region. This provides all social sectors with a good data foundation to understand and dig into the development of cross-border e-commerce.

2. 1. 2   Indication System

This section will introduce the indication system of the RCEP SMEs Cross-Border E-Commerce (B2B) Index, the RCEP Cross-Border E-Commerce Purchase (B2C) Index and the RCEP Cross-Border Payment Service Index one after another.

2. 1. 2. 1   RCEP SMEs Cross-Border E-Commerce (B2B) Index

The RCEP SMEs Cross-Border E-Commerce(B2B) Index (RCEP B2B Index) comprehensively measure the development of cross-border e-commerce of SMEs in the RCEP region from four dimensions: comprehensive results, supply and demand scale, supply-side development quality, and demand-side development quality. It consists of 4 primary indicators of trade scale, trade bodies, enterprise development, and market focus, 7 secondary indicators like the scale of inquiries, the number of sellers, the number of products, and 13 tertiary indicators like the number of inquiries from buyers to sellers, the number of orders, and the number of newly registered sellers in the RCEP region. The indication system is presented in Table 2-1.

Table 2-1   Indication System of RCEP SMEs Cross-Border E-Commerce(B2B) Index

Primary Indicators	Secondary Indicators	Tertiary Indicators
Trade scale	Inquiry scale	Number of inquiries from buyers in the RCEP region to sellers in the RCEP region
		Number of inquiries from buyers in the RCEP region to sellers outside the RCEP region
		Number of inquiries from buyers outside the RCEP region to sellers in the RCEP region
	Order size	Number of orders in the RCEP region
		Transaction amount of orders in the RCEP region
Trade bodies	Number of sellers	Number of newly registered sellers in the RCEP region
		Number of active sellers in the RCEP region
	Number of buyers	Number of newly registered buyers in the RCEP region
		Number of active buyers in the RCEP region
Enterprise development	Number of products	Average number of products of sellers in the RCEP region
	Number of new products	Average number of new products of sellers in the RCEP region
Market focus	China focus	Number of orders from Chinese sellers to buyers in the RCEP region
		Transaction amount of orders from Chinese sellers to buyers in the RCEP region

2. 1. 2. 2   RCEP Cross-Border E-Commerce Purchase(B2C) Index

The RCEP Cross-Border E-Commerce Purchase (B2C) Index (RCEP B2C Index) takes four dimensions into consideration—overall trade situation, supply side, demand side and platform intermediary, and comprehensively measure the development of cross-border e-commerce imports in the RCEP region. The indication system includes 4 primary indicators of trade scale, enterprise development, market demand and platform service, 9 secondary indicators such as order size, brand

132

development and order demand, and 11 tertiary indicators that include the number of orders on Tmall Global in the RCEP region, the transaction amount of orders and the number of new brands on Tmall Global in the RCEP region. The indication system is presented in Table 2-2.

Table 2-2   Indication System of RCEP Cross-Border E-Commerce Purchase (B2C) Index

Primary Indicators	Secondary Indicators	Tertiary Indicators
Trade scale	Order size	Number of orders on Tmall Global in the RCEP region
		Transaction amount of orders on Tmall Global in the RCEP region
	Number of brands	Number of brands on Tmall Global in the RCEP region
Enterprise development	Brand development	Number of new brands on Tmall Global in the RCEP region
	Business incubation	Number of successful incubation of new merchants on Tmall Global
	Product supply	Average number of brands' products on Tmall Global in the RCEP region
Market demand	Order demand	Average number of brands' orders on Tmall Global in the RCEP region
	Average unit price per customer transaction	Average unit price per customer transaction of brands on Tmall Global in the RCEP region
Platform service	Satisfaction	Average satisfaction score of brands on Tmall Global in the RCEP region
	Delivery time	Average delivery time of orders on Tmall Global in the RCEP region (overseas shipments only)
		Average delivery time of orders on Tmall Global in the RCEP region (domestic bonded warehouses shipments only)

2.1.2.3   RCEP Cross-Border Payment Service Index

The RCEP Cross-Border Payment Service Index starts with the scale and quality of cross border payment services and quantitatively assesses the development level of digital payment. It includes 2 primary indicators of cross-border payment service scale and cross-border payment service quality, 5 secondary indicators of cross-border payment scope, cross-border payment depth, cross-border payment activity, cross-border payment service efficiency, and cross-border payment service convenience, and 10 tertiary indicators that include the number of Chinese sellers and non-Chinese sellers and the cross-border transaction number of Chinese sellers in the RCEP region. It provides a factual basis for understanding the development to better promote the cross-border digital payment, help small- and medium-sized foreign trade enterprises in the RCEP region "go global" and accelerate the economic integration in the RCEP region. The indication system is presented in Table 2-3.

Table 2-3 Indication System of RCEP Cross-Border Payment Service Index

Primary Indicators	Secondary Indicators	Tertiary Indicators
Cross-border payment service scale	Cross-border payment scope	Number of Chinese sellers providing cross-border payments in the RCEP region
		Number of non-Chinese sellers providing cross-border payments in the RCEP region
	Cross-border payment depth	Cross-Border transaction amount of Chinese sellers in the RCEP region
		Cross-Border transaction amount of non-Chinese sellers in the RCEP region
	Cross-border payment Activity	Number of cross-border receipts of Chinese sellers in the RCEP region
		Number of cross-border receipts of non-Chinese sellers in the RCEP region
	Cross-border payment service efficiency	Average duration of cross-border receipts of Chinese sellers in the RCEP region
		Average duration of cross-border receipts of non-Chinese sellers in the RCEP region

Continued

Primary Indicators	Secondary Indicators	Tertiary Indicators
Cross-border payment service quality	Cross-border payment service convenience	Supported currencies in cross-border payments of Chinese sellers in the RCEP region
		Supported currencies in cross-border payments of non-Chinese sellers in the RCEP region

2. 1. 3　Calculation Method

The three indexes are gained through step-by-step, layered, and weighted calculations. The calculation steps are as follows.

2. 1. 3. 1　Positively Managing the Indicators

Indexes in this book are all the higher the better. But there exists some indicators whose original direction is opposite to the index direction. For example, the cross-border payment service efficiency is measured by average duration of cross-border receipts of Chinese sellers in RCEP region and number of cross-border receipts of non-Chinese sellers in the RCEP region. However, these two indicators are negative, which means the larger their value is, the lower the cross-border payment service efficiency is. Therefore, this book adopts the reciprocals of such indicators' values to keep them in line with the total direction.

2. 1. 3. 2　Standardizing the Data

The standardized scores for each indicator are obtained after data cleansing, data association, and dimension removal. The specific standardization formula is as follows.

$$X_{k,j}^{*} = \frac{X_{k,j}}{X_{k,1}}$$

$X_{k,j}$ represents the jth observation of the k indicator. $X_{k,j}^{*}$ represents the standardized score of the jth observation of the kth indicator.

2. 1. 3. 3   Weighting the Indicators

As described above, this book exploits a combination of subjective expert scoring method and objective coefficient of various method to determine the weight of each indicator.

2. 1. 3. 4   Calculating the Indexes

The results of each index, including the total indexes and the primary and secondary sub-indexes, are obtained by multiplying the standardized scores of the indicators and the weights of the indicators then adding up. The formula for index calculation is as follows.

$$\text{index value} = \sum_{j=1}^{N} X_{k,j}^{*} W_{k}.$$

W_k represents the weight of the kth indicator.

2. 1. 3. 5   Updating the Indexes

Based on the original analysis model, this book will make appropriate optimization and adjustments to the indication system, the statistical methods, and weights according to the actual situation to ensure the rationality, continuity, and consistency of the index evaluation results.

2. 2   RCEP SMEs Cross-Border E-Commerce (B2B) Index

This section shows the index analysis results and conclusions drawn from the RCEP B2B Index and the four primary indicators of trade scale, trade bodies, enterprise development, and market focus.

2.2.1   Index: Steady Growth Driven by the Strong Momentum of Cross-Border E-Commerce under the COVID-19 Pandemic

2.2.1.1   A General Perspective

Steady increase as a trend: The RCEP B2B Index from 2019Q1 to 2021Q4 showed a steady upward trend, except for a slight decline in 2020Q1 and 2021Q4 as a result of the pandemic. The rest quarters maintain the pace of growth(see Figure 2-1).

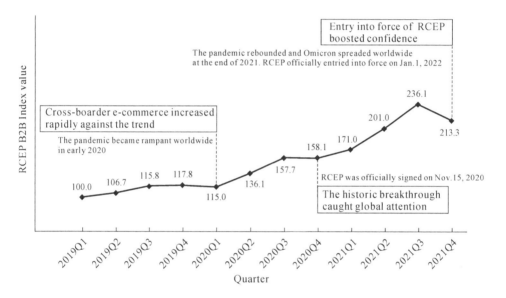

Figure 2-1   Trend of RCEP B2B Index from 2019 to 2021

Rapid growth in the total index: The index doubled within 3 years, with an average annual growth rate of 28.7%, 1.5 times the growth rate of the China-ASEAN Trade Index (19.6%) released by China's General Administration of Customs, which represents the overall trade situation in the same period. In addition, in terms of the ring growth rate, Q2 and Q3 of each year are the fastest growing stages of cross-border e-commerce for SMEs. The ring growth rate of the total index of Q2 and Q3 in 2020 and 2021 even exceeded 15%. In terms of the year-on-year growth rate, the growth rate in 2020 and 2021 remained high stable state, which were all above 25%, except for 2020Q1(only 15%).

2.2.1.2　A Structural Perspective

The external economic environment and emergencies have influenced the RCEP B2B Index.

Firstly, The COVID-19 pandemic has significantly contributed to the growth of cross-border e-commerce. However, the recurrent pandemic brings pressure to the long-term development of cross-border e-commerce because of the interdependent economic systems. Since the beginning of 2020, the pandemic has been rampant all over the world, causing difficulties to the traditional off-line trade. In March 2020, the WHO announced that the COVID-19 is a global pandemic. Its negative effects on traditional trade continued to expand while cross-border e-commerce was growing rapidly at the same time. However, the RCEP B2B total index of 2021Q4 declined for the first time after the fell in 2020Q1(-9.7%) influenced by the recurrent global pandemic, the spreading mutated virus Omicron, the weak economic recovery in the world and high shipping costs. This indicates that the development of small- and medium-sized cross-border e-commerce enterprises are also under great pressure. Therefore, 2022 is an important year to maintain the sustainable development of cross-border e-commerce.

Secondly, The RCEP will inject new vitality into the development of cross-border e-commerce in the region covered. The RCEP was formally signed on November 15, 2020. It will promote the regional development of cross-border e-commerce by eliminating tariff barriers, establishing flexible rules of origin, promoting e-commerce, improving the convenience level of trade, and encouraging technical cooperation and cooperation among SMEs. Such benefits are also reflected in the RCEP B2B Index. From Q1 to Q3 in 2021, the ring growth rates of the RCEP B2B Index were 8.1%, 17.5% and 17.5% respectively, much higher than the average growth rate(8.0%)

in 2020. In addition, the RCEP entered into force on January 1, 2022. It will greatly boost market confidence and enhance the economic resilience of various countries after the pandemic.

2.2.2 Primary Indicators: Impressive Performance of RCEP SMEs in Cross-Border E-Commerce Scale and Enterprise Development

This book draws the following conclusions by comparing the trend of the four primary indicators with the index (see Figure 2-2). On the one hand, the RCEP B2B trade scale indicator has the largest increase (3.1 times within 3 years), followed by the B2B enterprise development indicator (2.8 times within 3 years) which surged from Q1 to Q3 in 2021. The B2B trade bodies indicator ranked the third since its increase rate was 1.4 times in 3 years while the B2B market focus indicator increased the least (1.1 times within 3 years). On the other hand, all RCEP B2B primary indicators have declined to different extents in 2021Q4. And as mentioned above, the recurrent pandemic, the weak economic recovery in the world and high shipping costs all had negative impact on cross-border e-commerce for SMEs.

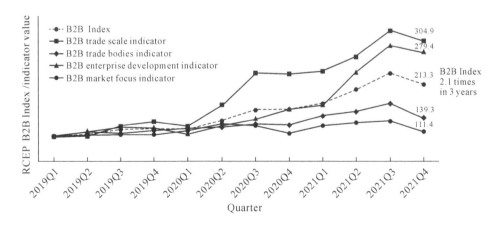

Figure 2-2　Trend of RCEP B2B Index and Primary Indicators from 2019 to 2021

2.2.2.1   Trade Scale: The Largest Increase in SMEs Cross-Border E-Commerce, More than 5 Times That of General Trade

Generally, from 2019Q1 to 2021Q4, the RCEP B2B trade scale indicator showed a stepwise growth, ranking the first among the four primary indicators with an average annual growth rate of 45.0% (see Figure 2-3). This was much higher than the annual growth rate (7%) of China's general trade to RCEP countries during the same period. Meanwhile, the B2B trade scale indicator of Q2 and Q3 grew relatively faster every year. The ring growth rates of the index of Q2 and Q3 in 2020 were up to 37.4% and 39.8% respectively.

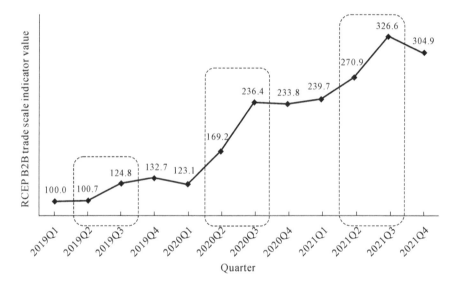

Figure 2-3   Trend of RCEP B2B Trade Scale Indicator from 2019 to 2021

Structurally, first of all, in terms of cross-border e-commerce inquiries inside and outside the RCEP region (more than 215 countries are involved), the number of inquiries from the outside was more than 6 times the number of inquiries from the inside in the past 3 years. But from the perspective of the average number of inquiries per country, the average number of inquiries per country inside the RCEP region has been maintained to be

140

more than 2 times the number of inquiries per country outside the RCEP region, which indicates the fact that the RCEP buyers attach great importance to cross-border trade.

Secondly, for both inside and outside the RCEP region, there was an increasing concentration on the inquiries of top 5 industries. The proportion of inquiries outside stepped up from 39. 0% in 2018 to around 43. 0% in 2021Q3, and rose from 36. 5% to 39. 0% as for the inquiries inside. The inquiries of top 5 industries outside the RCEP were slightly different from those of the inside. The outside focuses on consumer electronics, apparel, beauty & personal care, sports & entertainment, and home & garden. The machinery industry is out of the top 5. The inside focuses more on consumer electronics, home & garden, apparel, sports & entertainment, and machinery. It suggests that the preference for chinese products inside the RCEP was mainly in machinery, electrical equipment and supplies, cars & motorcycles and accessories, home & garden, health care, beauty & personal care, construction, apparel, lamps & lighting fittings, packaging & printing, consumer electronics, sports & entertainment, hardware. Transactions in these fields all accounted for more than 5% of the total in the past three years. Machinery and home & garden (top 2) transactions accounted for 12% and 8. 9% respectively and maintained a rapid increase, with their growth rates standing at 121. 3% and 150. 6% in 2021Q2 from the same period in 2020. Besides, security & protection and environmental protection industries saw negative growth.

Thirdly, sellers in the RCEP are mainly from China, Thailand, Vietnam, R. O. Korea, Malaysia, the Philippines, Japan, Indonesia, Singapore, Australia, New Zealand, and Myanmar. The top 5 RCEP countries with high enthusiasm for trade with China has changed from Australia, the Philippines, Malaysia, Indonesia and Thailand in 2018 to the Philippines, Australia, Indonesia, Malaysia and Singapore in 2021.

Fourthly, in the domestic market of China, Guangdong Province and Zhejiang Province have maintained the first echelon. Since 2018Q1, among the inquiries to China, the ones to the two provinces took up more than 60%, both from the outside and inside of the RCEP, and the transactions accounted for more than 50%. The second echelon were Jiangsu, Shandong, Fujian, and Hebei Provinces, accounting for more than 5% of total transactions. And Shandong and Jiangsu in particular, each accounted for over 10% of the transactions.

2.2.2.2   Trade Bodies: Steady Growth in spite of the Note-Worthy Decline in 2021Q4

Generally, the average annual growth rate of the RCEP B2B Index of trade bodies indicator in the 3 years was 11.7%, indicating a steady increase (see Figure 2-4). And it is worth noticing that the trade bodies index rapidly increased after the RCEP was signed in 2020Q4, representing positive influence brought by the policy dividends to the trade bodies. However, the B2B trade bodies indicator witnessed a great decline of ring growth rate in 2021Q4, which reached a peak of 19.0%. This is an alert

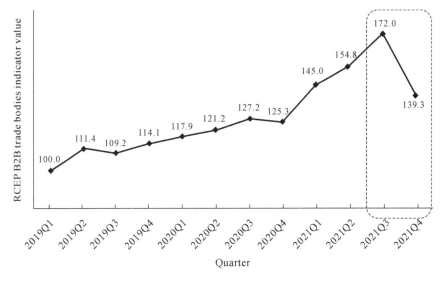

Figure 2-4   Trend of RCEP B2B Trade Bodies Indicator from 2019 to 2021

which calls for attention from all parties.

Structurally, the number of newly registered sellers in the RCEP region fluctuated greatly, with a 246. 6% increase in 2019Q2 and a 56. 2% decrease in 2021Q2. At the same time, the number of newly registered buyers in the region has shown a rapid growth, with an average annual growth rate of 13. 2%; only 4 quarters out of the total 12 declined quarter-on-quarter. It suggests that new sellers are more sensitive to changes in the external environment than buyers. In addition, although the number of active RCEP buyers was still more than that of active sellers, both of them shared the same tendency and had maintained an annual growth of more than 15%, reflecting the increasing recognition and participation in trade digitization of RCEP SMEs.

2. 2. 2. 3　Enterprise Development: The Transformation from Offline Trade
　　　　　　 to Online Trade Regardless of Quarterly Changes

Generally, the average annual growth rate of RCEP B2B enterprise development indicator in the 3 years was 40. 8% and its growth was less influenced by quarterly changes (see Figure 2-5). The B2B enterprise

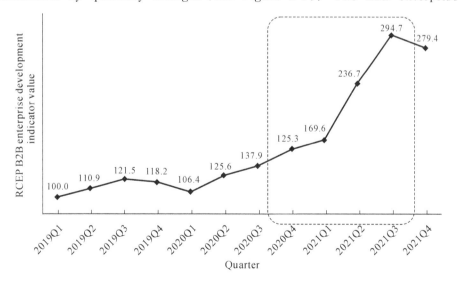

Figure 2-5　Trend of RCEP B2B Enterprise Development Indicator from 2019 to 2021

development indicator has risen sharply for three consecutive quarters after the official signature of RCEP in 2020Q4. The year-on-year growth rates of Q1, Q2 and Q3 in 2020 reached 59.5%, 88.5% and 113.6% respectively. This suggests that the RCEP has promoted the development of RCEP enterprises.

Structurally, digital cross-border trade has become the global focus since the pandemic spread at the beginning of 2020. Offline cross-border trade has fastened its pace to move into the online world in 2021 when the pandemic became a new normal. More RCEP enterprises have accelerated developing online cross-border e-commerce markets with their own targets. They began to sell their offline products and also innovated new products on online platforms. The average quarter-on-quarter growth of the average number of new products of sellers in RCEP region has been 44.9% in 2021Q3 and kept increasing. The average number of products sold by RCEP sellers has also increased steadily but the growth speed has slowed slightly recently. In particular, the average quarter-on-quarter growth rate of the average number of products sold by sellers in the region was 3.8% before 2020Q3. But from 2020Q4, the growth of the average number of products gradually staged onto a plateau phase.

2.2.2.4　Market Focus: Evident Fluctuation with More Emphasis on China since the Signing of RCEP

Generally, the RCEP B2B market focus indicator fluctuated with the quarterly change with a stronger growth in Q1 and Q2 every year and a general downward trend in Q4(see Figure 2-6). Besides, the B2B market focus indicator in 2021Q4 declined significantly. It was mainly affected by the recurrent pandemic, higher logistics costs and other factors, resulting in a simultaneous decline in the number of orders to China from buyers inside and outside the RCEP region.

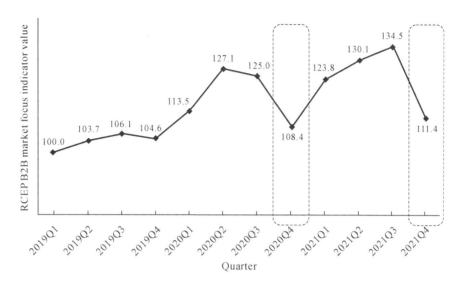

Figure 2-6 Trend of RCEP B2B Market Focus Indicator from 2019 to 2021

Structurally, the overall scale of orders from the RCEP buyers to Chinese sellers grew gradually. The transaction of orders by Chinese sellers to RCEP buyers in 2021Q4 was 3.5 times amount of 2019Q1 And the number of orders in 2021Q4 was 3.9 times that of 2019Q1. This suggests that the Chinese brands have gained a good reputation and a growing influence among the RCEP buyers. The outbreak of the COVID-19 pandemic has also boosted the increase in the transaction of Chinese sellers. Specifically, the transactions amount of Chinese sellers in 2021Q4 was 3.4 times that of 2020Q1 when the COVID-19 pandemic broke out. To a certain extent, it proved that the new lifestyle and way of working such as working from home and stay-at-home economy during the pandemic in the past two years has boosted the demand for fitness equipment, remote working supplies, and entertainment requisites in overseas markets. Therefore, those demands promoted the increase in the number of orders to Chinese sellers who possess pronounced advantages in these industries.

2.3 RCEP Cross-Border E-Commerce Purchase (B2C) Index

This section displays the index analysis results and conclusions drawn from the RCEP B2C Index and 4 primary indicators of trade scale, enterprise development, market demand, and platform service.

2.3.1 Index: Rapid Increase with Regular Fluctuation

2.3.1.1 A General Perspective

Firstly, It showed a gradual increase with fluctuation. From 2019Q1 to 2021Q4, though the RCEP B2C fluctuated within different quarters, it kept increasing gradually(see Figure 2-7).

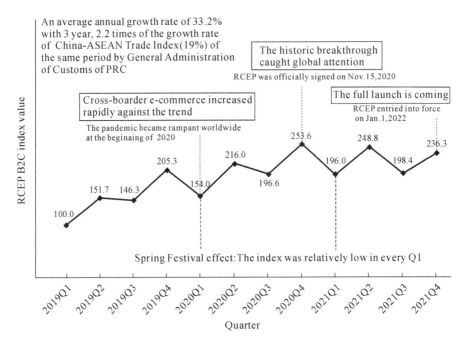

Figure 2-7 Trend of RCEP B2C Index from 2019 to 2021

Secondly, the index rose rapidly which increased 2. 4 times within 3 years with an average annual growth rate of 33. 2%. The growth rate of 2020 was 2. 2 times the growth rate of the China-ASEAN Trade Index (reflecting the overall trade situation) of the General Administration of Customs in the same period (19. 6%), which indicates the great vitality of cross-border e-commerce imports.

2. 3. 1. 2   A structural perspective

The RCEP B2C Index was affected by the economic cycle and emergencies.

Firstly, affected by the traditional Chinese New Year, the index is the lowest in Q1 each year.

Secondly, since the beginning of 2020 when the pandemic has been raging around the world, the development of traditional trade has stagnated while cross-border e-commerce has developed rapidly, showing strong resilience and potential.

Thirdly, after the RCEP was officially signed on November 15, 2020, the tariff reduction commitments such as immediate reduction to zero tariff and reduce to zero tariffs within ten years have attracted much attention. Particularly, the breakthrough of a bilateral tariff reduction arrangement between China and Japan for the first time rose the expectation and confidence to the development of market. RCEP entried into force on January 1, 2022. Although the influence of RCEP is not salient according to the index trend, it will definitely benefit millions of consumers and enterprises and shorten the "economic distance" of different countries. It will also further enhance the post-pandemic economic recovery capacity of various countries and promote a long-term development.

2.3.2　Primary Indicators: Increasing Together to Promote China's Cross-Border E-Commerce Import Prosperity

This book draws the following conclusion by comparing the trend of the four primary indicators of this index with the total index (see Figure 2-8). The spiraling RCEP B2C trade scale indicator has seen the largest increase (4.0 times within 3 years), followed by the steadily rising B2C enterprise development indicator (3.2 times within 3 years). The B2C market demand indicator came to the third (1.8 times within 3 years) with the largest fluctuation. Although the growth of B2C platform service indicator is less impressive (1.4 times within 3 years), it kept improving continuously.

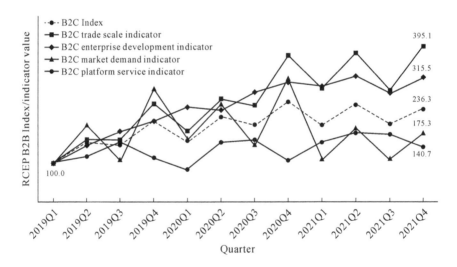

Figure 2-8　Trend of the RCEP B2C Index and Primary Indicators from 2019 to 2021

2.3.2.1　Trade Scale: Most Rapid Increase Driven by Vitality of Cross-Border E-Commerce than that of the Full Volume of Trade

Generally, the RECP B2C trade scale indicator has the fastest growth rate with an annual average growth rate of 58.1% in 3 years, which is similar to the overall index trend(see Figure 2-9). It also fluctuated within

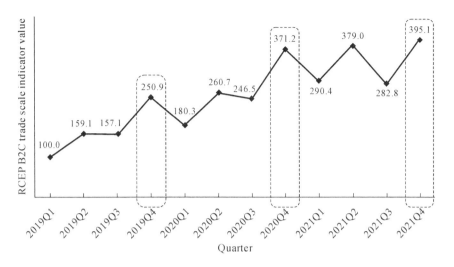

Figure 2-9 Trend of RCEP B2C Trade Scale Indicator from 2019 to 2021

different quarters. Particularly, influenced by "Double 11" shopping carnival (on November 11), the trade scale in Q4 grew rapidly every year, with an average growth rate of 50% compared with Q3. In addition, the trade scale index peaked at 395.1 in 2021Q4, showing the prosperity of cross-border e-commerce imports in the RCEP region.

Structurally, the order quantity, transactions and number of brands on Tmall Global in the RCEP region have all increased rapidly. The average year-on-year growth rates of 2020Q1 to 2021Q1 were 31.8%, 36.2% and 30.9%, exceeding the average annual growth rate (2.8%) of China's total merchandise imports from RCEP region from 2019 to 2020, which suggests strong vitality of cross-border e-commerce.

2.3.2.2　Enterprise Development: Strong Momentum with Increasing Brand Stickiness in the RCEP Region

Generally, on the one hand, the average annual growth rate of the RCEP (B2C) enterprise development indicator from 2019 to 2021 was 46.7%, indicating the strong development momentum of RCEP enterprises (brands) (see Figure 2-10). As the only one of the 4 primary indicators of

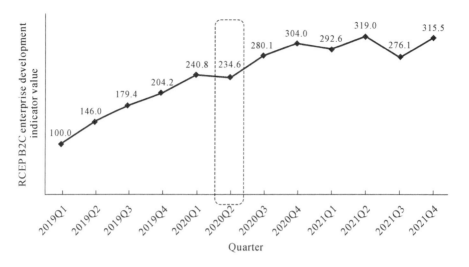

Figure 2-10　Trend of RCEP B2C Enterprise Development Indicator from 2019 to 2021

this index which is not influenced by quarters, it reflects that the confidence of RCEP enterprises in the Chinese market is not affected by economic cyclical fluctuations. On the other hand, the COVID-19 pandemic outbreak in 2021Q1 had a slight impact on the development of RCEP enterprises, but the substantial reversal in Q3 confirmed again the strong resilience of cross-border e-commerce.

　　Structurally, the average year-on-year growth rate of the number of new brands in the RCEP region was 31.5% from 2020Q1 to 2021Q2. Countries like Thailand and Malaysia provide popular products with the most significant growth rate; Thai latex pillows and Malaysian bird's nests have become well-received by Chinese consumers. Meanwhile, the settlement and development of these nationwide famous brands further facilitate the simultaneous growth of other local brands and enhance the regional influence and synchronous growth of enterprises. In addition, the average product output of brands in the RCEP region has grown steadily year on year by 8.4% quarterly on average, with expanding product categories and increasing brand stickiness. In the meanwhile, the number of Tmall Global's successful business incubation grows sharply year on year by

122. 2% quarterly, which is mainly attributed to the active influence of the platform. Tmall Global lowers the participation costs of merchants, provides merchants with horizontal capacity support, reversely inputs customer insights to brands, and thus formed a positive synergistic closed loop to constantly promote the successful incubation of new businesses.

2. 3. 2. 3　Market Demand: With the Greatest Seasonal Fluctuations, Chinese Consumers Have the Potential to Lead the Global Price

Generally, the average annual growth rate of the RECP B2C market demand indicator from 2019 to 2021 was 20. 6%, with the greatest seasonal fluctuations among the 4 primary indicators (see Figure 2-11). Due to various sales promotions, Q2 and Q4 were obviously the peak of relative market demand each year. In addition, under the pandemic, China's market demand for products in the RCEP region in 2020 increased, rather than decreased, and the B2C market demand indicator rose by an average of 25. 6% in 2020 compared to that in 2019. However, it is also worth noting that after the normalization of pandemic prevention, consumption became more rational, and the market demand in 2021 declined significantly

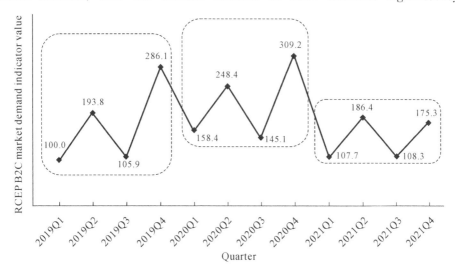

Figure 2-11　Trend of RCEP B2C Market Demand Indicator from 2019 to 2021

compared to that in 2020, though still better than that in 2019.

Structurally, the average number of orders of brands in the RCEP region rises and falls simultaneously with the per customer transaction, showcasing a similar trend. Specifically, the average per customer transaction of brands in the RCEP region rises in general, with an average year-on-year growth rate of 3.9% from 2020Q1 to 2021Q2, and the highest growth rate of 9.4%. This reflects that while the turnover of many European and American brands has declined due to geopolitics and global economic situation, the demand and recognition of Chinese consumers for RCEP brands have risen against the trend, which has stimulated the growth of the average per customer transaction, indicating Chinese customers' potential of leading the global market and shaping the trend of consumer goods prices.

2.3.2.4　Platform Services: Continually Improved Platform Services and Consumer Experience Despite the Pandemic and Other External Obstacles

Generally, although the B2C platform service indicator from 2019 to 2021 was only 12.1%, which is relatively low among the 4 primary indicators, the continually improved consumer experience was obvious(see Figure 2-12). It is worth noting that in the past, the platform service

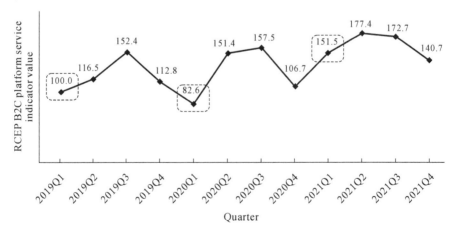

Figure 2-12　Trend of RCEP B2C Platform Service Indicator from 2019 to 2021

indicator in Q1 was always relatively low each year due to the logistic suspension during the Spring Festival. However, since the Spring Festival in 2021, more and more logistics companies and businesses have made great efforts to optimize their services during this holiday. "No closing during the spring festival" has gradually become a new trend, promoting the B2C platform service indicator in 2021Q1 to increase by 41.9%, rather than decrease. The decline of the B2C platform service indicator in Q3 and Q4 of 2021 was mainly attributed to the recurrence of the pandemic in China and other countries since the winter, resulting in the increasing average logistics time of both bonded warehouses and overseas shipments.

Structurally, on the one hand, as Chinese customers' satisfaction with the RCEP brands has steadily increased, and these brands have gained higher acceptance among them. On the other hand, though hindered by the pandemic worldwide, rising shipping costs and so on, the logistics time of bonded warehouses and overseas shipments still decreased in general with occasional rebounds. Compared with 2020Q1, the average logistics time of bonded warehouses in 2021Q1 decreased by 42%, and that of overseas shipments also decreased by 21%. To lower the logistics time, Tmall Global and Cainiao have cooperated to establish multiple storage sites overseas. Through the improvement of cooperation agreements with many bonded warehouses and various ways of cooperation with brands, the intelligent warehouse distribution network has been launched to store cross-border commodities in the warehouse closest to consumers in advance, so that the proportion of cross-border packages delivered the next day can be increased by up to 90%, further optimizing the consumer experience.

2. 4   RCEP Cross-Border Payment Service Index

This section reflects the analysis results and core conclusions of the RCEP Cross-Border Payment Service Index from surface to depth, based on the index itself and the 2 primary indicators — cross-border payment service scale and cross-border payment service quality.

2. 4. 1   Index: The Pandemic Catalyzed Trade Digitization and the Supporting Payment Services Grew Rapidly

2. 4. 1. 1   A General Perspective

Firstly, the overall trend steadily rised. From 2018Q1 to 2021Q4, despite the complex external economic situation, cross-border payment services in the RCEP region steadily developed. In 2021, the RCEP Cross-Border Payment Service Index scaled new heights. The index in 2021Q4 reached 214. 1, exceeding 200 for the first time(see Figure 2-13).

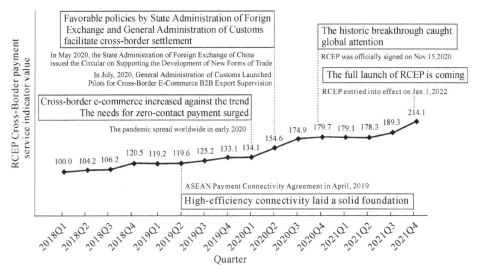

Figure 2-13   Trend of RCEP Cross-Border Payment Service Index from 2018 to 2021

Secondly, the index rapidly rised. RCEP Cross-Border Payment Service Index rose 2.1 times from 2018 to 2021, with an average annual growth rate of 21.0%. During this period, the index grew the fastest in 2020Q2, 2018Q4 and 2020Q3, with ring growth rates of 15.2%, 13.4% and 13.2% respectively, far higher than the average quarterly growth rate of 5.3% from 2018 to 2021. In 2021, Q4 was the quarter with the most obvious growth. Its ring growth rate was 13.1%, second only to that in 2020Q3, and ranked the fourth among all 16 quarters from 2018 to 2021. The year-on-year growth rate in 2021Q4 even reached up to 19.1%.

2.4.1.2　A Structural Perspective

Firstly, as the above-mentioned RCEP SMEs Cross-Border E-Commerce (B2B) Index and RCEP Cross-Border E-Commerce Purchase (B2C) Index reflect, since the beginning of 2020, cross-border e-commerce has grown rapidly despite the pandemic raging around the world. Digital payment, as a ancillary service for the cross-border e-commerce industry, took the opportunity of the convenient payment method, the spread of online consumption and procurement to quickly infuse every aspect of our lives after the pandemic, which led to the largest increase in RCEP Cross-Border Payment Service Index during the reporting period in 2020, and the rapid growth in 2021.

Secondly, in the spring of 2020, China's relevant economic and trade departments introduced a series of favorable policies to facilitate cross-border payment and settlement: supporting the innovation of new forms of cross-border trade; simplifying the process of foreign exchange; optimizing foreign exchange services; firmly supporting the resumption of work and production; and promoting the high-quality development of the foreign trade economy. As for China Customs, it has innovatively carried out a series of pilot customs for cross-border e-commerce B2B export, added customs supervision codes 9710 and 9810, extended the innovative achievements of cross-border e-commerce supervision from B2C to B2B, and implemented convenient measures for customs clearance. In this context, higher cross-border transaction volumes have naturally contributed to the prosperity of cross-border payments, leading to the substantial growth of RCEP Cross-Border Payment Service Index in 2020Q3, up 13.2% from 2020Q2.

Thirdly, the formal entry into force of the RCEP on 1 January 2022 will substantially promote the deepening of regional cooperation, which will inevitably bring about the sustained and vigorous development of cross-border payment services in the RCEP region.

2.4.2 Primary Indicators: Scale and Quality Went Hand in Hand, and Funds Flowed to RCEP Trade Enterprises

By comparing the index and the 2 primary indicators(see Figure 2-14), it is clear that, on the one hand, the increase of the scale cross-border payment service indicator was greater (rose by 2.5 times from 2018 to 2021), reflecting the stronger demand for cross-border payment services

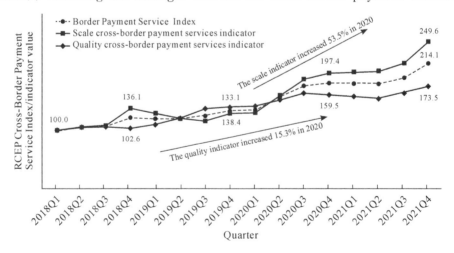

Figure 2-14 Trend of RCEP Cross-Border Payment Service Index and Primary Indicators from 2018 to 2021

over time; during these 4 years, the scale indicator rose the fastest in 2020 (with a year-on-year growth rate of 53. 5%), and rose relatively slowly in 2021 (with a year-on-year growth rate of 26. 4%). On the other hand, although the increase in the RCEP cross-border payment service quality indicator was small (rising by 1. 7 times from 2018 to 2021), it reflects the gradual optimization of cross-border payment services; during these 4 years, the quality indicator rose the fastest in 2020 (with a year-on-year growth rate of 15. 3%), and also increased significantly in 2021 (with a year-on-year growth rate of 8. 8%).

2. 4. 2. 1   Cross-Border Payment Service Ccale: Overseas Procurement Demand Remained Strong and Payment Transactions Kept Active

Generally, firstly, the vitality indicator of RCEP cross-border payment services grew the fastest, with an average annual growth rate of 38. 3% from 2018 to 2021, much higher than the other two secondary indicators (see Figure 2-15). During these 4 years, the number of payments in 2020Q2 grew the fastest, and the vitality indicator rose by 46. 7% month on

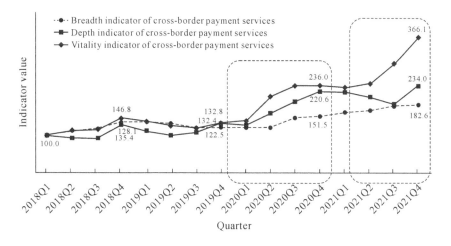

Figure 2-15   Trend of Breadth, Depth and Vitality Indicators of RCEP Cross-Border Payment Services from 2018 to 2021

month. Secondly, the depth indicator and the breadth indicator of RCEP cross-border payment services have also maintained a high above-double-digit growth rate, with average annual growth rates of 23.7% and 16.3% respectively from 2018 to 2021. During these 4 years, the number of sellers representing the breadth of cross-border payments declined slightly in 2020Q2, but then continued to rise as many new merchants (new sellers) started to do cross-border business online. At the same time, the depth indicator of RCEP cross-border payment services decreased first, and then increased in 2021. Thirdly, the comparison of the depth indicator and the vitality indicator in 2021 shows that, although the number of cross-border payments has increased, the payment amount has decreased or had a growth rate much lower than that of the number of payments. This indicates that orders tend to be fragmented and small, reflecting the distinctive characteristics of "micro multinational enterprises" to some extent.

Structurally, in terms of receiving regions, the receiving scale of cross-border e-commerce businesses (sellers) in China is larger than that in other regions. In other regions, Southeast Asian e-commerce ranks first in the number of sellers, receipts, and collection amounts, followed by Japan, R. O. Korea, Australia, and Singapore. The outbreak of the pandemic in 2020 led to an increase in the overall revenue of e-commerce worldwide. In 2021, however, many small- and medium-sized sellers were forced to close some of their stores due to the tax reform in Europe, rectification and closure of overseas Internet platforms, etc. However, the overseas procurement demand is still high, businesses gradually turned to other operation channels such as private operations and independent stations to seek development. Transactions in new forms of business feature higher frequency and small orders from the payment process.

2. 4. 2. 2   Cross-Border Payment Service Quality: Continuous Breakthrough in
              Efficiency and Maintenance of Convenience

Generally, traditional methods of cross-border payment and settlement
have common problems such as long waiting times, high costs, many
intermediate links, and hard-to-control risks(see Figure 2-16). However, it
can be concluded from the above figure that, on the one hand, the efficiency
of RCEP cross-border payment services grew at an average annual rate of
16. 9% from 2018 to 2021, which is more obvious than the growth rate of
payment convenience (with an average annual growth rate of 12. 4%).
During these 4 years, 2019 is the key period for optimizing the transfer
duration. In this year, the efficiency indicator in Q3 increased by 12. 1%
month on month, and that in Q4 increased by 33. 4% year on year. This
was mainly attributed to the rise of cross-border payment enterprises in
China at that time. As a result, the setting of payment licenses contributed
to the gradual establishment of industry standards and the gradual decline of
cross-border payment rates. At the same time, during the pandemic in
2020, promoted by surging demand for online payments, cross-border
payment efficiency continued to improve, with a year-on-year growth rate of

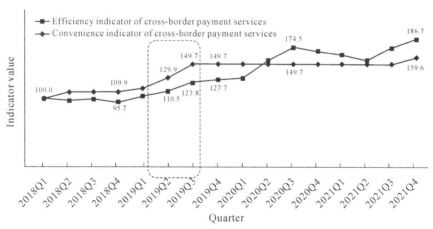

**Figure 2-16   Trend of Efficiency and Convenience Indicators of RCEP Cross-Border
Payment Services from 2018 to 2021**

39.1% in 2020Q2. On the other hand, from the beginning of 2018 to the end of 2019, cross-border payment platforms have added multiple currencies with technological means and channel connections to meet the multinational enterprises' more and better collection needs, thus constantly improving the convenience indicator of cross-border payment services. Since then, the convenience indicator has remained stable.

Structurally, service providers of cross-border payments have continued to improve the efficiency of capital turnover, and have reduced the financial pressure on merchants by opening more settlement channels with cooperative banks. Cash flow is very important for small multinational enterprises. In the past, money transfers took over "T+7" days. But now, thanks to the instant transfer, it is instantaneous to complete a transfer, facilitating the development of this industry. In addition, the transaction currencies of cross-border payments have remained relatively stable, meeting the demand for customary settlement currencies in the trade flow. In all links of cross-border e-commerce, merchants have also become more satisfied with the digitalization of payments.

3   Related Cases of Cross-Border E-Commerce

3. 1   Digital Cross-Border Trade Platform Connecting the World

In the past 20 years, the deep integration of new technologies and globalization has greatly promoted the development of cross-border e-commerce and given birth to a series of professional digital cross-border trade platforms. As time goes by, the services provided by relevant digital cross-border trade platforms have gradually expanded from the initial information interaction to all links in the process of cross-border trade, such as transactions, payments, and logistics, bringing significant convenience to sellers and consumers. The establishment of free trade zones has further reduced the tax costs of cross-border trade. With the combined effect of these factors, sellers have been able to engage in cross-border trade with the same costs and in a way similar to domestic trade.

The root cause is that digital cross-border trade platforms have integrated the markets of various countries through IT-based approaches and reduced the information asymmetry between buyers and sellers, thus expanding the breadth and depth of trade in the virtual space. For platforms, the marginal cost of attracting more sellers to engage in cross-border trade is almost zero; for cross-border trade sellers, the unique network effect of digital cross-border trade platforms can bring more business opportunities than traditional agency trade. Therefore, as an important carrier of cross-border e-commerce, digital cross-border trade platforms can improve the welfare of all market entities and, in turn, achieve Pareto improvement. The following are two typical cases of digital cross-border trade platforms.

3. 1. 1 AliExpress

AliExpress, established in 2010, is a global market-oriented cross-border e-commerce platform owned by Alibaba Group. AliExpress is mainly aimed at foreign retail buyers while sellers are mainly from China, so it is also called "the international version of Taobao". This platform guarantees transactions through international accounts of Alipay and delivers commodities using international logistics channels of its own or a third party. After years of development, AliExpress has set up 18 language sites, covering over 200 countries and regions in the world, and has become the largest cross-border retail e-commerce platform in China and the third largest English online shopping website in the world.

AliExpress not only creates enormous opportunities for small- and medium-sized cross-border e-commerce businesses around the world, but also provides a brand-new lifestyle for consumers in various countries or regions. For sellers, AliExpress provides one-stop shop services: sellers of small- and medium-sized businesses only need to fulfil the qualification requirements of the platform, and then they can open shops on the platform and expand their businesses all over the world. At the same time, the platform also provides a variety of services for them, such as dropshipping, capital settlement, cross-border logistics, and so on, which significantly lowers the threshold for cross-border trade. For buyers all over the world, they can buy almost everything they want at a lower price on AliExpress.

More importantly, AliExpress amazes many foreign consumers with the "Chinese speed" of the logistics industry. Thanks to the domestic preferred warehouses AliExpress established around the world, consumers in many countries and regions have been able to receive commodities from China within 5 working days, and in R. O. Korea, even within 72 hours.

To some extent, AliExpress can be regarded as the Chinese solution of B2C digital cross-border trade platforms. Similar to Taobao, Aliexpress does not directly sell commodities on its platform. Instead, it serves sellers of small- and medium-sized businesses as a carrier of digital cross-border trade, which endows the platform with inclusive properties. With RCEP provisions related to tariffs and cross-border e-commerce coming into force, AliExpress and related small- and medium-sized sellers will usher in more business opportunities and bring more convenience to consumers in the RCEP region.

3. 1. 2 Amazon

Amazon is a multinational e-commerce company headquartered in Seattle, USA. It is currently one of the world's largest online retailers and ranks third in the *Fortune* Global 500 in 2021. Amazon was founded in 1994. At that time, it only sold books online. But with the innovation of Internet business models and the progress of information technology, Amazon has kept expanding its business and gradually become a comprehensive digital cross-border trade platform integrating self-operated trading and third-party sales. The main markets of Amazon's e-commerce department include North America, Europe, the Middle East, Australia, etc. Among them, the share of the North American e-commerce market exceeded 40% in 2021 and is still growing rapidly.

Compared with other digital cross-border trade platforms in the market today, Amazon is quite different in two aspects. First, Amazon has invested substantial resources in the past 10-plus years to establish a complete logistics system of its own and storage facilities to improve the delivery efficiency and user experience. But at the same time, Amazon also faces the problem of high investment, low returns. Amazon has set up FBA (fulfillment by Amazon) warehouses around the world. Overseas sellers only need to transport commodities to these warehouses, and Amazon will provide subsequent services including packaging, delivery, and customer service, greatly lowering the participation threshold for cross-border e-commerce. Second, Amazon has also established a huge self-operated department, that is, the platform itself is also involved in the production and sales of commodities. Amazon has set up policies such as "Project Zero" and "Price Drop Refund" for its self-operated commodities, which is highly spoken of by consumers.

3.2　Continuously Innovative Logistics Services

China has become the largest online shopping market and the largest exporter. According to data from the National Bureau of Statistics, the total retail sales of consumer goods in China exceeded 44 trillion RMB yuan in 2021, of which the national online retail sales exceeded 13 trillion RMB yuan. However, the current ratio of China's annual total logistics costs to GDP is about 15%, higher than the 8% of most developed countries. Reducing domestic and foreign logistics costs through new technologies, new ideas, new structures, and reasonable policies is of important significance to promote cost-effectiveness of logistics, facilitate industrial restructuring, cultivate new economic growth drivers, and improve the overall efficiency of the national economy.

The prosperity of cross-border e-commerce is closely connected with fast, convenient, and low-cost logistics services. In the era of cross-border e-commerce, the distribution scale of products in China and around the world has increased exponentially, which also raises the requirements for logistics services. In recent years, Chinese logistics companies represented by Cainiao, SF Express, STO Express, YTO Express, ZTO Express, Best Express, and Yunda Express have also been improving the operational efficiency of the logistics industry through new technologies and new models, such as the Internet of Things, big data, and overseas warehouses. The following are two typical cases of the development of the logistics industry in the digital economy era.

3. 2. 1   Cainiao Logistics Contributes to Cross-Border Trade Development

Founded on May 28, 2013, Cainiao Logistics is a new kind of logistics company established by Alibaba Group, STO Express, YTO Express, ZTO Express, Yunda Express and so on. In the past years, in order to establish a safe and reliable international logistics supply chain, Cainiao Network has continoushy built a global intelligent backbone network. As of today, Cainiao has established an overseas logistics infrastructure network, including core airport hubs and overseas warehouses. This infrastructure network is equipped with 5 logistics hubs and overseas warehouses of over 2 million square meters. Cainiao has cooperated with shipping and aviation companies to operate over 500 international shipping lanes and over 900 international air lanes. Moreover, it has also cooperated with overseas postal and express companies to continuously improve overseas delivery services. In 2020, Cainiao Network handed 4 million cross-border packages per day, ranking first in the whole world.

At the same time, the application of a large number of new technologies has greatly improved the operational efficiency of Cainiao Logistics and promoted the rapid development of green logistics. For example, before the "Double 11" (November 11) in 2020, Cainiao has completed the transformation of the e-commerce logistics information processing system for 11 countries in Southeast Asia, which has a stronger capacity for carrying and processing information. At present, this system has met the connection needs of many e-commerce platforms, nearly 100 express delivery enterprises, tens of thousands of small- and medium-sized sellers, and millions of consumers in the Southeast Asian market. It can guarantee the operation of over 100 million packages every day. The average cost per order has decreased by 10%, and the peak package processing capacity of this system has increased by 10 times. Cainiao's intelligent packing algorithm can also directly reduce the phenomenon of "overuse and over-packaging". By optimizing the container size and recommending reasonable binning plans, Cainiao has managed to make the number of "slimmed" packages in its warehouses exceed 250 million. Now this technology has been promoted across the whole industry.

Driven by technologies and advocating win-win ecology, Cainiao Logistics perfectly fits the theme of cross-border trade development in the era of the digital economy, and to some extent, overturns people's perception of the traditional logistics industry. With the formal implementation of the RCEP, Cainiao Logistics will also usher in broader development space and provide logistics support for the development of digital cross-border trade in the RCEP region.

3.2.2 SF International

SF Holding Co., Ltd. (hereinafter referred to as SF) was established in 1993. After years of development, it has grown into the largest private logistics enterprise in China. In addition to providing high-quality logistics services at the distribution end, SF has also extended its services to front-end processes, including production, supply, marketing, and distribution, for the value chain. Moreover, it provides customers with integrated logistics services, including intelligent warehousing management, sales forecasting, and settlement management. In 2010, SF started to expand its international business and established the SF International Division (hereinafter referred as SF International).

SF International is committed to providing convenient and reliable international express services for domestic and foreign manufacturers, trading companies, cross-border e-commerce companies and consumers, aiming to help outstanding companies and products in China "go global" and "bring in" overseas high-quality companies and products. SF International's standard express and cost-effective economic express have covered 78 countries or regions, including the United States, the European Union countries, Russia, etc. ; cross-border e-commerce small parcel business has covered more than 200 countries or regions around the world, providing high-quality and reliable logistics services for cross-border e-commerce export sellers. At present, SF operates more than 3,500 international flights every year, and has established 12 overseas warehouses in Europe, North America and Southeast Asia. By leveraging on domestic and overseas collection and delivery networks, warehousing, customs clearance, agency and other resources, SF International provides one-stop import and export supply chain service for customers.

As a "top performer" in the traditional logistics industry, SF has long insisted on investing most of its profits in the research and development of logistics technologies and the layout of logistics infrastructures. It has always adhered to the customer-oriented business philosophy, which has won SF a significant reputation among consumers. With the continuous development of cross-border e-commerce under the framework of the RCEP, SF will also usher in more business opportunities and introduce the high-quality logistics services in China to enterprises and consumers in various countries.

3. 3 Cross-Border Payment Platform

Payment is an essential link in trade. In this sense, the diversified and digital development of the cross-border payment platforms is equivalent to building a convenient and safe channel for cross-border trade. Since then, everything has become easier. Enterprises in the RCEP region are able to enjoy safer and smoother payment and settlement services, and their capital allocation is also more flexible and guaranteed. Thanks to the rapid development of digital payment platforms, more and more small and micro businesses in various countries become able to participate in cross-border trade in the RCEP region at a lower cost. Inclusiveness driven by digitalization has truly been translated into reality.

Generally speaking, online cross-border payments include three links: acquiring, money transfer, and exchange: acquiring refers to the transfer of information flow and capital flow between overseas buyers and sellers; money transfer refers to the transfer of capital flow and information flow between cross-border banks or third-party payment institutions; exchange refers to the settlement after the enterprise receives money. At present, there are third-party payment institutions at every link in the cross-border payment chain. Various types of payment platforms have integrated financial services into their business scope by technological means to escort cross-border trade in the RCEP region. WorldFirst and Airwallex, as representative cross-border payment platforms in China and around the world, began with two different links—money transfer and exchange, respectively—and have actively integrated modern technologies. While dedicating on their own businesses, they have also gradually extended to other cross-border payment services to provide more professional and systematic cross-border payment services for cross-border e-commerce development in the RCEP region and the rest of the world.

3. 3. 1 WorldFirst

WorldFirst was established in London in 2004 and joined the Ant Group in 2019. Since then, it has become the fastest-growing cross-border financial service platform in the payment industry, along with Alipay, mainly providing payment services for cross-border enterprises. According to the "Technology-Empowered Digital Trade in Asia Pacific" report released by Deloitte in 2021, WorldFirst ranks first among cross-border e-commerce sellers from China, Japan, and R. O. Korea, occupying a share of above 40%.

Alipay once put forward the concept of "traveling around the world with a mobile phone", while WorldFirst helps merchants "sell globally with one account". Payment service-focused WorldFirst pays more attention to improving the quality of its cross-border payment services. The platform has also introduced the "N10" model, that is to "connect N currencies, N markets, and transfer money globally in 1 minute with 0 exchange rate loss". This innovation of payment model has reduced the overall transfer duration of foreign trade enterprises from 1—2 months to seconds, greatly easing the capital turnover pressure of foreign trade enterprises. At the same time, the fast, convenient, and economical cross-border payment services have also significantly lowered the capital threshold for enterprises to participate in cross-border trade. Leveraging on its own strengths in payment services, WorldFirst has successfully helped more cross-border e-commerce enterprises achieve the goal of "selling globally with zero threshold". According to the latest data from the platform, before the formal entry into force of RCEP, many sellers on the platform were eager to get a share of the global "New Year's Holiday Economy". Since July 1,

2021, Chinese sellers' demand for loans such as E-Commerce Loan and USD Loan has surged due to the capital gap of long-time stock during Christmas and New Year's Day. At the same time, with more and more products "created in China" delivered to overseas consumers, the "flow" of cross-border payments has also reached its annual peak.

3.3.2 Airwallex

Airwallex, established in Melbourne, Australia in 2015, is a third-party payment company that started out as foreign exchange hedging. The foreign exchange services that financial institutions can provide mainly include checking, locking, purchasing, settling, buying and selling forward foreign exchange. Bank exchange products are mainly standardized products. New exchange technology companies will help users predict exchange rate changes and operate exchange through more friendly methods such as real-time locking of exchange rates and control of exchange losses.

The establishment of Airwallex stemmed from the personal experience of its founders on the operational difficulties of small cross-border businesses. In cross-border trade activities, enterprises, especially SMEs, often need to face relatively high foreign exchange fees and bank payment service fees relative to their own size. Airwallex is committed to building a more streamlined, transparent and cost-effective cross-border payment solution. The platform's self-developed foreign exchange engine is directly connected to the interbank exchange rate market, providing the most competitive prices and foreign exchange trading and risk management technologies. which makes it highly competitive in foreign exchange business. Based on this solid exchange aggregation capability, Airwallex has gradually expanded its payment business scope and continued to launch rich financial products. At present, the platform gradually has the functions of acquiring, receiving, paying and issuing cards. Currently, Airwallex has set up offices in China, Singapore, Malaysia and other places, providing cross-border payment solutions for cross-border trade companies in 19 markets around the world. The business scope includes multi-currency exchange, global collection accounts, global payment, etc. The industries it serves cover cross-border e-commerce, online travel, logistics, education and study abroad, financial institutions, digital marketing, online entertainment, and so on.

3. 4   Small but Excellent Micro-Multinationals

With the comprehensive establishment and continuous advancement of RCEP, cross-border trade in the region will inevitably become more active. At the same time, the development of digital infrastructure in the region and the popularization of Internet technology also promote the prosperous symbiosis of cross-border e-commerce and SMEs in various countries. On the one hand, the development of cross-border e-commerce has greatly lowered the capital and personnel thresholds for enterprises to participate in cross-border trade, and more and more SMEs can participate in cross-border trade through online platforms more easily. Micro-multinational enterprises have become the norm, and the dream of digital inclusiveness will become reality. On the other hand, SMEs are crucial in developing the economy, creating jobs, activating the market, and improving people's livelihood. Take China as an example. Data from Sixlens show that by the end of 2020, the number of SMEs in operation in China exceeded 42 million, accounting for 98.5% of the total number of enterprises in the country (more than 43 million). A large number of SMEs will become the living force of cross-border e-commerce and promote the sustainable development of cross-border e-commerce in the RCEP region.

According to the *Annual Report of Overseas Development of Chinese Enterprises* (2020) jointly released by the Beijing Enterprise International Management Research Base of the University of International Business and Economics and the Social Sciences Academic Press, the transaction scale of global cross-border e-commerce exceeded $1 trillion in 2020, with an average annual growth rate of up to 30%, much higher than that of trade in goods. Under this circumstance, micro-multinational enterprises in the RCEP region have also actively employed cross-border e-commerce platforms for their self-fulfillment. Cross-border e-commerce has provided tailored solutions for inclusive development needs. These needs range from small and micro manufacturing enterprises that expand offline and online channels, cross-border e-commerce 2C (to costomers) merchants that originated from Internet platforms and emphasize the cultivation of dominant intellectual property (IP), to township enterprises that pursue the common prosperity of villages through cross-border trade.

3.4.1 Pegasus Official

Pegasus Official (hereinafter referred to as Pegasus) is a small family-owned enterprise in Thailand that specializes in luggage products. The outbreak of the COVID-19 pandemic has exposed Pegasus' sales to significant uncertainty. Such a challenge forced Pegasus' CEO Kanseenee Sapchotikul to pay closer attention to building its digital services and channels to mitigate the negative impacts of the pandemic and raise business resilience.

Pegasus actively launched products on Amazon and other e-commerce platforms, attempting to establish and maintain its digital marketing channels, expand and sustain the global business. Meanwhile, Pegasus conducted timely research on global customers' intention to shop online. Pegasus found that masks were in great demand internationally, so it began exporting masks to the United States and other countries. As a result, its sales increased by more than 300% within only six months. Since then, Pegasus has launched its luggage products on the e-commerce platforms in succession. It is estimated that sales from Amazon alone would account for 50% of its total revenues.

In conclusion, in addition to Pegasus's active exploration of marketing opportunities, the cross-border e-commerce platforms also contributed to its success in surviving the pandemic. Pegasus has successfully moved the offline business to the online world through the development of cross-border e-commerce, which expanded its market space rapidly. Such practice is worthy of reference for other small and micro enterprises.

3. 4. 2　Dongqi Group

A large number of micro-multinational enterprises that started from e-commerce businesses sell goods to consumers. The "old three" of portable batteries, data cables, and lighters have been unable to meet the personalized consumer demands with the rapid change of the times. Consequently, growing e-commerce entrepreneurs began to focus on niche products. Dongqi Group from Hangzhou started with only three members in charge of operation, design, and cooperation with factories, yet they had insightful views on cross-border e-commerce.

Sun Dongqi, the founder of Dongqi Group, suggests that niche products featuring personality and support for customization are more likely to be welcomed than mass-market goods. Dongqi Group has launched several novel and distinctive products that sell out immediately when they go online, including tatami-style gaming chairs for Japanese otaku men, cartoon owl door stops for American stay-at-home dads, and colorful haute couture sweaters for turtles favored by Japanese and European customers. While this was a great encouragement to Sun Dongqi, it also made him realize the importance of innovating new products and building unique IPs. The pandemic did not hamper the development of Dongqi Group. Instead, it stimulated new ideas for product design. White-collar workers in Europe, the United States, Japan, and R. O. Korea started to concern about how to look good in Zoom meetings since the pandemic made remote work a trend. Therefore, products like laptop stands and wall decorations are selling well. Accordingly, Dongqi Group quickly launched beauty magnifying lamps that make the face more three-dimensional and the skintone more beautiful. Dongqi Group is now building an independent foreign trade station, which allows it to develop the Direct to Consumer (D2C) model beyond the Business to Customer (B2C) model.

Dongqi Group's success derives from its precise sensitivity to individualized consumer demands and benefits from extensive cross-border e-commerce platforms and big data analysis techonology. Cross-border e-commerce has built a closer relationship between global customers and producers and opened the door to wealth for innovative entrepreneurs.

3. 5　Government-Enterprise Cooperation and Government Innovation Management

RCEP is the world's most populous and promising free trade zone with the largest scale of economic and trade coverage. RCEP has fully demonstrated the confidence and determination of its members to jointly uphold multilateralism and free trade, and promote regional economic integration. It will make significant contributions to the regional or even global development of cross-border e-commerce. And the development of cross-border e-commerce has also profoundly promoted government-enterprise cooperation, inter-governmental cooperation, and government innovation management of members, thus promoting regional economic and social development.

Win-win cooperation strengthens the country and enriches the people. Government-enterprise cooperation has become an inclination in the era of cross-border e-commerce, with governments taking the lead in integrating resources and enterprises providing technical support, jointly promoting the rapid development of cross-border e-commerce. Joint contribution leads to shared benefits. Inter-governmental cooperation breaks through the traditional barriers to international trade by reducing tariffs and driving the movement of trade factors. This gives rise to cross-border data circulation and digitalization of the customs system, hence improving efficiency, reducing costs, and boosting development. Innovative cooperation constructs a digital government. Government innovation management has become a major trend in the digital era. Digital technology is now widely applied to facilitate scientific decision-making in the government, introduce policies, laws and regulations, implement intelligent construction, and enhance the effectiveness and efficiency of government management and services.

3.5.1 China (Hangzhou) Cross-Border E-Commerce Comprehensive Pilot Area

On March 7, 2015, the State Council approved the establishment of the China (Hangzhou) Cross-Border E-Commerce Comprehensive Pilot Zone (CPZ), which is also the first comprehensive pilot zone in China. As the national e-commerce hub, Hangzhou plans to transform CPZ into a comprehensive platform characterized by "online integration + cross-border trade + comprehensive services" through 3 to 5 years of reform and experimentation. With "logistics clearance channels + online comprehensive service platform information system + financial value-added services" as its core competitiveness, CPZ aims to integrate "customs" "taxation" "foreign exchange" "inspection" "commerce" "logistics" and "finance" into a distinctive whole. It seeks to combine online comprehensive service platforms with offline comprehensive park platforms to become a national hub for cross-border e-commerce entrepreneurship, innovation, service and big data center.

CPZ provides free registration, online archival filing, and real-time declaration for the RCEP e-commerce enterprises through the online comprehensive services platform. It also connects regulatory authorities (like customs, foreign exchange, taxation, trade and industry, and public security) and financial and logistics enterprises. The interconnection and information sharing between government and enterprise departments realize completely paperless customs clearance with its efficiency improved and costs reduced, thereby optimizing the import and export modes of cross-border e-commerce. Sticking to the principles of "data management, ports release, efficient entry and exit, and full control", CPZ attempts to innovate "a digital fence" and explore a new supervision system of "more data flow, less human intervention, quick customs clearance, and convenient item return" to stimulate accessible customs clearance and free trade.

Under the RCEP framework, zero-tariff products accounted for 90% of the trade in goods. The RCEP members have simplified the customs clearance process and improved its efficiency through system or policy coordination and the application of digital technology. Consequently, cross-border imports and exports have embraced new development opportunities and growth points. CPZ has become the first one to enjoy the dividends brought by RCEP economic and trade rules, develop the new infrastructure of cross-border e-commerce, and create a quality business environment. Hangzhou Municipal Government, Malaysia Digital Economy Corporation

(MDEC) and Alibaba Group signed a memorandum of understanding (MoU) in 2017. Cainiao Network officially launched its first Hangzhou-Kuala Lumpur flight in 2020. CPZ will further strengthen its close cooperation with the RCEP countries and intensify the competitive advantages of China and Asia-Pacific supply chains around the globe.

3.5.2 Electronic World Trade Platform

The marriage between new technologies and globalization has created a whole new form of trade that requires new rules. The Electronic World Trade Platform (eWTP) Initiative emerged on the scene. The eWTP was officially initiated at the Boao Forum for Asia (BFA) in March 2016, intending to help SMEs, developing countries, and youth access global markets. As an open, transparent, and non-profit platform, eWTP is dedicated to coordinating the cooperation and input of stakeholders among RCEP members in cross-border trade. It has fostered the joint development of cross-border electronic trade.

In October 2017, the Electronic World Trade initiated the construction of a trial zone in Hangzhou, China, strongly supporting the international development of major domestic e-commerce platforms within the RCEP region. By establishing an intelligent logistics network, improving cross-border payment systems and expanding third-party services, the two-way import and export channels of global electronic trade are broadened. Leveraging the dual convenience of infrastructure interconnectivity and cross-border e-commerce, the trial zone promotes innovative exploration and coordinated development at both the market and institutional levels, aiming to build a free, convenient, open and efficient global electronic trade corridor, and accelerate the establishment of a hub for the online Silk Road. The trial zone has developed a comprehensive data management system based on data, achieving sub-second customs clearance through the "three-way collision" of transaction, payment, and logistics information.

The first overseas eHub was officially launched in Malaysia under the eWTP initiative in November 2017. This marked high appreciation and widespread acceptance of the eWTP platform in RCEP members. Since the launch of eWTP, Malaysia's exports of goods to China have increased dramatically, ranking at the top among countries along the Belt and Road. Vast small- and medium-sized sellers in Malaysia have benefited from the convenience and dividends of cross-border e-commerce. For example, a small enterprise in Malaysia selling bird's nests shortened its clearance duration after the China-Malaysia customs clearance system took effect. Its turnover on Tmall Global surged from 20 million RMB yuan to 100 million RMB yuan within a year.

4　Cross-Border E-Commerce Development of RCEP Members

4. 1　Cross-Border E-Commerce Development of China

4. 1. 1　Overview of Social Economy and Cross-Border E-Commerce Development of China

In 2020, China's Gross Domestic Product (GDP) was worth $14722. 7 billion, representing year-on-year growth of 2. 3%. China was then home to 1. 41 billion people, of which 17. 9% were aged 14 years or younger, 68. 6% between 15 and 64 years, and only 13. 5% over 65 years. Its birth rate was 8. 52‰, while the death rate was 7. 07‰, with the natural increase rate standing at 1. 45‰. The urban per capita disposable income came in at 43,834 RMB yuan, while that in rural areas stood at 17,131 RMB yuan. And the average annual wage of employed persons was 79,854 RMB yuan.

In 2020, the population of Internet users in China hits 989 million, with an Internet availability rate of 70%. In particular, mobile phone Internet users reached 986 million, and its proportion was up to 99. 7%; users accessing the Internet via their televisions, desktops, laptops, and tablet PCs occupied 24. 0%, 32. 8%, 28. 2%, and 22. 9% respectively. The amount of rural Internet users reached 309 million, making up for 31.3% of the total Internet users; while the number of urban Internet users was 680 million, accounting for the rest 68.7%. Online shopping users numbered 782 million, accounting for 79.1% of the overall Internet users. Specifically, mobile online shopping users amounted to 781 million, constituting 79.2% of the total(see Figure 4-1).

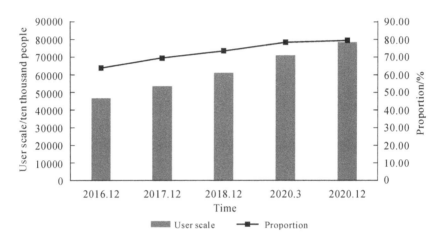

Figure 4-1 User Scales and Proportion from 2016 to 2020

Source: The 47th China Statistical Report on Internet Development.

In 2021, cross-border e-commerce managed to develop against the economic recession and functioned as an essential channel to facilitate trade. In 2021, the import and export volume of cross-border e-commerce totaled 1.98 trillion RMB yuan, up 15% year-on-year, according to statistics from China Customs. Particularly, the e-commerce exports stood at 1.44 trillion RMB yuan, an increase of 24.5% yearly. In terms of market procurement, the export scales have exceeded 900 billion RMB yuan. With the expansion of national pilot programs, China's market procurement export volumes added up to 930.39 billion RMB yuan in 2021, a rise of 32.1%, accounting for 4.3% of the gross export value of the same period in 2020 and contributing to 1.3% of the export growth. A new batch of 46 cross-border e-commerce comprehensive pilot zones have been established nationwide. China has also added two export regulatory codes "9710" and "9810" (for cross-border e-commerce B2B direct export and export overseas warehouses) to facilitate customs clearance. The COVID-19 pandemic has struck the biggest blow to the global economy. Its worldwide spread resulted in increasing instability and uncertainty in the international situation. The world economy remained complicated and grim. Therefore, the 5th Plenary Session of the 19th Central Committee of the CPC, the 14th Five-Year Plan, and Long-Range Objectives through the Year 2035 all point out that China should forcefully promote the profound integration of digital economy and real economy; accelerate the construction of a new development structure with domestic circulation in the lead and the dual domestic and international circulations mutually advancing each other; and speed up its digital development by forging new advantages of the digital economy. The "dual circulations" based on the "dual integration" will together support China's construction of the new development pattern.

4.1.2 Comparison between General Trade and Cross-Border E-Commerce of China

4.1.2.1 China Exports by Country(or Region)

Table 4-1 shows top 10 export countries or regions in general trade and cross-border e-commerce of China.

Table 4-1 Top 10 Export Countries or Regions in General Trade and Cross-Border E-Commerce of China

Rank	General Trade (Top 10 Export Countries or Regions)			Cross-Border E-Commerce (Top 10 Countries or Regions of Export Demand)		
	2019	2020	2021	2019	2020	2021
1	US	US	US	US	US	US

Continued

Rank	General Trade (Top 10 Export Countries or Regions)			Cross-Border E-Commerce (Top 10 Countries or Regions of Export Demand)		
	2019	2020	2021	2019	2020	2021
2	Hong Kong, China	Hong Kong, China	Hong Kong, China	India	India	India
3	Japan	Japan	Japan	Canada	UK	Brazil
4	R. O. Korea	R. O. Korea	Vietnam	UK	Canada	UK
5	Germany	Vietnam	R. O. Korea	Russia	Peru	Canada
6	Vietnam	Germany	Germany	Australia	Australia	Philippines
7	India	India	Netherlands	Brazil	Philippines	Pakistan
8	Netherlands	Netherlands	UK	Nigeria	Mexico	Peru
9	UK	UK	India	Mexico	Brazil	Mexico
10	Singapore	Singapore	Singapore	Germany	Pakistan	Australia

Source: Data of general trade is from China General Administration of Customs and data of cross-border e-commerce is from Alibaba. com.

4.1.2.2 China Imports by Country(or Region)

Table 4-2 shows top 10 import countries or regions in general trade and cross-border e-commerce of China.

Table 4-2 Top 10 Import Countries or Regions in General Trade and Cross-Border E-Commerce of China

Rank	General Trade (Top 10 Import Countries or Regions)			Cross-Border E-Commerce (Top 10 Countries or Regions of Import Demand)		
	2019	2020	2021	2019	2020	2021
1	R. O. Korea	R. O. Korea	Japan	India	Vietnam	India
2	Japan	Japan	R. O. Korea	Thailand	Malaysia	Vietnam
3	US	US	US	US	India	US
4	Germany	Australia	Australia	Vietnam	Thailand	South Africa
5	Taiwan, China	Germany	Germany	Pakistan	US	Thailand
6	Australia	Brazil	Brazil	Taiwan, China	South Africa	France

Continued

Rank	General Trade (Top 10 Import Countries or Regions)			Cross-Border E-Commerce (Top 10 Countries or Regions of Import Demand)		
	2019	2020	2021	2019	2020	2021
7	Brazil	Malaysia	Vietnam	South Africa	Turkey	Ukraine
8	Russia	Vietnam	Malaysia	Turkey	Pakistan	UK
9	Singapore	Russia	Russia	R. O. Korea	R. O. Korea	Germany
10	Vietnam	Saudi Arabia	Thailand	Malaysia	Ukraine	Pakistan

Source: Data of general trade is from China General Administration of Customs and data of cross-border e-commerce is from Alibaba. com.

4.1.2.3   China Exports by Category

Table 4-3 shows top 10 categories of exported goods in general trade and cross-border e-commerce of China.

Table 4-3   Top 10 Categories of Exported Goods in General Trade and Cross-Border E-Commerce of China

Rank	General Trade (Top 10 Categories of Exported Goods)			Cross-Border E-Commerce(Top 10 Categories of Export Demand)		
	2019	2020	2021	2019	2020	2021
1	Broadcasting equipment	Electric motors	Electrical & electronic equipment	Consumer electronics	Security & protection	Consumer electronics
2	Computers	Industrial machinery	Machinery, nuclear reactors & boilers	Beauty & personal care	Medicines & health care	Apparel
3	Office machine parts	Furniture	Furniture, lighting signs & prefabricated buildings	Apparel	Beauty & personal care	Beauty & personal care
4	Integrated circuits	Plastics	Plastics	Household supplies	Consumer electronics	Sports & entertainment

Continued

Rank	General Trade (Top 10 Categories of Exported Goods)			Cross-Border E-Commerce (Top 10 Categories of Export Demand)		
	2019	2020	2021	2019	2020	2021
5	Telephones	Cars & vehicle parts	Optical, photographic, technical, medical & surgical apparatus	Machinery	Machinery	Home & garden
6	Vehicle parts	Precision instruments	Vehicles other than railway or tramway rolling-stock	Cars & motorcycles	Apparel	Machinery
7	Refined petroleum	Apparel (knitted)	Other textiles, suits & worn clothing	Sports & entertainment	Sports & entertainment	Cars & motorcycles
8	Power transformers	Articles of iron & steel	Toys, games & sports requisites	Packaging & printing	Household supplies	Packaging & printing
9	Semiconductors	Apparel (not knitted)	Articles of iron & steel	Watches, jewelry & glasses	Packaging & printing	Furniture
10	Lamps & lighting fittings	Toys & sports requisites	Apparel (not knitted or crocheted)	Luggage, bags & cases	Cars & motorcycles	Health & medical care

Source: Data of general trade is from China General Administration of Customs and data of cross-border e-commerce is from Alibaba. com.

4.1.2.4 China Imports by Category

Table 4-4 shows top 10 categories of imported goods in general trade and cross-border e-commerce of China.

Table 4-4 Top 10 Categories of Imported Goods in General Trade and Cross-Border E-Commerce of China

Rank	General Trade (Top 10 Categories of Imported Goods)			Cross-Border E-Commerce (Top 10 Categories of Import Demand)		
	2019	2020	2021	2019	2020	2021
1	Crude petroleum	Electric motors	Electrical & electronic equipment	Household supplies	Health & medical care	Home & garden
2	Integrated circuits	Petroleum & mineral fuels	Mineral fuels, mineral oils & products of their distillation	Machinery	Household supplies	Sports & entertainment
3	Iron ores	Industrial machinery	Machinery, nuclear reactors, & boilers	Consumer electronics	Machinery	machinery
4	Liquefied petroleum gas	Ores	Slag & ash	Apparel	Consumer electronics	Consumer electronics
5	Cars	Precision instruments	Optical, photographic, technical, medical & surgical apparatus	Minerals & metals	Security & protection	Cars & motorcycles
6	Gold	Cars & vehicle parts	Vehicles other than railway or tramway rolling-stock	Food & beverage	Sports & entertainment	Apparel
7	Copper	Plastics	Plastics	Medicines & health care	Packaging & printing	Packaging & printing
8	Vehicle parts	Gemstones & metals	Copper	Packaging & printing	Construction	Beauty & personal care
9	Machinery	Organic chemicals	Organic chemicals	Agriculture	Apparel	Hardware

Continued

Rank	General Trade (Top 10 Categories of Imported Goods)			Cross-Border E-Commerce (Top 10 Categories of Import Demand)		
	2019	2020	2021	2019	2020	2021
10	Refined petroleum	Copper	Oilseeds, oleaginous fruits, cereals, seeds & fruit	Sports & entertainment	Cars & motorcycles	Furniture

Source: Data of general trade is from China General Administration of Customs and data of cross-border e-commerce is from Alibaba. com.

4. 2 Cross-Border E-Commerce Development of Japan

4. 2. 1 Overview of Social Economy and Cross-Border E-Commerce Development of Japan

In 2020, Japan's GDP amounted to $5.06 trillion dollars, down 4.59% from a year earlier, and its GDP per capita dropped by 4.26% to $40,200 dollars, according to official data from the World Bank. Meanwhile, Japan's total population reached 126 million, with an overall high educational level. Statistics from the Organization for Economic Cooperation and Development (OECD) show that 31.3% of Japanese aged between 25 and 64 years had attained a bachelor's or equivalent higher education degree by 2020, 1.7 times the average of OECD members (18.2%). As a developed country, Japan has a well-developed digital economic infrastructure. In 2021, the population of Internet users in Japan rose to 117 million, with an Internet availability rate of 93%. Japan had 201 million mobile subscribers and 94 million social media users by January 2021, with each availability rate standing at 159% and 74%, according to DataReportal. Statistics from Japan's Ministry of Economy, Trade, and

Industry (METI) indicate that Japanese retail industry recorded 146.46 trillion JPN yen (around $1271.354 billion dollars) in sales in 2020, of which online retailing took up 13.18%.

To develop its digital economy, Japan focuses on digital technology innovation and digitalization of industries, trade, and society. The government of Japan is actively supporting the deep integration of digital technology with economic growth and social governance. **Firstly, digital technology innovation.** The Ministry of Internal Affairs and Communication Integrated Innovation Strategy Promotion Conference of Japan released the final report on its Quantum Technology Innovation Strategy in January 2020. This report put forward that Japan aims to develop the following four aspects: quantum communications and encryption link technology, trusted node technology, quantum relay technology, and wide-area network construction and operation technology. **Secondly, digitalization of industries.** In 2017, Ministry of Economy, Trade and Industry (METI) announced the Connected Industries Strategy that encourages the application of artificial intelligence, the Internet of things, cloud computing, and other technologies to manufacturing. It is to break through the bottlenecks of the aging population, labor shortage, and insufficient industrial competitiveness. Since then, Japan has successively issued the *White Paper on Japanese Manufacturing Industry*, Comprehensive Innovation Strategy, Integrated Innovation Strategy, and 2nd Strategic Innovation Promotion Program (SIP) to advance the digitalization of industries. **Thirdly, digitalization of trade.** In 2013, the government of Japan launched the Japan Revitalization Strategy, which proposes to improve the Japanese economy through digital trade, promote tax preferential system, and introduce instant depreciation for particular information and communication devices. These measures have greatly stimulated the vitality for the development of enterprise informatization.

Fourthly, digitalization of society. In 2016, the Japanese government first proposed the concept of super-smart Society 5.0 in the 5th Science and Technology Basic Plan (2016-2020) and Science, Technology and Innovation Strategy 2016. And Japan further paved the way for Society 5.0 and Connected Industries from the perspective of strategic planning, institutional development, and talent cultivation, under the guidance of documents like the Next Generation Artificial Intelligence Promotion Strategy, Science, Technology, and Innovation Comprehensive Strategy 2017 and Integrated Innovation Strategy, Japan began to implement its Digital New Deal Strategy in 2019. Japan spent more budget on "post 5G" information and communication infrastructure, ICT facilities in schools, and informatization of SMEs to promote its society to be more digital and intelligent.

The scale of e-commerce in Japan has seen an evidently upward trend both domestically and internationally. Domestically, Japan's B2C and B2B market reached 19.3 trillion JPN yen and 334.9 trillion JPN yen respectively in 2020. The overall scale has generally maintained growth momentum in the past 5 years despite its slow growth (see Figure 4-2). Internationally, Japan's sales to Chinese customers alone were up to 19,499 trillion JPN yen in 2020, up 17.8% from that in 2019.

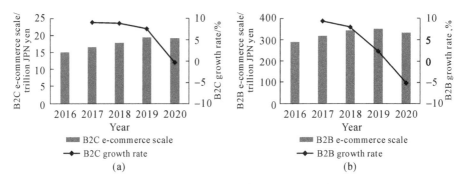

Figure 4-2   Domestic Scales of E-Commerce of Japan

Source: METI of Japan.

4. 2. 2 Comparison between General Trade and Cross-Border E-Commerce of Japan

4. 2. 2. 1 Japan Exports by Country(or Region)

Table 4-5 shows top 10 export countries or regions in general trade and cross-border e-commerce of Japan.

Table 4-5 Top 10 Export Countries or Regions in

General Trade and Cross-Border E-Commerce of Japan

Rank	General Trade (Top 10 Export Countries or Regions)			Cross-Border E-Commerce (Top 10 Countries or Regions of Export Demand)		
	2019	2020	2021	2019	2020	2021
1	US	China	China	Philippines	Philippines	Philippines
2	China	US	US	China	Indonesia	Indonesia
3	R. O. Korea	R. O. Korea	Taiwan, China	Indonesia	Malaysia	Malaysia
4	Taiwan, China	Taiwan, China	R. O. Korea	Australia	China	Vietnam
5	Hong Kong, China	Hong Kong, China	Hong Kong, China	Malaysia	Australia	Australia
6	Thailand	Thailand	Thailand	Vietnam	Vietnam	Thailand
7	Germany	Singapore	Germany	Thailand	Thailand	China
8	Singapore	Germany	Singapore	R. O. Korea	Singapore	Cambodia
9	Vietnam	Vietnam	Vietnam	Singapore	Cambodia	Singapore
10	Australia	Malaysia	Malaysia	Cambodia	R. O. Korea	R. O. Korea

Source: Data of general trade is from Japan Customs, and data of cross-border e-commerce is from Alibaba. com.

4. 2. 2. 2 Japan Imports by Country(or Region)

Table 4-6 shows top 10 import countries or regions in general trade and cross-border e-commerce of Japan.

Rank	General Trade (Top 10 Import Countries or Regions)			Cross-Border E-Commerce (Top 10 Countries or Regions of Import Demand)		
	2019	2020	2021	2019	2020	2021
1	China	China	China	China	China	China
2	US	US	US	Vietnam	Vietnam	Vietnam
3	Australia	Australia	Australia	Thailand	Thailand	R. O. Korea
4	R. O. Korea	Taiwan, China	Taiwan, China	R. O. Korea	R. O. Korea	Thailand
5	Saudi Arabia	R. O. Korea	R. O. Korea	Philippines	Malaysia	Philippines
6	Taiwan , China	Thailand	Saudi Arabia	Malaysia	Philippines	Malaysia
7	UAE	Vietnam	UAE	Indonesia	Indonesia	Singapore
8	Thailand	Germany	Thailand	Singapore	Singapore	Indonesia
9	Germany	Saudi Arabia	Germany	Australia	Australia	New Zealand
10	Vietnam	UAE	Vietnam	New Zealand	New Zealand	Australia

Source: Data of general trade is from Japan Customs, and data of cross-border e-commerce is from Alibaba. com.

4.2.2.3   Japan Exports by Category

Table 4-7 shows top 10 categories of exported goods in general trade and cross-border e-commerce of Japan.

Table 4-7   Top 10 Categories of Exported

Goods in General Trade and Cross-Border E-Commerce of Japan

Rank	General Trade (Top 10 Categories of Exported Goods)			Cross-Border E-Commerce (Top 10 Categories of Export Demand)		
	2019	2020	2021	2019	2020	2021
1	Vehicles other than railway or tramway rolling-stock & parts & accessories thereof	Vehicles other than railway or tramway rolling-stock & parts & accessories thereof	Nuclear reactors, boilers, machinery and mechanical appliances & parts thereof	Cars & motorcycles	Cars & motorcycles	Cars & motorcycles

Continued

Rank	General Trade (Top 10 Categories of Exported Goods)			Cross-Border E-Commerce (Top10 Categories of Export Demand)		
	2019	2020	2021	2019	2020	2021
2	Nuclear reactors, boilers, machinery and mechanical appliances & parts thereof	Consumer electronics	Vehicles other than railway or tramway rolling-stock & parts & accessories thereof	Consumer electronics	Sports & entertainment	Household appliances
3	Electrical & electronic equipment	Electrical & electronic equipment	Electrical & electronic equipment	Apparel	Apparel	Food & beverage
4	Cocoa & cocoa preparations	Nuclear reactors, boilers, machinery and mechanical appliances & parts thereof	Unclassified goods	Hardware	Food & beverage	Sports & entertainment
5	Precision instruments & apparatus	Optical, photographic, technical, medical & surgical apparatus	Optical, photographic, technical, medical & surgical apparatus	Medicines & health care	Consumer electronics	Consumer electronics
6	Iron & steel	Vessels & associated transport equipment	Iron & steel	Sports & entertainment	Hardware	Hardware
7	Plastics & articles thereof	Semiconductor materials	Plastics & articles thereof	Machinery	Household appliances	Apparel
8	Organic chemicals	Precious metals	Organic chemicals	Food & beverage	Beauty & personal care	Health & medical care
9	Mineral fuels, mineral oils & products of their distillation	Household appliances	Chemical products	Household appliances	Medicines & health care	Beauty & personal care
10	Vessels & associated transport equipment	Unclassified goods	Pearls, gemstones, metals & coins	Household supplies	Health & medical care	Home & garden

Source: Data of general trade is from globalEDGE, Trading Economics, and Tracking Docket. Data of cross-border e-commerce is from Alibaba.com.

4.2.2.4　Japan Imports by Category

Table 4-8 shows top 10 categories of imported goods in general trade and cross-border e-commerce of Japan.

Table 4-8　Top 10 Categories of Imported Goods in General Trade and Cross-Border E-Commerce of Japan

Rank	General Trade (Top 10 Categories of Imported Goods)			Cross-Border E-Commerce (Top 10 Categories of Import Demand)		
	2019	2020	2021	2019	2020	2021
1	Mineral fuels, mineral oils & products of their distillation	Mineral fuels, mineral oils & products of their distillation	Mineral fuels, mineral oils & products of their distillation	Consumer electronics	Consumer electronics	Apparel
2	Electrical & electronic equipment	Electrical & electronic equipment	Electrical & electronic equipment	Household supplies	Apparel	Consumer electronics
3	Nuclear reactors, boilers, machinery and mechanical appliances & parts thereof	Nuclear reactors, boilers, machinery and mechanical appliances & parts thereof	Nuclear reactors, boilers, machinery and mechanical appliances & parts thereof	Apparel	Beauty & personal care	Home & garden
4	Precision instruments & apparatus	Optical, photographic, technical, medical & surgical apparatus	Pharmaceutical products	Sports & entertainment	Sports & entertainment	Sports & entertainment
5	Pharmaceutical products	Pharmaceutical products	Ores, slag & ash	Cars & motorcycles	Packaging & printing	Packaging & printing
6	Vehicles other than railway or tramway rolling-stock & parts & accessories thereof	Ores, slag & ash	Optical, photographic, technical, medical & surgical apparatus	Machinery	Cars & motorcycles	Beauty & personal care
7	Ores, slag & ash	Vehicles other than railway or tramway rolling-stock & parts & accessories thereof	Pearls, gemstones, metals & coins	Beauty & personal care	Machinery	Machinery

Continued

Rank	General Trade (Top 10 Categories of Imported Goods)			Cross-Border E-Commerce (Top 10 Categories of Import Demand)		
	2019	2020	2021	2019	2020	2021
8	Plastics & articles thereof	Natural or cultured pearls & precious or semi-precious stones	Vehicles other than railway or tramway rolling-stock & parts & accessories thereof	Packaging & printing	Security & protection	Cars & motorcycles
9	Organic chemicals	Organic chemicals	Plastics & articles thereof	Watches, jewelry & glasses	Home & garden	Health & medical care
10	Articles of apparel & clothing accessories (not knitted or crocheted)	Plastics & articles thereof	Organic chemicals	Luggage, bags & cases	Medicines & health care	Furniture

Source: Data of general trade is from globalEDGE, Trading Economics, and Tracking Docket. Data of cross-border e-commerce is from Alibaba. com.

4.3 Cross-Border E-Commerce Development of R. O. Korea

4.3.1 Overview of Social Economy and Cross-Border E-Commerce Development of R. O. Korea

R. O. Korea's GDP was worth $ 1. 63 trillion in 2020, and its GDP per capita was $ 31,489, a 0. 61% decline from that in 2019. Its population grew by only 0. 14% to 51. 78 million from 2019 to 2020. R. O. Korea has the lowest birth rate in the world amid the fast growth of its elderly population.

R. O. Korea has ranked first in the world for 3 consecutive years in terms of its information and communication technology (ICT) penetration, according to the World Economic Forum(WEF). R. O. Korea had around 49 million Internet users and 39. 2 million mobile subscribers in 2020, with the penetration rates standing at 97% and 76% respectively. A survey reveals that almost 99% of R. O. Koreans go online at least once a week, spending an average of 14. 3 hours a week on the Internet. R. O. Korea's e-commerce market ranks the fifth largest in the world and the third largest in the Asia-Pacific region, next only to China and Japan. In 2020, the total retail sales in R. O. Korea were $413. 4 billion dollars, a rise of 0. 41% from that of the previous year. In contrast, its online retail sales surged by 19. 11% to $140. 2 billion dollars, accounting for 34% of the total (see Figure 4-3). The well-established digital infrastructure in R. O. Korea provides robust support for its development of cross-border e-commerce. Its cross-border e-commerce market totaled $3. 5 billion dollars in 2020.

Figure 4-3   Total Retail Sales and Online Retail Sales of R. O. Korea (2017—2020)

Source: Statistics Korea.

In July 2020, the R. O. Korean government launched The Korean New Deal, in which the Digital New Deal gives strong support to cross-border e-commerce. In 2020, R. O. Korea's top 3 e-commerce platforms were Coupang Corp, Naver Corp and eBay Inc, with market shares of 19. 2%, 13. 6% and 12. 8% respectively. Other e-commerce platforms include 11ST, Lotteen and SSG. The credit card is the commonest payment tool in

R. O. Korea, and one inhabitant owns on average 3. 9 credit cards. Over 70% of online transactions are settled by credit card, followed by debit card and transfer. With the development of quick payment, methods such as PayPal, Samsung Pay and Alipay have attracted a large number of users. Online retailers and enterprises also offer their own payment systems, such as Coupang's Rocket Pay, Shinsegae's SSG Pay and Lotte Group's L. Pay. As the competition among e-commerce platforms intensifies, quick delivery service has become the key to attract customers. To meet this demand, Coupang invested $1. 3 billion to build logistics infrastructure for its famous Rocket Delivery, so as to provide same-day or next-day delivery services. Following the success of Coupang's Rocket Delivery, other e-commerce platforms have gradually established their logistics systems.

4. 3. 2 Comparison between General Trade and Cross-Border E-Commerce of R. O. Korea

4. 3. 2. 1 R. O. Korea Exports by Country(or Region)

Table 4-9 shows top 10 export countries or regions in general trade and cross-border e-commerce of R. O. Korea.

Table 4-9 Top 10 Export Countries or Regions in General Trade and Cross-Border E-Commerce of R. O. Korea

Rank	General Trade (Top 10 Export Countries or Regions)			Cross-Border E-Commerce (Top 10 Countries or Regions of Export Demand)		
	2019	2020	2021	2019	2020	2021
1	China	China	China	US	US	US
2	US	US	US	India	India	India
3	Vietnam	Vietnam	Vietnam	Russia	Philippines	Philippines
4	Hong Kong, China	Hong Kong, China	Hong Kong, China	Canada	Russia	Mexico
5	Japan	Japan	Japan	China	UK	Russia

Rank	General Trade (Top 10 Export Countries or Regions)			Cross-Border E-Commerce (Top 10 Countries or Regions of Export Demand)		
	2019	2020	2021	2019	2020	2021
6	Taiwan, China	India	India	UK	Canada	Peru
7	India	Singapore	Singapore	Pakistan	Mexico	Brazil
8	Mexico	Mexico	Germany	Vietnam	Peru	Chile
9	Singapore	Malaysia	Malaysia	Indonesia	Indonesia	Indonesia
10	Philippines	Germany	Mexico	Philippines	Chile	UK

Source: Data of general trade is from Korea Customs Service, and data of cross-border e-commerce is from Alibaba. com.

4. 3. 2. 2 R. O. Korea Imports by Country(or Region)

Table 4-10 shows top 10 import countries or regions in general trade and cross-border e-commerce of R. O. Korea.

Table 4-10 Top 10 Import Countries or Regions in General Trade and Cross-Border E-Commerce of R. O. Korea

Rank	General Trade (Top 10 Import Countries or Regions)			Cross-Border E-Commerce (Top 10 Countries or Regions of Import Demand)		
	2019	2020	2021	2019	2020	2021
1	China	China	China	China	China	China
2	US	US	US	Vietnam	Vietnam	Vietnam
3	Japan	Japan	Japan	India	India	India
4	Saudi Arabia	Saudi Arabia	Germany	Thailand	Pakistan	Pakistan
5	Germany	Vietnam	Vietnam	US	Thailand	US
6	Vietnam	Australia	Australia	Pakistan	US	Thailand
7	Russia	Germany	Saudi Arabia	Taiwan, China	Taiwan, China	Taiwan, China
8	Taiwan, China	Russia	Russia	Philippines	UK	South Africa
9	Qatar	Qatar	Malaysia	Hong Kong, China	Malaysia	UK
10	Kuwait	Kuwait	Singapore	Indonesia	South Africa	France

Source: Data of general trade is from Korea Customs Service, and data of cross-border e-commerce is from Alibaba. com.

4.3.2.3 R.O. Korea Exports by Category

Table 4-11 shows top 10 categories of exported goods in general trade and cross-border e-commerce of R.O. Korea.

Table 4-11 Top 10 Categories of Exported Goods in General Trade and Cross-Border E-Commerce of R.O. Korea

Rank	General Trade (Top 10 Categories of Exported Goods)			Cross-Border E-Commerce (Top 10 Categories of Export Demand)		
	2019	2020	2021	2019	2020	2021
1	Electromechanical equipment	Electromechanical equipment	Electromechanical equipment	Beauty & personal care	Beauty & personal care	Beauty & personal care
2	Industrial machinery	Industrial machinery	Industrial machinery	Cars & motorcycles	Cars & motorcycles	Consumer electronics
3	Vehicles & parts	Vehicles & parts	Vehicles & parts	Medicines & health care	Machinery	Food & beverage
4	Petroleum & mineral fuels	Petroleum & mineral fuels	Plastics	Machinery	Health & medical care	Health & medical care
5	Plastics	Plastics	Petroleum & mineral fuels	Consumer electronics	Medicines & health care	Cars & motorcycles
6	Precision instruments	Iron & steel	Medical devices	Household appliances	Consumer electronics	Apparel
7	Organic chemicals	Precision instruments	Iron & steel	Food & beverage	Household appliances	Machinery
8	Iron & steel	Organic chemicals	Ships	Hardware	Apparel	Household appliances
9	Ships	Ships	Organic chemicals	Sports & entertainment	Security & protection	Packaging & printing
10	Articles of iron & steel	Articles of iron & steel	Articles of iron & steel	Textiles & leather products	Household supplies	Sports & entertainment

Source: Data of general trade is from Korea Customs Service, and data of cross-border e-commerce is from Alibaba.com.

4.3.2.4 R.O. Korea Imports by Category

Table 4-12 shows top 10 categories of imported goods in general trade and cross-border e-commerce of R.O. Korea.

Table 4-12　Top 10 Categories of Imported Goods in General

Trade and Cross-Border E-Commerce of R. O. Korea

Rank	General Trade (Top 10 Categories of Imported Goods)			Cross-Border E-Commerce (Top 10 Categories of Import Demand)		
	2019	2020	2021	2019	2020	2021
1	Petroleum & mineral fuels	Petroleum & mineral fuels	Electromechanical equipment	Household supplies	Consumer electronics	Home & garden
2	Electromechanical equipment	Electromechanical equipment	Petroleum & mineral fuels	Consumer electronics	Machinery	Consumer electronics
3	Industrial machinery	Industrial machinery	Industrial machinery	Machinery	Sports & entertainment	Machinery
4	Precision instruments	Precision instruments	Medical devices	Sports & entertainment	Home & garden	Sports & entertainment
5	Vehicles & parts	Vehicles & parts	Vehicles & parts	Medicines & health care	Hardware	Packaging & printing
6	Iron & steel	Iron & steel	Ores	Cars & motorcycles	Packaging & printing	Cars & motorcycles
7	Organic chemicals	Ores	Organic chemicals	Packaging & printing	Security & protection	Apparel
8	Plastics	Organic chemicals	Plastics	Hardware	Cars & motorcycles	Hardware
9	Inorganic chemicals	Plastics	Iron & steel	Beauty & personal care	Household supplies	Health care
10	Apparel (not knitted)	Chemical products	Medication	Electrical equipment & products	Beauty & personal care	Construction

Source: Data of general trade is from Korea Customs Service, and data of cross-border e-commerce is from Alibaba. com.

4. 4　Cross-Border E-Commerce Development of Australia

4. 4. 1　Overview of Social Economy and Cross-Border E-Commerce Development of Australia

In 2020, Australia's GDP was $ 1,330. 9 billion, a decrease of $ 65. 7

billion from the previous year with a year-on-year growth of -0.28%. Compared with 2010, Australia's GDP in 2020 increased by $184.8 billion. Due to the COVID-19 pandemic, Australia suffered from its first recession in about 30 years. In 2020, Australia's GDP per capita was $51,812, a decrease of $3,245 from the previous year with a year-on-year growth of -1.53%. Compared with 2010, Australia's GDP per capita decreased by $210. Australia's Gross National Income (GNI) in 2020 was $1,380.2 billion. And GNI per capita was $53,730, a decrease of $1,370 compared with that in 2019, and an increase of $7,100 compared with that in 2010.

Australia, with a population of about 25 million, ranks 6th in the world in terms of territory. With a population density of 2 people per square kilometer, Australia has an urbanization rate of about 90%. Australia owns 21 million Internet users, with an Internet penetration rate of about 81% and an Internet availability rate of about 88%, of which smartphone users account for 48%. By 2025, Australia's Internet users are expected to exceed 21.5 million.

Australia is the world's 10th e-commerce market with about 80% of inhabitants purchasing online, and Australia's annual e-commerce expenditure per capita is $1,527. At present, eBay and Amazon dominate Australia's e-commerce market. Surveys show that consumers pay more attention to brand value and product quality. Currently, paying by card is major among Australia's online payment methods with a proportion of 42%, followed by online bank transfer, e-wallet, etc. POLi, a local payment agency in Australia and a real-time transfer tool for Australia Post, has become the main online payment tool besides credit cards and PayPal.

4.4.2 Comparison between General Trade and Cross-Border E-Commerce of Australia

4.4.2.1 Australia Exports by Country(or Region)

Table 4-13 shows top 10 export countries or regions in general trade and cross-border e-commerce of Australia.

Table 4-13   Top 10 Export Countries or Regions in General
Trade and Cross-Border E-Commerce of Australia

Rank	General Trade (Top 10 Export Countries or Regions)			Cross-Border E-Commerce (Top 10 Countries or Regions of Export Demand)		
	2019	2020	2021	2019	2020	2021
1	China	China	China	US	US	US
2	Japan	Japan	Japan	India	India	India
3	R.O. Korea	R.O. Korea	R.O. Korea	UK	UK	Brazil
4	India	UK	US	China	Canada	UK
5	US	US	UK	Nigeria	Australia	Canada
6	Taiwan, China	India	Singapore	Canada	Philippines	Philippines
7	Hong Kong, China	Singapore	New Zealand	Australia	Brazil	France
8	Malaysia	New Zealand	India	Russia	Nigeria	Saudi Arabia
9	New Zealand	Malaysia	Hong Kong, China	Brazil	Saudi Arabia	Pakistan
10	Singapore	Hong Kong, China	Malaysia	France	France	Spain

Source: Data of general trade is from globalEDGE, OEC and Trading Economics. Data of cross-border e-commerce is from Alibaba.com.

4.4.2.2 Australia Imports by Country(or Region)

Table 4-14 shows top 10 import countries or regions in general trade and cross-border e-commerce of Australia.

Table 4-14 Top 10 Import Countries or Regions in General Trade and Cross-Border E-Commerce of Australia

Rank	General Trade (Top 10 Import Countries or Regions)			Cross-Border E-Commerce (Top 10 Countries or Regions of Import Demand)		
	2019	2020	2021	2019	2020	2021
1	China	China	China	China	China	China
2	US	US	US	India	India	India
3	Japan	Japan	Japan	Pakistan	Pakistan	Pakistan
4	Germany	Thailand	Thailand	Vietnam	Vietnam	Vietnam
5	Thailand	Germany	Germany	US	US	US
6	R. O. Korea	R. O. Korea	Malaysia	Taiwan, China	Taiwan, China	UK
7	Singapore	Malaysia	R. O. Korea	Hong Kong, China	Turkey	South Africa
8	Malaysia	Singapore	Singapore	Thailand	South Africa	France
9	New Zealand	New Zealand	UK	R. O. Korea	R. O. Korea	Taiwan, China
10	UK	UK	New Zealand	Turkey	UK	Spain

Source: Data of general trade is from globalEDGE, OEC and Trading Economics. Data of cross-border e-commerce is from Alibaba. com.

4.4.2.3 Australia Exports by Category

Tbale 4-15 shows top 10 categories of exported goods in general trade and cross-border e-commerce of Australia.

Table 4-15 Top 10 Categories of Exported Goods in General Trade and Cross-Border E-Commerce of Australia

Rank	General Trade (Top 10 Categories of Exported Goods)			Cross-Border E-Commerce (Top 10 Categories of Export Demand)		
	2019	2020	2021	2019	2020	2021
1	Briquettes	Ores	Slag & ash	Food & beverage	Apparel	Food & beverage
2	Iron ores	Petroleum & mineral fuels	Commodities not specified by category	Apparel	Food & beverage	Home & garden

Continued

Rank	General Trade (Top 10 Categories of Exported Goods)			Cross-Border E-Commerce (Top 10 Categories of Export Demand)		
	2019	2020	2021	2019	2020	2021
3	Liquefied petroleum gas	Other commodities	Mineral fuels, mineral oils & products of their distillation	Agriculture	Sports & entertainment	Sports & entertainment
4	Gold	Gemstones & metals	Pearls, gemstones, metals & coins	Sports & entertainment	Household supplies	Agriculture
5	Alumina	Meat	Meat & edible offal	Beauty & personal care	Beauty & personal care	Consumer electronics
6	Copper	Industrial machinery	Machinery, nuclear reactors & boilers	Medicines & health care	Agriculture	Business services
7	Frozen beef	Medication	Cereals	Household supplies	Consumer electronics	Beauty & personal care
8	Wheat	Electric motors	Pharmaceutical products	Cars & motorcycles	Minerals & metals	Packaging & printing
9	Aluminum	Precision instruments	Electrical & electronic equipment	Packaging & printing	Health & medical care	Cars & motorcycles
10	Wool	Cereals	Aluminum	Minerals & metals	Packaging & printing	Apparel

Source: Data of general trade is from globalEDGE, OEC and Trading Economics. Data of cross-border e-commerce is from Alibaba. com.

4. 4. 2. 4　Australia Imports by Category

Table 4-16 shows top 10 categories of imported goods in general trade and cross-border e-commerce of Australia.

Table 4-16　Top 10 Categories of Imported Goods in General Trade and Cross-Border E-Commerce of Australia

Rank	General Trade (Top 10 Categories of Imported Goods)			Cross-Border E-Commerce (Top 10 Categories of Import Demand)		
	2019	2020	2021	2019	2020	2021
1	Refined petroleum	Industrial machinery	Machinery, nuclear reactors & boilers	Household supplies	Home & garden	Home & garden
2	Cars	Petroleum & mineral fuels	Vehicles other than railway or tramway rolling-stock	Apparel	Packaging & printing	Apparel
3	Crude petroleum	Cars & vehicle parts	Electrical & electronic equipment	Packaging & printing	Apparel	Packaging & printing
4	Delivery trucks	Electric motors	Mineral fuels, mineral oils & products of their distillation	Beauty & personal care	Beauty & personal care	Beauty & personal care
5	Broadcasting equipment	Medication	Pharmaceutical products	Sports & entertainment	Sports & entertainment	Sports & entertainment
6	Computers	Precision instruments	Pearls, gemstones, metals & coins	Consumer electronics	Gifts & crafts	Cars & motorcycles
7	Packaged medication	Gemstones & metals	Optical, photographic, technical & medical apparatus	Cars & motorcycles	Cars & motorcycles	Gifts & crafts
8	Gold	Other commodities	Plastics	Machinery	Consumer electronics	Consumer electronics
9	Medical devices	Plastics	Furniture, illuminated signs & pre-fabricated building	Gifts & crafts	Machinery	Machinery
10	Vehicle parts & accessories	Furniture	Articles of iron & steel	Luggage, bags & cases	Health & medical care	Furniture

Source: Data of general trade is from globalEDGE, OEC and Trading Economics. Data of cross-border e-commerce is from Alibaba. com.

4.5 Cross-Border E-Commerce Development of New Zealand

4.5.1 Overview of Social Economy and Cross-Border E-Commerce Development of New Zealand

According to the World Bank, New Zealand's GDP reached $21.07 billion in 2020, representing a year-on-year growth of 1.86%. GDP per capita was $41,400, representing a year-on-year decrease of 0.24%. New Zealand's population reached 5.0843 million with an overall high educational level. According to OECD statistics, as of 2020, among the inhabitants aged 25—64, 29.1% have obtained a bachelor's degree or an equivalent higher education degree.

New Zealand has a relatively complete digital economy infrastructure. As of 2021, the Internet availability rate in New Zealand hit 94%. According to DataReportal, by January 2021, the country's mobile phone users reached 6.56 million, which is 135.6% of the total population. Data shows that New Zealand's daily Internet usage duration per capita is 6h 39min. According to eCommerceDB statistics, in 2020, New Zealand's online retail market ranked 39th in the world, with a year-on-year growth rate of 31%, contributing 29% of the global online retail market growth. In 2020, New Zealand's online consumption per capita was $1,529. 72% of the inhabitants once visited online retail stores, and 61% ordered at least 1 product online.

As is reported by New Zealand Post, since 2019, New Zealand's e-commerce has witnessed steady growth year by year. In the first 10 months of 2021, New Zealand's online spending increased by 18% compared with the same period in 2020, and nearly 50% compared with the same period in

2019. The development of e-commerce also benefits e-payment and e-commerce platforms. In 2020, the top 5 payment platforms in New Zealand were Flo2Cash, Paystation, Windcave, Bambora and Stripe. In terms of sales, the top 3 e-commerce platforms were Countdown, Apple and Mitre10. Owing to the boom of e-commerce, New Zealand's logistics and transportation industry has witnessed rapid expansion in recent years, but great potential still remains as no category defining company has ever emerged yet.

The government, encouraging the digital economy, is optimistic about the commercial and social benefits the industry brings. In June 2020, New Zealand, together with Chile and Singapore, proposed the Digital Economy Partnership Agreement (DEPA), which is the world's first fully digital trade agreement. DEPA is to help small- and medium-sized countries build a beneficial cross-border digital trade scheme through cooperation. Additionally, the government explores what impact the new technologies (such as AR, VR, IoT and AI) will exert on New Zealand's society and economy. New Zealand endeavors to build a digital government, and encourage companies to maximize digital technology to enhance productivity.

4.5.2 Comparison between General Trade and Cross-Border E-Commerce of New Zealand

4.5.2.1 New Zealand Exports by Country(or Region)

Table 4-17 shows top 10 export countries or regions in general trade and cross-border e-commerce of New Zealand.

Table 4-17 Top 10 Export Countries or Regions in General Trade and Cross-Border E-Commerce of New Zealand

Rank	General Trade (Top 10 Export Countries or Regions)			Cross-Border E-Commerce (Top 10 Countries or Regions of Export Demand)		
	2018	2019	2020	2019	2020	2021
1	China	China	China	China	China	Australia

Continued

Rank	General Trade (Top 10 Export Countries or Regions)			Cross-Border E-Commerce (Top 10 Countries or Regions of Export Demand)		
	2018	2019	2020	2019	2020	2021
2	Australia	Australia	Australia	Australia	Australia	Philippines
3	US	US	US	Malaysia	Philippines	Malaysia
4	Japan	Japan	Japan	R. O. Korea	Malaysia	Japan
5	UK	UK	UK	Indonesia	Thailand	Thailand
6	R. O. Korea	R. O. Korea	R. O. Korea	Vietnam	Indonesia	Vietnam
7	India	Germany	Singapore	Thailand	Vietnam	Singapore
8	Singapore	Hong Kong, China	Taiwan, China	Philippines	Singapore	R. O. Korea
9	Germany	India	Hong Kong, China	Singapore	R. O. Korea	China
10	Hong Kong, China	Singapore	Germany	Japan	Japan	Indonesia

Source: Data of general trade is from Stats NZ, and data of cross-border e-commerce is from Alibaba. com.

4.5.2.2 New Zealand Imports by Country(or Region)

Table 4-18 shows top 10 import countries or regions in general trade and cross-border e-commerce of New Zealand.

Table 4-18 Top 10 Import Countries or Regions in General Trade and Cross-Border E-Commerce of New Zealand

Rank	General Trade (Top 10 Import Countries or Regions)			Cross-Border E-Commerce (Top 10 Countries or Regions of Import Demand)		
	2018	2019	2020	2019	2020	2021
1	Australia	Australia	China	China	China	China
2	China	China	Australia	Vietnam	Vietnam	Vietnam
3	US	US	US	Thailand	Thailand	Thailand
4	Japan	Singapore	Singapore	Philippines	Malaysia	R. O. Korea
5	Germany	Germany	Germany	R. O. Korea	R. O. Korea	Indonesia
6	Singapore	Japan	Japan	Indonesia	Indonesia	Malaysia
7	Thailand	UK	R. O. Korea	Japan	Japan	Japan

Continued

Rank	General Trade (Top 10 Import Countries or Regions)			Cross-Border E-Commerce (Top 10 Countries or Regions of Import Demand)		
	2018	2019	2020	2019	2020	2021
8	R. O. Korea	Thailand	Thailand	Malaysia	Philippines	Philippines
9	UAE	UAE	UK	Singapore	Singapore	Singapore
10	UK	R. O. Korea	Malaysia	Australia	Australia	Australia

Source: Data of general trade is from Stats NZ, and data of cross-border e-commerce is from Alibaba. com.

4. 5. 2. 3　New Zealand Exports by Category

Table 4-19 shows top 10 categories of exported goods in general trade and cross-border e-commerce of New Zealand.

Table 4-19　Top 10 Categories of Exported Goods in General

Trade and Cross-Border E-Commerce of New Zealand

Rank	General Trade (Top 10 Categories of Exported Goods)			Cross-Border E-Commerce (Top 10 Categories of Export Demand)		
	2018	2019	2020	2019	2020	2021
1	Tourism	Dairy products	Dairy products	Food & beverage	Food & beverage	Beauty & personal care
2	Dairy products	Tourism	Tourism	Consumer electronics	Security & protection	Health & medical care
3	Meat	Meat	Meat	Medicines & health care	Cars & motorcycles	Packaging & printing
4	Timber	Timber	Timber	Cars & motorcycles	Sports & entertainment	Lamps & lighting fittings
5	Traffic	Traffic	Fruits & nuts	Agriculture	Agriculture	Food & beverage
6	Fruits & nuts	Fruits & nuts	Cereal products	Office & school supplies	Consumer electronics	Sports & entertainment
7	Beverage	Cereal products	Beverage	Packaging & printing	Household supplies	Agriculture
8	Business services	Beverage	Business services	Household supplies	Office & school supplies	Construction
9	Cereal products	Business services	Traffic	Beauty & personal care	Packaging & printing	Home & garden
10	Machinery	Machinery	Machinery	Sports & entertainment	Medicines & health care	Machinery

Source: Data of general trade is from Stats NZ, and data of cross-border e-commerce is from Alibaba. com.

4.5.2.4　New Zealand Imports by Category

Table 4-20 shows top 10 categories of imported goods in general trade and cross-border e-commerce of New Zealand.

Table 4-20　Top 10 Categories of Imported Goods in General Trade and Cross-Border E-Commerce of New Zealand

Rank	General Trade (Top 10 Categories of Imported Goods)			Cross-Border E-Commerce (Top 10 Categories of Import Demand)		
	2018	2019	2020	2019	2020	2021
1	Means of transport	Machinery	Machinery	Household supplies	Sports & entertainment	Apparel
2	Machinery	Means of transport	Means of transport	Sports & entertainment	Apparel	Home & garden
3	Fuels & crude petroleum	Fuels & crude petroleum	Electronic machines	Packaging & printing	Packaging & printing	Sports & entertainment
4	Tourism	Tourism	Fuels & crude petroleum	Apparel	Cars & motorcycles	Cars & motorcycles
5	Electronic machines	Electronic machines	Other business services	Machinery	Machinery	Packaging & printing
6	Traffic	Traffic	Traffic	Cars & motorcycles	Beauty & personal care	Machinery
7	Other business services	Other business services	Information technology	Consumer electronics	Consumer electronics	Consumer electronics
8	Plastics & articles thereof	Plastics & articles thereof	Tourism	Beauty & personal care	Home & garden	Beauty & personal care
9	Information technology	Insurance & pension	Plastics & articles thereof	Construction	Household supplies	Furniture
10	Optical, medical & measuring apparatus	Information technology	Insurance & pension	Hardware	Hardware	Gifts & crafts

Source: Data of general trade is from Stats NZ, and data of cross-border e-commerce is from Alibaba. com.

4. 6　Cross-Border E-Commerce Development of Indonesia

4. 6. 1　Overview of Social Economy and Cross-Border E-Commerce Development of Indonesia

According to the World Bank, Indonesia's GDP in 2020 was $1.06 trillion, a year-on-year decrease of 2.07%. Its GDP per capita was $3,900, a year-on-year decrease of 3.11%. Meanwhile, Indonesia's population in 2020 reached 274 million. As is suggested by OECD statistics, as of 2020, among Indonesia's inhabitants aged 25—64, 4.9% have obtained a bachelor's degree or an equivalent higher education degree, which is lower than the OECD members' average of 18.2%. Indonesia has made progress on the infrastructure of digital economy. As of 2021, Indonesia's Internet users were 204 million, and its Internet availability rate reached 74%. According to DataReportal, by January 2021, Indonesia's mobile phone users reached 347 million with an availability rate of mobile communication at 126%. The country's social media users were 171 million with an availability rate of 62%.

Indonesia's e-commerce trade is also on the rise. In 2020, Indonesia's e-commerce market had a total size of $44 billion, accounting for 2.82% of the total retail sales of consumer goods. As is estimated by the US International Trade Administration, the market size of Indonesia's e-commerce will reach $83 billion by 2025. According to research on cross-border e-commerce by JP Morgan, in 2017—2019, Indonesia's e-commerce imports increased by 814% from 6.1 million to 49.7 million. China is one of Indonesia's major partners of cross-border e-commerce. As is reported by PPRO (a famous payment services provider from UK), by January 2020,

41% of cross-border e-commerce trade in Indonesia was made with China.

Indonesia attaches great importance to the advantage of digital technology and digital economy in promoting and multiplying the national economic growth, and has set the target of building Indonesia into the largest digital economy in Southeast Asia by 2020. Currently, there are 3 trends in Indonesia's digital economy. First, financial technology is booming. In 2016, the growth rate of start-ups in the financial sector was up to 78%, and the volume of e-payment transactions reached $1.45 billion. A number of prominent fintech companies emerged, such as Dompetku, Doku and Kartuk. Second, unicorn companies of sharing economy are flourishing. For example, Go-Jek, valued at $153 million, is able to process on average 8 orders per second. Other representatives include Grab, Ruangguru, and Sejasa. com. Third, the e-commerce is vigorously developing, and large platform companies are Tokopedia, Bukalapak, and Bhinneka. The Indonesian government takes e-commerce as its focus to develop digital economy with a goal set: as of the end of 2019, Indonesia's e-commerce volume is to exceed $130 billion with an annual growth rate of 50%, and technology companies valued over $10 billion are to reach 1,000. To promote the development of e-commerce, the Indonesian government has formulated an e-commerce roadmap, planning to provide support to Indonesia's e-commerce in 8 aspects: Funding, taxation, consumer protection, education, human resources, telecommunications infrastructure, logistics, Internet security, management and implementation. In April 2018, the Indonesian government issued a roadmap of Made in Indonesia 4.0 to exploit the potential of the 4th industrial revolution, and to enhance economic competitiveness.

4. 6. 2 Comparison between General Trade and Cross-Border E-Commerce of Indonesia

4. 6. 2. 1 Indonesia Exports by Country(or Region)

Table 4-21 shows top 10 export countries or regions in general trade and cross-border e-commerce of Indonesia.

Table 4-21 Top 10 Export Countries or Regions in General Trade and Cross-Border E-Commerce of Indonesia

Rank	General Trade (Top 10 Export Countries or Regions)			Cross-Border E-Commerce (Top 10 Countries or Regions of Export Demand)		
	2019	2020	2021	2019	2020	2021
1	China	China	China	China	Philippines	Australia
2	US	US	US	Australia	Malaysia	Philippines
3	Japan	Japan	Japan	Malaysia	Singapore	Malaysia
4	Singapore	Singapore	India	Philippines	China	China
5	India	India	Malaysia	R. O. Korea	Australia	Vietnam
6	Malaysia	Malaysia	Singapore	Vietnam	Thailand	Thailand
7	R. O. Korea	R. O. Korea	R. O. Korea	Singapore	Vietnam	Singapore
8	Philippines	Philippines	Philippines	Thailand	R. O. Korea	New Zealand
9	Thailand	Thailand	Thailand	New Zealand	Cambodia	R. O. Korea
10	Vietnam	Vietnam	Vietnam	Japan	New Zealand	Cambodia

Source: Data of general trade is from Statistics Indonesia, and data of cross-border e-commerce is from Alibaba. com.

4. 6. 2. 2 Indonesia Imports by Country(or Region)

Table 4-22 shows top 10 import countries or regions in general trade and cross-border e-commerce of indonesia.

Table 4-22　Top 10 Import Countries or Regions in General

Trade and Cross-Border E-Commerce of Indonesia

Rank	General Trade (Top 10 Import Countries or Regions)			Cross-Border E-Commerce (Top 10 Countries or Regions of Import Demand)		
	2019	2020	2021	2019	2020	2021
1	China	China	China	China	China	China
2	Singapore	Singapore	Singapore	Thailand	Thailand	Vietnam
3	Japan	Japan	Japan	R. O. Korea	Vietnam	Thailand
4	Thailand	US	US	Vietnam	R. O. Korea	R. O. Korea
5	US	Malaysia	Malaysia	Malaysia	Japan	Japan
6	R. O. Korea	R. O. Korea	R. O. Korea	Philippines	Malaysia	Malaysia
7	Malaysia	Thailand	Australia	Japan	Singapore	Philippines
8	Australia	Australia	Thailand	Singapore	Philippines	Singapore
9	India	India	India	Australia	Australia	Cambodia
10	Vietnam	Vietnam	Vietnam	New Zealand	New Zealand	Myanmar

Source: Data of general trade is from Statistics Indonesia, and data of cross-border e-commerce is from Alibaba. com.

4. 6. 2. 3　Indonesia Exports by Category

Table 4-23 shows top 10 categories of exported goods in general trade and cross-border e-commerce of Indonesia.

Table 4-23　Top 10 Categories of Exported Goods in General

Trade and Cross-Border E-Commerce of Indonesia

Rank	General Trade (Top 10 Categories of Exported Goods)			Cross-Border E-Commerce (Top 10 Categories of Export Demand)		
	2018	2019	2020	2019	2020	2021
1	Electrical & electronic equipment	Mineral fuels, mineral oils & products of their distillation	Mineral fuels, mineral oils & products of their distillation	Furniture & home decor	Furniture	Furniture

Continued

Rank	General Trade (Top 10 Categories of Exported Goods)			Cross-Border E-Commerce (Top 10 Categories of Export Demand)		
	2018	2019	2020	2019	2020	2021
2	Vehicles other than railway or tramway rolling-stock & parts & accessories thereof	Gums, resins & other vegetable saps and extracts	Resins & other vegetable saps and extracts	Food & beverage	Medicines & health care	Food & beverage
3	Nuclear reactors, boilers, machinery and mechanical appliances & parts thereof	Electrical & electronic equipment	Iron & steel	Agriculture	Food & beverage	Agriculture
4	Iron & steel	Vehicles other than railway or tramway rolling-stock & parts & accessories thereof	Electrical & electronic equipment	Apparel	Beauty & personal care	Beauty & personal care
5	Natural or cultured pearls, precious or semi-precious stones, precious metals, metals clad with precious metal & articles thereof	Iron & steel	Natural or cultured pearls, precious or semi-precious stones, precious metals, metals clad with precious metal & articles thereof	Beauty & personal care	Agriculture	Home & garden
6	Footwear, headgear, umbrellas, sun umbrellas, walking-sticks, seat-sticks, whips, riding-crops & parts thereof	Natural or cultured pearls, precious or semi-precious stones, precious metals, metals clad with precious metal & articles thereof	Vehicles other than railway or tramway rolling-stock & parts & accessories thereof	Household supplies	Consumer electronics	Energy

Continued

Rank	General Trade (Top 10 Categories of Exported Goods)			Cross-Border E-Commerce (Top 10 Categories of Export Demand)		
	2018	2019	2020	2019	2020	2021
7	Miscellaneous chemical products	Rubber & articles thereof	Rubber & articles thereof	Energy	Energy	Apparel
8	Articles of apparel & clothing accessories (not knitted or crocheted)	Nuclear reactors, boilers, machinery and mechanical appliances & parts thereof	Nuclear reactors, boilers, machinery and mechanical appliances & parts thereof	Construction	Cars & motorcycles	Construction
9	Paper, paperboard & articles thereof	Articles of apparel & clothing accessories (not knitted or crocheted)	Footwear, headgear, umbrellas, sun umbrellas, walking-sticks, seat-sticks, whips, riding-crops & parts thereof	Medicines & health care	Household supplies	Gifts & crafts
10	Articles of apparel & clothing accessories (knitted or crocheted)	Footwear, headgear, umbrellas, sun umbrellas, walking-sticks, seat-sticks, whips, riding-crops & parts thereof	Paper, paperboard & articles thereof	Sports & entertainment	Home & garden	Chemical industry

Source: Data of general trade is from globalEDGE, World's Top Exports, Connect2India. Data of cross-border e-commerce is from Alibaba. com.

4. 6. 2. 4   Indonesia Imports by Category

Table 4-24 shows top 10 categories of imported goods in general trade and cross-border e-commerce of indonesia.

Table 4-24   Top 10 Categories of Imported Goods in General Trade and Cross-Border E-Commerce of Indonesia

Rank	General Trade (Top 10 Categories of Imported Goods)			Cross-Border E-Commerce (Top 10 Categories of Import Demand)		
	2018	2019	2020	2019	2020	2021
1	Nuclear reactors, boilers, machinery and mechanical appliances & parts thereof	Nuclear reactors, boilers, machinery and mechanical appliances & parts thereof	Nuclear reactors, boilers, machinery and mechanical appliances & parts thereof	Consumer electronics	Consumer electronics	Consumer electronics
2	Electrical & electronic equipment	Mineral fuels, mineral oils & products of their distillation	Electrical & electronic equipment	Machinery	Sports & entertainment	Apparel
3	Iron & steel	Electrical & electronic Equipment	Mineral fuels, mineral oils & products of their distillation	Household supplies	Machinery	Sports & entertainment
4	Plastics & articles thereof	Iron & steel	Plastics & articles thereof	Cars & motorcycles	Cars & motorcycles	Cars & motorcycles
5	Vehicles other than railway or tramway rolling-stock & parts & accessories thereof	Plastics & articles thereof	Iron & steel	Sports & entertainment	Apparel	Machinery
6	Organic chemicals	Vehicles other than railway or tramway rolling-stock & parts & accessories thereof	Organic chemicals	Apparel	Hardware	Home & garden
7	Mineral fuels, mineral oils & products of their distillation	Organic chemicals	Vehicles other than railway or tramway rolling-stock & parts & accessories thereof	Hardware	Medicines & health care	Hardware

Continued

Rank	General Trade (Top 10 Categories of Exported Goods)			Cross-border E-Commerce(Top 10 Categories of Export Demand)		
	2018	2019	2020	2019	2020	2021
8	Iron & steel	Iron & steel	Cereals	Medicines & health care	Security & protection	Gifts & crafts
9	Residues and waste from the food industries; prepared animal fodder	Cereals	Other chemical products	Beauty & personal care	Packaging & printing	Footwear & parts thereof
10	Optical, photographic, technical, medical & surgical apparatus	Precision instruments & apparatus	Straw & fodder	Electrical equipment & products	Home & garden	Health care

Source: Data of general trade is from globalEDGE, World's Top Exports, Connect2India. Data of cross-border e-commerce is from Alibaba. com.

4.7 Cross-Border E-Commerce Development of Thailand

4.7.1 Overview of Social Economy and Cross-Border E-Commerce Development

In 2020, Thailand's GDP was $ 501.8 billion, with its per capita GDP of $7,189, down 7.8% year on year. In 2020, Thailand's population was 69.8 million, up 0.25% year on year. Among them, 52% of the population live in urban areas and 48% in rural areas.

In 2021, the number of Internet users in Thailand was 48.59 million, up 7.4% year on year. The Internet availability rate was 70%, while the number of smartphone users was about 53.57 million, with an availability rate of 77%. According to the Southeast Asia E-Commerce Report 2020

216

jointly released by Google, Temasek and Bain, the average daily online time of Thai residents rose from about 3. 7 hours before the pandemic to 4. 3 hours during the pandemic.

According to the data from Thailand's Electronic Transaction Development Agency (ETDA), Thailand's e-commerce platforms are divided into three categories: B2B, B2C and B2G, with market shares of 55%, 29% and 16% respectively. In 2020, the scale of Thailand's e-commerce market was $ 113. 6 billion, down 6. 6% year on year, while the scale of cross-border e-commerce was about $ 34. 1 billion, accounting for nearly 30% of Thailand's e-commerce market share(See Figure 4-4).

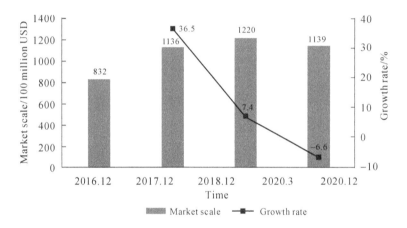

Figure 4-4   E-Commerce Market Scales and Its Growth Rates of Thailand 2016—2020

Source: National Statistical Office of Thailand.

The top three e-commerce platforms in Thailand are Shopee, Lazada and Facebook Fanpage. In addition to e-commerce platforms, Thai consumers also like to buy products on social media platforms such as Line, Instagram and Twitter. Online payment methods for Thai consumers are scattered. Credit cards and bank transfers are the most commonly used methods, with market shares of 26% and 27% respectively. According to statistics, Thailand has 0. 93 debit cards and 0. 34 credit cards per capita. The market shares of cash payment and digital wallet are 20% and 19%

respectively. In the context of the government's encouragement of electronic payment and high smartphone availability rate, the utilization of digital wallets is steadily on the rise. Electronic payment brands with high market shares in Thailand include TrueMoney and PayPal. Thai consumers like to shop on social media platforms, but compared with e-commerce platforms, these channels do not have comprehensive logistics support. Enterprises must manage their own logistics systems or outsource them to other third-party logistics (3PL) providers. Major logistics enterprises in Thailand include Thailand Post, Kerry Express, DHL and Honestbee GoodShip.

4.7.2   Comparison between General Trade and Cross-Border E-Commerce of Thailand

4.7.2.1   Thailand Exports by Country(or Region)

Table 4-25 shows top 10 export countries or regions in general trade and cross-border e-commerce of Thailand.

Table 4-25   Top 10 Export Countries or Regions in General Trade and Cross-Border E-Commerce of Thailand

Rank	General Trade (Top 10 Export Countries or Regions)			Cross-Border E-Commerce (Top 10 Countries or Regions of Export Demand)		
	2019	2020	2021	2019	2020	2021
1	China	US	US	India	India	India
2	US	China	China	US	US	US
3	Japan	Japan	Japan	Pakistan	Pakistan	Pakistan
4	Vietnam	Vietnam	Hong Kong, China	China	Philippines	Brazil
5	Hong Kong, China	Hong Kong, China	Vietnam	Russia	Malaysia	Bangladesh
6	Malaysia	Malaysia	Australia	UK	UK	Philippines
7	Indonesia	Australia	Singapore	Egypt	Bangladesh	Saudi Arabia
8	Singapore	Indonesia	Malaysia	Canada	Brazil	Indonesia

Rank	General Trade (Top 10 Export Countries or Regions)			Cross-Border E-Commerce (Top 10 Countries or Regions of Export Demand)		
	2019	2020	2021	2019	2020	2021
9	Philippines	Singapore	Indonesia	Turkey	Indonesia	Egypt
10	India	India	Switzerland	Bangladesh	Saudi Arabia	Turkey

Source: Data of general trade is from Thailand Customs and globalEDGE. Data of cross-border e-commerce is from Alibaba. com.

4.7.2.2 Thailand Imports by Country(or Region)

Table 4-26 shows top 10 import countries or regions in general trade and cross-border e-commerce of Thailand.

Table 4-26 Top 10 Import Countries or Regions in General Trade and Cross-Border E-Commerce of Thailand

Rank	General Trade (Top 10 Import Countries or Regions)			Cross-Border E-Commerce (Top 10 Countries or Regions of Import Demand)		
	2019	2020	2021	2019	2020	2021
1	China	China	China	China	China	China
2	Japan	Japan	Japan	India	India	Vietnam
3	Malaysia	US	US	Vietnam	Vietnam	India
4	US	Malaysia	Malaysia	US	Pakistan	US
5	Singapore	R. O. Korea	R. O. Korea	R. O. Korea	US	Pakistan
6	UAE	UAE	Singapore	Pakistan	UK	South Africa
7	R. O. Korea	Singapore	Indonesia	Taiwan, China	R. O. Korea	Hong Kong, China
8	Indonesia	Indonesia	UAE	Hong Kong, China	South Africa	UK
9	Taiwan, China	Germany	Vietnam	Philippines	Taiwan, China	France
10	Saudi Arabia	Saudi Arabia	Germany	UK	Japan	Taiwan, China

Source: Data of general trade is from Thailand Customs and globalEDGE. Data of cross-border e-commerce is from Alibaba. com.

4.7.2.3 Thailand Exports by Category

Table 4-27 shows top 10 categories of exported goods in general trade and cross-border e-commerce of Thailand.

Table 4-27 Top 10 Categories of Exported Goods in General Trade and Cross-Border E-Commerce of Thailand

Rank	General Trade (Top 10 Categories of Exported Goods)			Cross-Border E-Commerce (Top 10 Categories of Export Demand)		
	2019	2020	2021	2019	2020	2021
1	Industrial machinery	Industrial machinery	Industrial machinery	Agriculture	Consumer electronics	Agriculture
2	Electromechanical equipment	Electromechanical equipment	Electromechanical equipment	Office & school supplies	Agriculture	Food & beverage
3	Vehicles & parts	Vehicles & parts	Vehicles & parts	Consumer electronics	Food & beverage	Consumer electronics
4	Rubber & articles thereof	Rubber & articles thereof	Precious metal	Food & beverage	Cars & motorcycles	Office & school supplies
5	Plastics	Precious metal	Rubber & articles thereof	Cars & motorcycles	Office & school supplies	Cars & motorcycles
6	Precious metal	Plastics	Plastics	Minerals & metals	Beauty & personal care	Beauty & personal care
7	Petroleum & mineral fuels	Petroleum & mineral fuels	Meat & fish	Beauty & personal care	Security & protection	Minerals & metals
8	Meat & fish	Meat & fish	Petroleum & mineral fuels	Rubber plastics raw materials & articles thereof	Minerals & metals	Footwear & parts thereof
9	Organic chemicals	Precision instruments	Medical machinery	Medicines & health care	Health & medical care	Machinery
10	Wood & articles thereof	Organic chemicals	Fruits	Household supplies	Medicines & health care	Vehicles & traffic

Source: Data of general trade is from Thailand Customs and globalEDGE. Data of cross-border e-commerce is from Alibaba. com.

4.7.2.4 Thailand Imports by Category

Table 4-28 shows top 10 categories of imported goods in general trade and cross-border e-commerce of Thailand.

Table 4-28 Top 10 Categories of Imported Goods in General Trade and Cross-Border E-Commerce of Thailand

Rank	General Trade (Top 10 Categories of Imported Goods)			Cross-Border E-Commerce (Top 10 Categories of Import Demand)		
	2019	2020	2021	2019	2020	2021
1	Petroleum & mineral fuels	Electromechanical equipment	Electromechanical equipment	Consumer electronics	Machinery	Consumer electronics
2	Electromechanical equipment	Petroleum & mineral Fuels	Petroleum & mineral fuels	Machinery	Security & protection	Machinery
3	Industrial machinery	Industrial machinery	Industrial machinery	Household supplies	Consumer electronics	Sports & entertainment
4	Precious metal	Precious metal	Vehicles & parts	Cars & motorcycles	Medicines & health care	Home & garden
5	Iron & steel	Iron & steel	Iron & steel	Apparel	Cars & motorcycles	Cars & motorcycles
6	Vehicles & parts	Vehicles & parts	Plastics	Sports & entertainment	Hardware	Apparel
7	Plastics	Plastics	Precious metal	Packaging & printing	Packaging & printing	Packaging & printing
8	Precision instruments	Articles of iron & steel	Articles of iron & steel	Hardware	Sports & entertainment	Health & medical care
9	Organic chemicals	Precision instruments	Medical machinery	Beauty & personal care	Household supplies	Hardware
10	Fish & crustaceans	Organic chemicals	Miscellaneous chemical products	Electrical equipment & articles thereof	Health & medical care	Beauty & personal care

Source: Data of general trade is from Thailand Customs and globalEDGE. Data of cross-border e-commerce is from Alibaba. com.

4. 8 Cross-Border E-Commerce Development of the Philippines

4. 8. 1 Overview of Social Economy and Cross-Border E-Commerce Development of the Philippines

In 2020, the GDP of the Philippines was $361. 489 billion, up

-9.57% year on year, down $ 15.334 billion from 2019. The per capita GDP of the Philippines was $ 3298.83, up -10.78% year on year, down $ 186.51 from 2019. The GNI (Gross National Income) of the Philippines in 2020 was $ 375.998 billion, with per capita GNI of $ 3430, a growth rate of 12.58% and a decrease of $ 420 compared to 2019.

The banking facilities in the Philippine are relatively sound but not inclusive, resulting in low usage of electronic payments in the country. The Philippines has a population of 107 million, of which 73 million are mobile users and 67 million are online 24 hours a day. The reality of low financial inclusion has also hindered the popularization of electronic payment methods in the country. During the pandemic, the digital payment transactions in the Philippines surged due to concerns about contact infection and the government's request to "strengthen community quarantine". Retail e-commerce, takeaway delivery and digital goods have become new growth points for digital payment. Digital payments in the Philippines are gradually changing the country's businesses and consumers. Digital payment in the Philippine increased from $ 3.711 billion in 2016 to $ 7.861 billion in 2020, with the digital commerce reaching $ 310 million and mobile sales terminal payment reaching $ 4.98 billion in 2020.

Digital transformation has always been a major theme in the Philippines. Enterprises across the country are seeking to take advantage of the technological progress of 4IR (Fourth Industrial Revolution) to enter a new stage of development. The launch of 5G service in the Philippines will accelerate digital transformation and bring considerable benefits to enterprises. At the same time, consumers are also eagerly looking forward to the launch of 5G services to enhance the consumer experience on their personal devices. Consumers in the Philippines have spent billions of dollars on streaming media and e-commerce, and 5G service will not only provide them with a better experience, but also enhance digital connectivity nationwide. These trends will play a key role in the Philippines' future economic growth.

4. 8. 2　Comparison between General Trade and Cross-Border E-Commerce of the Philippines

4. 8. 2. 1　Philippines Exports by Country(or Region)

Table 4-29 shows top 10 export countries or regions in general trade and cross-border e-commerce of the Philippines.

Table 4-29　Top 10 Export Countries or Regions in General
Trade and Cross-Border E-Commerce of the Philippines

Rank	General Trade (Top 10 Export Countries or Regions)			Cross-Border E-Commerce (Top 10 Countries or Regions of Export Demand)		
	2019	2020	2021	2019	2020	2021
1	Hong Kong, China	US	Japan	India	US	US
2	US	Japan	US	US	India	India
3	China	China	China	Pakistan	UK	Brazil
4	Japan	Hong Kong, China	Hong Kong, China	China	France	Italy
5	Singapore	Singapore	Singapore	UK	Saudi Arabia	Pakistan
6	Germany	R. O. Korea	Thailand	Canada	Canada	Indonesia
7	R. O. Korea	Thailand	R. O. Korea	Saudi Arabia	South Africa	France
8	Thailand	Germany	Germany	Turkey	Brazil	Peru
9	Taiwan, China	Netherlands	Netherlands	Russia	UAE	Russia
10	Netherlands	Malaysia	Malaysia	Nigeria	Pakistan	Spain

Source: Data of general trade is from globalEDGE, OEC and Trading Economics. Data of cross-border e-commerce is from Alibaba. com.

4. 8. 2. 2　Philippines Imports by Country(or Region)

Table 4-30 shows top 10 Import countries or regions in general trade and cross-border e-commerce of the Philippines.

223

Rank	General Trade (Top 10 Import Countries or Regions)			Cross-Border E-Commerce (Top 10 Countries or Regions of Import Demand)		
	2019	2020	2021	2019	2020	2021
1	China	China	China	China	China	China
2	R. O. Korea	Japan	Japan	Thailand	Japan	Pakistan
3	Japan	R. O. Korea	US	Pakistan	Pakistan	India
4	Taiwan, China	US	R. O. Korea	India	India	US
5	US	Indonesia	Indonesia	R. O. Korea	Vietnam	Vietnam
6	Thailand	Thailand	Singapore	Taiwan, China	US	South Africa
7	Singapore	Singapore	Thailand	US	R. O. Korea	UK
8	Indonesia	Malaysia	Malaysia	Vietnam	South Africa	Germany
9	Malaysia	Vietnam	Vietnam	Hong Kong, China	Thailand	Taiwan, China
10	Vietnam	Hong Kong, China	Hong Kong, China	Japan	Hong Kong, China	France

Source: Data of general trade is from globalEDGE, OEC and Trading Economics. Data of cross-border e-commerce is from Alibaba. com.

4. 8. 2. 3   Philippines Exports by Category

Table 4-31 shows top 10 categories of exported goods in general trade and cross-border e-commerce of the Philippines.

Table 4-31   Top 10 Categories of Exported Goods in General

Trade and Cross-Border E-Commerce of the Philippines

Rank	General Trade (Top 10 Categories of Exported Goods)			Cross-Border E-Commerce (Top 10 Categories of Export Demand)		
	2019	2020	2021	2019	2020	2021
1	Electromechanical equipment	Electric motor	Electrical & electronic equipment	Agriculture	Food & beverage	Cars & motorcycles
2	Industrial machinery	Industrial machinery	Machinery, nuclear reactors & boilers	Food & beverage	Beauty & personal care	Consumer electronics

Continued

Rank	General Trade (Top 10 Categories of Exported Goods)			Cross-Border E-Commerce(Top 10 Categories of Export Demand)		
	2019	2020	2021	2019	2020	2021
3	Precision instrument	Fruits & nuts	Edible fruits, nuts, citrus fruit skins & melons	Cars & motorcycles	Agriculture	Agriculture
4	Edible fruits	Precision instrument	Optical, photographic, technical, medical & surgical apparatus	Minerals & metallurgy	Consumer electronics	Machinery
5	Precious metal	Gemstones & metal	Slag & ash	Office & school supplies	Cars & motorcycles	Food & beverage
6	Petroleum & mineral fuels	Copper	Copper	Beauty & personal care	Hardware	Beauty & personal care
7	Copper & cooper products	Ores	Pearls, gemstones, metals & coins	Consumer electronics	Machinery	Minerals & metallurgy
8	Animal & vegetable oil	Petroleum & mineral fuels	Vehicles other than railway or tramway rolling-stock	Medical & health care	Office & school supplies	Hardware
9	Ore sand	Plastics	Animal fats & vegetable oil & cleavage products	Rubber plastics raw material & articles thereof	Minerals & metallurgy	Sports & entertainment
10	Ships	Vehicles & parts thereof	Plastics	Household supplies	Home & garden	Health & medical care

Source: Data of general trade is from globalEDGE, OEC and Trading Economics. Data of cross-border e-commerce is from Alibaba. com.

4.8.2.4 Philippines Imports by Category

Table 4-32 shows top 10 categories of imported goods in general trade and cross-border e-commerce of the Philippines.

Table 4-32 Top 10 Categories of Imported Goods in General Trade and Cross-Border E-Commerce of the Philippines

Rank	General Trade (Top 10 Categories of Imported Goods)			Cross-Border E-Coomerce(Top 10 Categories of Import Demand)		
	2019	2020	2021	2019	2020	2021
1	Electromechanical equipment	Electric motor	Electrical & electronic equipment	Consumer electronics	Consumer electronics	Consumer electronics
2	Petroleum and mineral fuels	Petroleum and mineral fuels	Machinery, nuclear reactors & boilers	Machinery	Sports & entertainment	Home & garden
3	Industrial machinery	Industrial machinery	Mineral fuels, mineral oils & products of their distillation	Cars & motorcycles	Household supplies	Apparel
4	Vehicles & parts	Automobiles & parts	Vehicles other than railway or tramway rolling-stock	Household supplies	Apparel	Cars & motorcycles
5	Iron & steel	Iron & steel	Iron & steel	Apparel	Packaging & printing	Sports & entertainment
6	Plastics	Plastics	Plastics	Sports & entertainment	Cars & motorcycles	Furniture
7	Precision instruments	Cereals	Cereals	Beauty & personal care	Health & Medical care	Machinery
8	Cereals	Aircraft	Optics, photographic, technical & medical & surgical apparatus	Packaging & printing	Machinery	Packaging & printing
9	Paper	Precision instruments	Articles of iron & steel	Medical & health care	Beauty & personal care	Footwear & parts thereof
10	Miscellaneous food	Articles of iron & steel	Pharmaceutical products	Luggage, bags & cases	Household appliances	Toys

Source: Data of general trade is from globalEDGE, OEC and Trading Economics. Data of cross-border e-commerce is from Alibaba. com.

4. 9   Cross-Border E-Commerce Development of Singapore

4. 9. 1   Overview of Social Economy and Cross-Border E-Commerce Development of singapore

Singapore is a fast-growing international business center with per capita GDP ranking first in Asia. In 2020, Singapore's GDP was $ 340 billion and its per capita GDP was $ 59758, down 9. 2% year on year. Singapore is a fully urbanized country, with a population of 5. 68 million in 2020, down 0. 31% year on year.

In 2021, there was 5. 29 million Internet users in Singapore, up 2. 8% year on year. The Internet availability rate was 90%, while the number of smartphone users was about 5. 17 million, with a penetration rate of 88%. According to "Southeast Asia E-Commerce Report 2020" jointly released by Google, Temasek and Bain, the average daily online time of residents in Singapore rose to 4. 1 hours in 2020 from about 3. 6 hours before the COVID-19 pandemic.

Singapore is the hub of many cross-border e-commerce platforms in the Asia-Pacific region. Thanks to Singapore's preferential tax policies and the friendly and open business environment, many e-commerce companies such as Shopee, Lazada, Amazon, and Zalora have established headquarters here. In 2020, Singapore's total social retail sales were $ 38. 1 billion, down 15% year on year. However, Singapore's total online retail sales in 2020 reached $ 4. 8 billion, up 86% year on year, accounting for 12. 7% of the total social retail sales(See Figure 4-5). Cross-border online shopping is an important feature of Singapore's e-commerce market, with about 78% of online shoppers choosing to buy goods from abroad. In 2020, the scale of cross-border e-commerce in Singapore reached $ 2. 4 billion and occupied 55% of the e-commerce market, surpassing the domestic e-commerce market.

Figure 4-5   Total Retail Sales and Online Retail Sales of Singapore from 2018 to Nov. 2021

Source: Singapore Department of Statistics.

The digital economy agreements (DEA) are treaties that establish digital trade rules and digital economy cooperation between two or more economies to promote the participation of domestic enterprises in international cross-border e-commerce and e-commerce activities. By 2021, Singapore had completed negotiations on four digital economy agreements. The top three e-commerce companies in Singapore by traffic are Shopee, Lazada and Amazon, with monthly network visits of 12 million, 7. 3 million and 6. 46 million respectively. Other e-commerce platforms include Qoo10 and EZBuy. The overall availability rates of cards in Singapore are very high, with about 1. 6 debit cards and 1. 5 credit cards per capita. At present, credit cards are still the most popular online payment method in Singapore, accounting for about 63% of the market share, while digital wallets and bank transfers account for 21% and 10% market shares respectively. At the same time, PayNow, a national real-time electronic payment plan, is developing rapidly, with about 18. 2% of Singapore citizens taking it as their preferred payment method. Located at the crossroads of international shipping routes, Singapore is the transportation and logistics center of Southeast Asia. The developed logistics infrastructure has attracted international logistics companies such as FedEx, UPS and DHL to set up major freight hubs here.

4. 9. 2 Comparison between General Trade and Cross-Border E-Commerce of Singapore

4. 9. 2. 1   Singapore Exports by Country(or Region)

Table 4-33 shows top 10 export countries or regions in general trade and cross-border e-commerce of Singapore.

Table 4-33   Top 10 Export Countries or Regions in General
Trade and Cross-Border E-Commerce of Singapore

Rank	General Trade (Top 10 Export Countries or Regions)			Cross-Border E-Commerce (Top 10 Countries or Regions of Export Demand)		
	2019	2020	2021	2019	2020	2021
1	China	China	China	US	US	US
2	Hong Kong, China	Hong Kong, China	Hong Kong, China	India	India	India
3	Malaysia	Malaysia	US	China	UK	Brazil
4	US	US	Malaysia	Russia	Philippines	Vietnam
5	Indonesia	Indonesia	Indonesia	UK	Canada	Pakistan
6	India	Japan	Japan	Canada	Pakistan	Bangladesh
7	Japan	Thailand	R. O. Korea	Indonesia	Indonesia	Peru
8	Taiwan, China	R. O. Korea	Thailand	Brazil	Saudi Arabia	Egypt
9	Thailand	Vietnam	Vietnam	Pakistan	Brazil	Philippines
10	Australia	India	Netherlands	Malaysia	Malaysia	Colombia

Source: Data of general trade is from Singapore Customs and globalEDGE. Data of cross-border e-commerce is from Alibaba. com.

4. 9. 2. 2   Singapore Imports by Country(or Region)

Table 4-34 shows top 10 import countries or regions in general trade and cross-border e-commerce of Singapore.

Table 4-34　Top 10 Import Countries or Regions in General

Table 4-34　Top 10 Import Countries or Regions in General

Trade and Cross-Border E-Commerce of Singapore

Rank	General Trade (Top 10 Import Countries or Regions)			Cross-Border E-Commerce (Top 10 Countries or Regions of Import Demand)		
	2019	2020	2021	2019	2020	2021
1	China	China	China	China	China	China
2	Malaysia	US	Malaysia	India	India	India
3	US	Malaysia	US	Thailand	Vietnam	Vietnam
4	Taiwan, China	Japan	Japan	R. O. Korea	Thailand	Pakistan
5	Japan	Indonesia	R. O. Korea	Vietnam	Malaysia	Thailand
6	Indonesia	R. O. Korea	Indonesia	Malaysia	Pakistan	Taiwan, China
7	R. O. Korea	France	France	Taiwan, China	R. O. Korea	R. O. Korea
8	Saudi Arabia	UAE	Thailand	Pakistan	Indonesia	US
9	France	Germany	Germany	US	Taiwan, China	South Africa
10	India	UK	UK	Hong Kong, China	US	Hong Kong, China

Source: Data of general trade is from Singapore Customs and globalEDGE. Data of cross-border e-commerce is from Alibaba. com.

4. 9. 2. 3　Singapore Exports by Category

Table 4-35 shows top 10 categories of exported goods in general trade and cross-border e-commerce of Singapore.

Table 4-35　Top 10 Categories of Exported Goods in General

Trade and Cross-Border E-Commerce of Singapore

Rank	General Trade (Top 10 Categories of Exported Goods)			Cross-Border E-Commerce (Top 10 Categories of Export Demand)		
	2019	2020	2021	2019	2020	2021
1	Electromechanical equipment	Electromechanical equipment	Electromechanical equipment	Agriculture	Agriculture	Agriculture
2	Petroleum & mineral fuels	Industrial machinery	Industrial machinery	Food & beverage	Food & beverage	Food & beverage
3	Industrial machinery	Petroleum & mineral fuels	Petroleum & mineral fuels	Cars & motorcycles	Machinery	Machinery

Continued

Rank	General Trade (Top 10 Categories of Exported Goods)			Cross-Border E-Commerce (Top 10 Categories of Export Demand)		
	2019	2020	2021	2019	2020	2021
4	Organic chemicals	Other heterocyclic compounds	Medical machinery	Household supplies	Consumer electronics	Consumer electronics
5	Precision instruments	Precision instruments	Precious metal	Machinery	Cars & motorcycles	Cars & motorcycles
6	Precious metal	Precious metal	Unclassified	Consumer electronics	Security & protection	Home & garden
7	Plastics	Plastics	Plastics	Medical & health care	Hardware	Commercial services equipment
8	Medication	Organic chemicals	Organic chemicals	Energy source	Household supplies	Rubber raw materials & articles thereof
9	Ships	Cosmetics	Cosmetics	Electrical equipment & products	Health & medical care	Health & medical care
10	Miscellaneous food	Medication	Medication	Gifts & crafts	Medicines & health care	Energy source

Source: Data of general trade is from Singapore Customs and globalEDGE. Data of cross-border e-commerce is from Alibaba. com.

4.9.2.4 Singapore Imports by Category

Table 4-36 shows top 10 categories of imported goods in general trade and cross-border e-commerce of Singapore.

Table 4-36 Top 10 Categories of Imported Goods in General Trade and Cross-Border E-Commerce of Singapore

Rank	General Trade (Top 10 Categories of Imported Goods)			Cross-Border E-Commerce (Top 10 Categories of Import Demand)		
	2019	2020	2021	2019	2020	2021
1	Petroleum & mineral fuels	Electromechanical equipment	Electromechanical equipment	Household supplies	Packaging & printing	Packaging & printing
2	Electromechanical equipment	Petroleum & mineral	Industrial machinery	Packaging & printing	Consumer electronics	Home & garden

Continued

Rank	General Trade (Top 10 Categories of Imported Goods)			Cross-border Trade (Top 10 Categories of Impoert Demand)		
	2019	2020	2021	2019	2020	2021
3	Industrial machinery	Industrial machinery	Petroleum & mineral fuels	Consumer electronics	Beauty & personal care	Consumer electronics
4	Precious metal	Precious metal	Precious metal	Apparel	Security & protection	Machinery
5	Precision instruments	Precision instruments	Medical & surgical apparatus	Beauty & personal care	Apparel	Apparel
6	Ships	Aircraft	Plastics	Machinery	Medicines & health care	Furniture
7	Plastics	Plastics	Organic chemicals	Luggage, bags & cases	Home & garden	Sports & entertainment
8	Aircraft	Organic chemicals	Aircraft	Gifts & crafts	Machinery	Beauty & personal care
9	Organic chemicals	Vehicles & parts	Cosmetics	Sports & entertainment	Sports & entertainment	Health & medical care
10	Miscellaneous chemical products	Cosmetics	Miscellaneous chemical products	Construction	Household supplies	Gifts & crafts

Source: Data of general trade is from Singapore Customs and global EDGE. Data of cross-border e-commerce is from Alibaba. com.

4. 10　Cross-Border E-Commerce Development of Malaysia

4. 10. 1　Overview of Social Economy and Cross-Border E-Commerce Development of Malaysia

In 2020, Malaysia's GDP was $336.7 billion and its per capita GDP was $10402, down 8.2% year on year. Malaysia's population was 32.37 million in 2020, an increase of 1.3% year on year. 77% of the population live in urban areas, and 23% live in rural areas.

In 2021, the number of Internet users in Malaysia was 27.43 million, up 2.8% year on year. The Internet availability rate was 84%, while the number of smartphone users reached 28.36 million, with an availability rate of 87%. According to "Southeast Asia E-Commerce Report 2020" jointly released by Google, Temasek and Bain, the average daily online time of Malaysian residents rose from about 3.7 hours before the COVID-19 pandemic to 4.2 hours during the pandemic in 2020. In 2020, Malaysia's e-commerce market was $7.2 billion, up 24.8% year on year(see Figure 4-6), while cross-border e-commerce reached $3.3 billion, accounting for 45% of the e-commerce market.

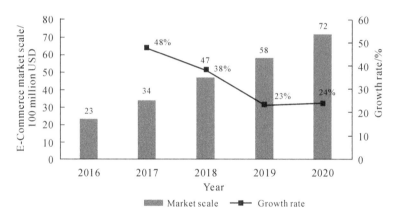

Figure 4-6   E-Commerce Market Scales and Growth Rates of Malaysia 2016—2020

Source: Department of Statistics Malaysia.

In order to promote the development of e-commerce, the Malaysian government approved the National eCommerce Strategic Roadmap 2.0 (NESR 2.0) in 2021, aiming to improve economic competitiveness and build a digital society through digitalization. The top three e-commerce companies by traffic in Malaysia are Shopee, Lazada, and PG Mall. The number of monthly network visitors for each is 54 million, 13.75 million, and 7.06 million, respectively. Other e-commerce platforms include LeLong and Qoo10, etc.

Bank transfer is the most important payment method in Malaysia, which owns approximately 45% of market share. The second is card payment, accounting for about 36% of the market share. According to statistics, Malaysia has 1.33 debit cards and 0.32 credit card per capita. Although the proportion of cash payment is gradually decreasing, it still accounts for 10% of the market share. However, digital wallets account for only 6% of the market share. PayPal, Visa Checkout and Masterpass are all popular electronic payment methods. Operating a digital wallet in Malaysia requires a government-issued digital currency license. Alipay, WeChat and Google Pay are licensed international payment brands in Malaysia. The supply chain and logistics sectors in Malaysia are very scattered, involving a large number of SMEs as well as large logistics enterprises include NEC, Fujitsu, DHL and Pos Malaysia, etc.

4.10.2   Comparison between General Trade and Cross-Border E-Commerce of Malaysia

4.10.2.1   Malaysia Exports by Country(or Region)

Table 4-37 shows top 10 export countries or regions in general trade and cross-border e-commerce of Malaysia.

Table 4-37   Top 10 Export Countries or Regions in General Trade and Cross-Border E-Commerce of Malaysia

Rank	General Trade (Top 10 Export Countries or Regions)			Cross-Border E-Commerce (Top 10 Countries or Regions of Export Demand)		
	2019	2020	2021	2019	2020	2021
1	Singapore	China	China	US	US	US
2	China	Singapore	Singapore	India	India	India
3	US	US	US	China	China	France
4	Hong Kong, China	Hong Kong, China	Hong Kong, China	Canada	France	Brazil
5	Japan	Japan	Japan	UK	UK	Philippines

Continued

Rank	General Trade (Top 10 Export Countries or Regions)			Cross-Border E-Commerce (Top 10 Countries or Regions of Export Demand)		
	2019	2020	2021	2019	2020	2021
6	Thailand	Thailand	Thailand	Saudi Arabia	Philippines	Pakistan
7	India	India	R. O. Korea	Indonesia	Turkey	Indonesia
8	R. O. Korea	Vietnam	Vietnam	France	Pakistan	Egypt
9	Mexico	R. O. Korea	India	Russia	Italy	Canada
10	Taiwan, China	Indonesia	Indonesia	Pakistan	Canada	UK

Source: Data of general trade is from Malaysia Customs and global EDGE. Data of cross-border e-commerce is from Alibaba. com.

4.10.2.2 Malaysia Imports by Country(or Region)

Table 4-33 shows top 10 import countries or regions in general trade and cross-border e-commerce of Malaysia.

Table 4-38 Top 10 Import Countries or Regions in General Trade and Cross-Border E-Commerce of Malaysia

Rank	General Trade (Top 10 Import Countries or Regions)			Cross-Border E-Commerce (Top 10 Countries or Regions of Import Demand		
	2019	2020	2021	2019	2020	2021
1	China	China	China	China	China	China
2	Singapore	Singapore	Singapore	India	India	India
3	Japan	US	US	Thailand	Thailand	Vietnam
4	US	Japan	Japan	Pakistan	Vietnam	South Africa
5	Thailand	Thailand	R. O. Korea	Vietnam	Pakistan	Pakistan
6	Taiwan, China	Indonesia	Indonesia	R. O. Korea	US	Thailand
7	Indonesia	R. O. Korea	Thailand	US	UK	US
8	R. O. Korea	Germany	India	Taiwan, China	South Africa	UK
9	India	India	Germany	Philippines	R. O. Korea	France
10	Germany	Australia	Australia	UK	Japan	Germany

Source: Data of general trade is from Malaysia Customs and global EDGE. Data of cross-border e-commerce is from Alibaba. com.

4.10.2.3 Malaysia Exports by Category

Table 4-39 shows top 10 categories of exported goods in general trade and cross-border e-commerce of Malaysia.

Table 4-39 Top 10 Categories of Exported Goods in General Trade and Cross-Border E-Commerce of Malaysia

Rank	General Trade (Top 10 Categories of Exported Goods)			Cross-Border E-Commerce (Top 10 Categories of Export Demand)		
	2019	2020	2021	2019	2020	2021
1	Electromechanical equipment	Electromechanical equipment	Electromechanical equipment	Food & beverage	Health & medical care	Food & beverage
2	Petroleum & mineral fuels	Petroleum & mineral fuels	Petroleum & mineral fuels	Cars & motorcycles	Food & beverage	Machinery
3	Industrial machinery	Industrial machinery	Industrial machinery	Medicines & health care	Security & protection	Agriculture
4	Animal fats & vegetable oil	Animal fats & vegetable oil	Animal fats & vegetable oil	Machinery	Machinery	Cars & motorcycles
5	Precision instruments	Precision instruments	Rubber & articles thereof	Agriculture	Medicines & health care	Health & medical care
6	Plastics	Plastics	Medical & surgical apparatus	Consumer electronics	Cars & motorcycles	Home & garden
7	Rubber & articles thereof	Rubber & articles thereof	Plastics	Household supplies	Agriculture	Furniture
8	Organic chemicals	Iron & Steel	Iron & Steel	Beauty & personal care	Beauty & personal care	Architecture
9	Wood & articles thereof	Miscellaneous chemical products	Miscellaneous chemical products	Architecture	Household supplies	Consumer electronics
10	Aluminum & articles thereof	Organic chemicals	Aluminum & articles thereof	Furniture & home decor	Consumer electronics	Beauty & personal care

Source: Data of general trade is from Malaysia Customs and global EDGE. Data of cross-border e-commerce is from Alibaba.com.

4.10.2.4 Malaysia Import by Category

Table 4-40 shows top 10 import categories in general trade and cross-border e-commerce of Malaysia.

Table 4-40　Top 10 Import Categories in General Trade and Cross-Border E-Commerce of Malaysia

Rank	General Trade (Top 10 Categories of Imported Goods)			Cross-Border E-Commerce (Top 10 Categories of Export Demand)		
	2019	2020	2021	2019	2020	2021
1	Electromechanical equipment	Electromechanical equipment	Electromechanical equipment	Consumer electronics	Machinery	Consumer electronics
2	Petroleum & mineral fuels	Petroleum & mineral fuels	Petroleum & mineral fuels	Machinery	Consumer electronics	Machinery
3	Industrial machinery	Industrial machinery	Industrial machinery	Household supplies	Packaging & printing	Home & garden
4	Plastics	Plastics	Plastics	Apparel	Security & protection	Cars & motorcycles
5	Vehicles & parts	Iron & steel	Medical & surgical apparatus	Packaging & printing	Cars & motorcycles	Sports & entertainment
6	Iron & steel	Vehicles & parts	Iron & steel	Cars & motorcycles	Medicines & health care	Apparel
7	Precision instruments	Precision instruments	Aluminum & articles thereof	Beauty & personal care	Apparel	Packaging & printing
8	Precious metals	Precious metals	Vehicles & parts	Sports & entertainment	Beauty & personal care	Furniture
9	Organic chemicals	Organic chemicals	Precious metals	Medicines & health Care	Sports & entertainment	Beauty & personal care
10	Rubber & articles thereof	Miscellaneous chemical products	Rubber & articles thereof	Hardware	Household supplies	Health care

Source: Data of general trade is from Malaysia Customs and globalEDGE. Data of cross-border e-commerce is from Alibaba.com.

4.11 Cross-Border E-Commerce Development of Vietnam

4.11.1 Overview of Social Economy and Cross-Border E-Commerce Development of Vietnam

In 2020, Vietnam's GDP reached $271.2 billion, with a growth rate of 2.91 %. GDP of Vietnam in 2020 is about 1.4 times higher than that in 2015 (according to the International Monetary Fund, Vietnam may become the fourth largest economy in ASEAN in 2020), making Vietnam rank among the countries of highest GDP growth. In 2020, the GDP per capita in Vietnam was about $2750. Meanwhile, Vietnam's total imports and exports increased by 3.6 times, from $157.1 billion in 2010 to $517 billion in 2019. In 2020, due to the severe impact of the COVID-19 pandemic, the total import and export volume was about $527 billion, equivalent to more than 190% of GDP. Exports grew rapidly from $72.2 billion in 2010 to about $267 billion in 2020 with an average annual increase of 14%. Therefore, the merchandise trade surplus reached a new peak of $19.1 billion. In 2020, the total population of Vietnam was 97.3386 million, which has increased by 876,500 over 2019, and the population growth rate was 0.9%. In 2020, Vietnam's population aged 65 and above accounted for 8%, making it an aging society; in terms of gender, the population of women is relatively more than that of men. In 2020, Vietnam's urbanization rate was 37.3%, and the rate has been increasing steadily year by year.

Vietnam's Internet development is at the forefront of developing countries. At present, more than 70% of the people are using smartphones. The Internet penetration rate is about 66%, while the e-commerce penetration rate (among Internet users) is about 77%. The number of e-commerce users reached 50 million, exceeding the global average of 46.5%. According to "Southeast Asia Internet Economic Report 2021" jointly released by Google, Temasek and Bain, Vietnam's Internet economy is expected to grow by 31% this year, reaching $ 21 billion, of which e-commerce revenue will be $ 13 billion, the same as Malaysia.

A study by Visa showed a significant increase in e-wallet users and payment applications in 2020, indicating that more than 85% of consumers have at least 1 cashless payment method, with 71% of consumers using it at least once a week. Although the most popular payment method is still cash on delivery: a survey by Statista shows that 78% of online shoppers still prefer to pay for online shopping by cash; however, with the strong development of e-wallets such as Momo and Zalopay, the prosperity of digital payment is just around the corner. Looking ahead, Vietnam's e-commerce revenue is expected to reach $ 39 billion in 2025, surpassing the $ 35 billion of Thailand, ranking the second in Southeast Asia. According to the iPrice report, the most commonly used e-commerce platforms in Vietnam are Shopee, Lazada, Tiki, and Sendo. The report shows that Vietnam's e-commerce market is gradually maturing, which means that the channels and methods for platforms to obtain traffic are more diversified without restriction of discount forms.

4.11.2　Comparison between General Trade and Cross-Border E-Commerce of Vietnam

4.11.2.1　Vietnam Exports by Country(or Region)

Table 4-41 shows top 10 export countries or regions in general trade and cross-border e-commerce of Vietnam.

Table 4-41 Top 10 Export Countries or Regions in General

Trade and Cross-Border E-Commerce of Vietnam

Rank	General Trade (Top 10 Export Countries or Regions)			Cross-Border E-Commerce (Top 10 Countries or Regions of Export Demand)		
	2019	2020	2021	2019	2020	2021
1	US	US	US	US	US	US
2	China	China	China	India	India	India
3	Japan	Japan	Japan	UK	UK	Brazil
4	R. O. Korea	R. O. Korea	R. O. Korea	China	Canada	UK
5	Germany	Hong Kong, China	Hong Kong, China	Nigeria	Australia	Canada
6	Hong Kong, China	Netherlands	Netherlands	Canada	Philippines	Philippines
7	India	India	Germany	Australia	Brazil	France
8	Netherlands	Germany	India	Russia	Nigeria	Saudi Arabia
9	UAE	UK	UK	Brazil	Saudi Arabia	Pakistan
10	Thailand	Thailand	Thailand	France	France	Spain

Source: Data of general trade is from globalEDGE, OEC and Trading Economics. Data of cross-border e-commerce is from Alibaba. com.

4. 11. 2. 2   Vietnam Imports by Country(or Region)

Table 4-42 shows top 10 import countries or regions in general trade and cross-border e-commerce of Vietnam.

Table 4-42 Top 10 Import Countries or Regions in General

Trade and Cross-Border E-Commerce of Vietnam

Rank	General Trade (Top 10 Import Countries or Regions)			Cross-Border E-Commerce (Top 10 Countries or Regions of Import Demand)		
	2019	2020	2021	2019	2020	2021
1	China	China	China	China	China	China
2	R. O. Korea	R. O. Korea	R. O. Korea	Thailand	Thailand	US
3	Japan	Japan	Japan	India	US	France
4	Thailand	US	US	US	South Africa	India

Continued

Rank	General Trade (Top 10 Import Countries or Regions)			Cross-Border E-Commerce (Top 10 Countries or Regions of Import Demand)		
	2019	2020	2021	2019	2020	2021
5	Taiwan, China	Thailand	Thailand	R. O. Korea	India	Pakistan
6	US	Malaysia	Malaysia	Taiwan, China	R. O. Korea	South Africa
7	Malaysia	Indonesia	Indonesia	Germany	Pakistan	Thailand
8	Singapore	India	Australia	Hong Kong, China	Malaysia	UK
9	India	Australia	India	Malaysia	UK	Germany
10	Germany	Singapore	Ireland	Pakistan	Taiwan, China	Japan

Source: Data of general trade is from globalEDGE, OEC and Trading Economics. Data of cross-border e-commerce is from Alibaba. com.

4. 11. 2. 3   Vietnam Exports by Category

Table 4-43 shows top 10 categories of exported goods in general trade and cross-border e-commerce of Vietnam.

Table 4-43   Top 10 Export Categories in General Trade and

Cross-Border E-Commerce of Vietnam

Rank	General Trade (Top 10 Categories of Exported Goods)			Cross-Border E-Commerce (Top 10 Categories of Export Demand)		
	2019	2020	2021	2019	2020	2021
1	Electromechanical equipment	Electric motors	Electrical & electronic equipment	Beauty & personal care	Beauty & personal care	Beauty & personal care
2	Shoes and boots	Shoes	Machinery, nuclear reactor, boiler	Consumer electronics	Consumer electronics	Home & garden
3	Apparel (not knitted)	Apparel (not knitted)	Shoes, leggings etc.	Food & beverage	Household supplies	Food & beverage
4	Industrial machinery	Apparal (knitted)	Apparal (knitted or crocheted)	Household supplies	Food & beverage	Agriculture
5	Apparel (knitted)	Industrial machinery	Apparel (not knitted or crocheted)	Agriculture	Agriculture	Furniture

Continued

Rank	General Trade (Top 10 Categories of Exported Goods)			Cross-Border E-Commerce (Top 10 Categories of Export Demand)		
	2019	2020	2021	2019	2020	2021
6	Furniture	Furniture	Furniture, illuminated sign, prefabricated buildings	Apparel	Apparel	Apparel
7	Fish	Seafood	Fish, crustaceans, mollusks, aquatic invertebrate	Construction	Furniture	Machinery
8	Fruit	Fruit and nuts	Iron & steel	Luggage, bags & cases	Security & protection	Consumer electronics
9	Precision instruments	Precision instruments	Plastics	Furniture & home decor	Health & medical care	Architecture
10	Plastics	Plastics	Edible fruits, nuts, citrus fruit peels, melons	Machinery	Machinery	Sports & entertainment

Source: Data of general trade is from globalEDGE, OEC and Trading Economics. Data of cross-border e-commerce is from Alibaba. com.

4. 11. 2. 4　Vietnam Imports by Category

Table 4-44 shows top 10 import categories in general trade and cross-border e-commerce of Vietnam.

Table 4-44　Top 10 Categories of Imported Goods in General Trade and Cross-Border E-Commerce of Vietnam

Rank	General Trade (Top 10 Categories of Import Goods)			Cross-Border E-Commerce (Top 10 Categories of Import Demand)		
	2019	2020	2021	2019	2020	2021
1	Electromechanical equipment	Electric motors	Slag & ash	Consumer electronics	Medical & health care	Consumer electronics
2	Industrial machinery	Industrial machinery	Products not specified by category	Machinery	Machinery	Machinery

242

Continued

Rank	General Trade (Top 10 Export Countries or Regions)			Cross-Border E-Commerce (Top 10 Countries or Regions of Export Demand)		
	2019	2020	2021	2019	2020	2021
3	Petroleum & mineral fuels	Plastics	Mineral fuels, mineral oils & products of their distillation	Electrical equipment & articles thereof	Consumer electronics	Cars & motorcycles
4	Plastics	Petroleum & mineral fuels	Pearls, gemstones, metals & coins	Cars & motorcycles	Security & protection	Sports & entertainment
5	Iron & steel	Iron & steel	Meat & edible offal	Household supplies	Hardware	Hardware
6	Precision instruments	Precision instruments	Machinery, nuclear reactors, boilers	Hardware	Cars & motorcycles	Home & garden
7	Vehicles & parts	Cars & parts	Cereals	Medicines & health care	Household supplies	Beauty & personal care
8	Fruit	Knitted fabric	Pharmaceutical products	Sports & entertainment	Sports & entertainment	Health & medical care
9	Fish	Cotton	Electrical, electronic equipment	Beauty & personal care	Electrical equipment & articles thereof	Electrical equipment & articles thereof
10	Organic chemicals	Articles of iron & steel	Aluminum	Packaging & printing	Packaging & printing	Apparel

Source: Data of general trade is from globalEDGE, OEC and Trading Economics. Data of cross-border e-commerce is from Alibaba. com.

4. 12   Cross-Border E-Commerce Development of Myanmar

4. 12. 1   Overview of Social Economy and Cross-Border E-Commerce Development of Myanmar

Based on the data from World Bank, Myanmar's GDP reached

$ 79. 852 billion in 2020, increased by 3. 17% over the previous year; and the GDP per capita was $ 1467. 60, increased by 2. 48% over the previous year. At the same time, the total population of Myanmar reached 54,409,800 in 2020.

The digital economy infrastructure of Myanmar still needs to be improved. By the time of January 2021, Myanmar had 23. 65 million Internet users, increased by 12% over the previous year, with an Internet availability rate of 43%. The number of mobile phone users was 69. 43 million, decreased by 0. 9% over the previous year, and the availability rate of mobile phones reached 127%. The development of online retail in Myanmar is lagging behind. By 2019, the online retail scales of Myanmar were only $ 6 million, accounting for less than 1% of the total retail scales. However, analysts from Statista believe that there is huge potential for its online retail development. In 2015, 2C2P and MPU launched the first online payment platform in Myanmar. In 2020, the Central Bank of Myanmar launched online banking services for the first time. At present, the top three e-commerce platforms in Myanmar are Shop MM, Spree, and 365Myanmar.

The Myanmar government has gradually realized the importance of cross-border e-commerce and has begun to encourage its development. In 2020, the Myanmar Government established the Sub-Committee on Digital Trade and Electronic Commerce Development(DTECD). The Committee actively connects the private and public sectors, and adjusts relevant regulatory measures based on feedbacks from the private sectors to encourage companies to achieve digital transformation. In addition, the main objectives of the Committee include increasing the income of the rural population through e-commerce.

4. 12. 2   Comparison between General Trade and Cross-Border E-Commerce of Myanmar

4. 12. 2. 1   Myanmar Exports by Country(or Region)

Table 4-45 shows top 10 export countries or regions in general trade and cross-border e-commerce of Myanmar.

Table 4-45   Top 10 Export Countries or Regions in General Trade and Cross-Border E-Commerce of Myanmar

Rank	General Trade (Top 10 Export Countries or Regions)			Cross-Border E-Commerce (Top 10 Countries or Regions of Export Demand)		
	2018	2019	2020	2019	2020	2021
1	China	China	China	China	China	Philippines
2	Thailand	Thailand	Thailand	Vietnam	Thailand	Indonesia
3	Japan	Japan	Japan	Thailand	Philippines	Malaysia
4	India	US	US	Indonesia	Malaysia	Australia
5	Hong Kong	Germany	India	Malaysia	Vietnam	Vietnam
6	Germany	India	UK	R. O. Korea	Australia	Cambodia
7	Singapore	Spain	Spain	Singapore	R. O. Korea	China
8	US	UK	Germany	Philippines	Indonesia	Thailand
9	R. O. Korea	R. O. Korea	Netherlands	Australia	Singapore	Singapore
10	UK	Netherlands	R. O. Korea	Cambodia	Japan	Japan

Source: Data of general trade is from Central Statistical Organization of Myanmar, and data of cross-border e-commerce is from Alibaba. com.

4. 12. 2. 2   Myanmar Imports by Country(or Region)

Table 4-46 shows top 10 import countries or regions in general trade and cross-border e-commerce of Myanmar.

Table 4-46 Top 10 Import Countries or Regions in General
Trade and Cross-Border E-Commerce of Myanmar

Rank	General Trade (Top 10 Import Countries or Regions)			Cross-Border E-Commerce (Top 10 Countries or Regions of Import Demand)		
	2018	2019	2020	2019	2020	2021
1	China	China	China	China	China	China
2	Singapore	Singapore	Singapore	Thailand	Thailand	Thailand
3	Thailand	Thailand	Thailand	Vietnam	Vietnam	Vietnam
4	India	Malaysia	Indonesia	R. O. Korea	Japan	Japan
5	Indonesia	Indonesia	Malaysia	Japan	R. O. Korea	R. O. Korea
6	Malaysia	India	India	Malaysia	Malaysia	Malaysia
7	Japan	Vietnam	R. O. Korea	Philippines	Philippines	Singapore
8	Vietnam	Japan	Vietnam	Singapore	Singapore	Indonesia
9	R. O. Korea	R. O. Korea	Japan	Indonesia	Indonesia	Philippines
10	US	US	US	Australia	Australia	Australia

Source: Data of general trade is from Central Statistical Organization of Myanmar, and data of cross-border e-commerce is from Alibaba. com.

4. 12. 2. 3 Myanmar Exports by Category

Table 4-47 shows top 10 categories of exported goods in general trade and cross-border e-commerce of Myanmar.

Table 4-47 Top 10 Categories of Exported Goods in General
Trade and Cross-Border E-Commerce of Myanmar

Rank	General Trade (Top 10 Categories of Exported Goods)			Cross-Border E-Commerce (Top 10 Categories of Export Demand)		
	2018	2019	2020	2019	2020	2021
1	Apparel	Apparel	Apparel	Agriculture	Apparel	Apparel
2	Gas fuel	Gas fuel	Gas fuel	Beauty & personal care	Agriculture	Consumer electronics
3	Base metal	Base metal	Base metal	Food & beverage	Luggage, bags & cases	Agriculture

Continued

Rank	General Trade (Top 10 Categories of Exported Goods)			Cross-Border E-Commerce (Top10 Categories of Export Demand)		
	2018	2019	2020	2019	2020	2021
4	Rice	Rice	Rice	Cars, motorcycles	Food & beverage	Cars, motorcycles
5	Jadeite	Jadeite	Fish & fish Products	Minerals & metals	Beauty & personal care	Furniture
6	Fish & fish products	Fish & fish products	Black gram	Consumer electronics	Cars & motorcycles	Vehicles & traffic
7	Black gram	Mung bean	Mung bean	Business services	Security & protection	Household appliances
8	Mung bean	Black gram	Corn	Luggage, bags & cases	Business services	Fabric & textile raw materials
9	Corn	Raw rubber	Raw rubber	Architecture	Fabric & textile raw materials	Hardware
10	Raw rubber	Peanut seeds	Peanut seeds	Watches, jewelry & glasses	Furniture	Food & beverage

Source: Data of general trade is from Central Statistical Organization of Myanmar, and data of cross-border e-commerce is from Alibaba. com.

4. 12. 2. 4　Myanmar Imports by Category

Table 4-48 shows top 10 import categories in general trade and cross-border e-commerce of Myanmar.

Table 4-48　Top 10 Import Categories in General Trade and

Cross-Border E-Commerce of Myanmar

Rank	General Trade (Top 10 Categories of Imported Goods)			Cross-Border E-Commerce (Top 10 Categories of Import Demand)		
	2018	2019	2020	2019	2020	2021
1	Mineral fuels	Mineral fuels	Non-electric machinery and transportation equipment	Consumer electronics	Consumer electronics	Consumer electronics

Continued

Rank	General Trade (Top 10 Categories of Imported Goods)			Cross-Border E-Commerce (Top 10 Categories of Import Demand)		
	2018	2019	2020	2019	2020	2021
2	Nuclear reactors, boilers, machinery and mechanical appliances & parts thereof	Non-electric machinery and transportation equipment	Refined mineral oil	Machinery	Machinery	Toys
3	Non-electric machinery & transportation equipment	Base metals & articles thereof	Electrical & electronic equipment	Cars & motorcycles	Cars & motorcycles	Apparel
4	Electrical & electronic equipment	Electrical & electronic equipment	Base metals & articles thereof	Apparel	Apparel	Health & health care
5	Man-made fiber	Man-made fiber	Man-made fiber	Household supplies	Packaging & printing	Machinery
6	Plastics & articles thereof	Plastics & articles thereof	Plastics & articles thereof	Medicines & health care	Sports & entertainment	Sports & entertainment
7	Edible vegetable oil	Edible vegetable oil	Edible vegetable oil	Hardware	Sports & entertainment	Cars & motorcycles
8	Medication	Medication	Medication	Electrical equipment & products	Health & medical care	Home & garden
9	Fertilizer	Fertilizer	Fertilizer	Packaging & printing	Medicines & health care	Beauty & personal care
10	Paper, paperboard & articles thereof	Paper, paperboard & articles thereof	Coal & coke	Beauty & personal care	Home & garden	Packaging & printing

Source: Data of general trade is from Central Statistical Organization of Myanmar, and data of cross-border e-commerce is from Alibaba.com.

4. 13　Cross-Border E-Commerce Development of Cambodia

4. 13. 1　Overview of Social Economy and Cross-Border E-Commerce Development of Cambodia

In 2020, Cambodia's GDP was $ 25. 29 billion and its GDP per capita was $ 1512. 73, decreased by 6. 6% over the previous year. In 2020, Cambodia's population was 16. 72 million, increased by 1. 4% over the previous year. Among them, 24. 5% of the population live in urban areas, and 75. 5% of the population live in rural areas.

In 2021, the number of Internet users in Cambodia was 8860, 000, which a year-on-year increase of 14%, and the Internet penetration rate was 53%. In addition, Cambodia has more than 10 million smartphones connected to the Internet. Mobile Internet access is affordable with the lowest price in the world, about $ 0. 13/GB. Cambodia's e-commerce market is relatively underdeveloped in Southeast Asia due to restrictions such as imperfect Internet infrastructure, backward development of the logistics industry, less consumers, and backward electronic payment systems such as credit cards. In 2021, Cambodia's annual e-commerce market is $ 971 million, increased by 19% over the previous year(see Figure 4-7).

In 2020, Cambodia launched the E-Commerce Strategy with the aim of develeping the digital economy and promoting the trade development. The most popular e-commerce platforms in Cambodia are Glad Market, Mall855 and MAIO Mall. Other e-commerce platforms include RoseRb, Aliexpress, and Taobao, etc. The inhabitants also like to shop online on social media such as Facebook. In Cambodia, the vast majority of transactions are settled in cash, but in recent years, with the rapid development of financial

Figure 4-7　E-Commerce Market Scales and Growth Rates of Cambodia

Source: National Institute of Statistics of Cambodia.

technology, more and more Cambodians began to use smartphones for e-payments, including QR code, e-wallet, bank transfer, mobile phone top up, bill payment, car hailing and shopping. Therefore, many third-party payment platforms have emerged, such as ABA PAY, Dura Pay, and M pay, etc.

Cambodia's relatively poor transportation infrastructure and high logistics costs have greatly hindered the development of e-commerce. Road transportation is Cambodia's main transportation method, accounting for about 90% of passenger and freight transportation, while water transportation and railway transportation account for smaller proportions. Although water transportation takes up a small proportion of Cambodia's freight sector, two international ports, Phnom Penh Autonomous Port (PPAP) and Sihanoukville Autonomous Port (SAP), play an important role in the country's export trade and economic development.

4. 13. 2　Comparison between General Trade and Cross-Border E-Commerce of Cambodia

4. 13. 2. 1　Cambodia's Exports by Country(or Region)

Table 4-49 shows top 10 export countries or regions in general trade and cross-border e-commerce of Cambodia.

Table 4-49 Top 10 Export Countries or Regions in General

Trade and Cross-Border E-Commerce of Cambodia

Rank	General Trade (Top 10 Export Countries or Regions)			Cross-Border E-Commerce (Top 10 Countries or Regions of Export Demand)		
	2019	2020	2021	2019	2020	2021
1	US	US	US	US	US	US
2	Germany	Japan	Singapore	India	Peru	Peru
3	Japan	Germany	China	China	India	Egypt
4	UK	China	Japan	Saudi Arabia	Saudi Arabia	Chile
5	China	UK	Germany	Russia	UK	Brazil
6	France	Canada	UK	Egypt	Canada	Indonesia
7	Canada	Belgium	Canada	Peru	Russia	Canada
8	Vietnam	Spain	Hong Kong, China	Australia	Nigeria	Colombia
9	Spain	Thailand	Thailand	Canada	Egypt	Saudi Arabia
10	Thailand	Netherlands	Belgium	UK	China	Philippines

Source: Data of general trade is from General Department of Customs and Excise of Cambodia, and globalEDGE. Data of cross-border e-commerce is from Alibaba. com.

4.13.2.2 Cambodia's Imports by Country(or Region)

Table 4-50 shows top 10 import countries or regions in general trade and cross-border e-commerce of Cambodia.

Table 4-50 Top 10 Import Countries or Regions in General

Trade and Cross-Border E-Commerce of Cambodia

Rank	General Trade (Top 10 Import Countries or Regions)			Cross-Border E-Commerce (Top 10 Countries or Regions of Import Demand)		
	2019	2020	2021	2019	2020	2021
1	Thailand	China	China	China	China	China
2	China	Thailand	Thailand	Thailand	Thailand	Vietnam
3	Singapore	Vietnam	Vietnam	R.O. Korea	Vietnam	Pakistan

Continued

Rank	General Trade (Top 10 Import Countries or Regions)			Cross-Border E-Commerce (Top 10 Countries or Regions of Import Demand)		
	2019	2020	2021	2019	2020	2021
4	Vietnam	Japan	Singapore	Vietnam	R. O. Korea	US
5	Taiwan, China	Indonesia	Indonesia	US	India	Thailand
6	R. O. Korea	R. O. Korea	Japan	India	US	India
7	Hong Kong, China	Singapore	R. O. Korea	Hong Kong, China	Pakistan	R. O. Korea
8	Indonesia	Malaysia	Hong Kong, China	Japan	UK	UK
9	US	Hong Kong, China	Switzerland	Pakistan	Japan	Japan
10	Malaysia	US	Malaysia	Taiwan, China	South Africa	France

Source: Data of general trade is from General Department of Customs and Excise of Cambodia, and globalEDGE. Data of cross-border e-commerce is from Alibaba. com.

4. 13. 2. 3 Cambodia's Exports by Category

Table 4-51 shows top 10 categories of exported goods in general trade and cross-border e-commerce of cambodia.

Table 4-51 Top 10 Export Categories of Exported Goods in
General Trade and Cross-Border E-Commerce of Cambodia

Rank	General Trade (Top 10 Categories of Exported Goods)			Cross-Border E-Commerce(Top 10 Categories of Export Demand)		
	2019	2020	2021	2019	2020	2021
1	Apparel (knitted)	apparel (knitted)	apparel (knitted)	Machinery	Machinery	Machinery
2	Apparel (not knitted)	Apparel (not knitted)	Precious metals	Electronic components, modules, accessories & communication	Electronic components, modules, accessories & communication	Electronic components, modules, accessories & communication

Continued

Rank	General Trade (Top 10 Categories of Exported Goods)			Cross-Border E-Commerce(Top 10 Categories of Export Demand)		
	2019	2020	2021	2019	2020	2021
3	Footwear	Footwear	Apparel (not knitted)	Communication	Beauty & personal care	Beauty & personal care
4	Leather products	Leather products	Footwear	Beauty & personal care	Agriculture	Material handling
5	Electromechanical equipment	Electromechanical equipment	Leather products	Agriculture	Food & beverage	Food & beverage
6	Vehicles & parts	Vehicles & parts	Electromechanical equipment	Food & beverage	Consumer electronics	Health & medical care
7	Cereals	Precious metals	Furniture	Consumer electronics	Health & medical care	Home textile
8	Vegetables	Cereals	Vehicles & parts	Mechanical equipment	Medicines & health care	Consumer electronics
9	Fruits	Furniture	Cereals	Architecture	Cars & motorcycles	Apparel
10	Plastics	Fur	Printed Books	Medicines & health care	Home textile	Agriculture

Source: Data of general trade is from General Department of Customs and Excise of Cambodia, and globalEDGE. Data of cross-border e-commerce is from Alibaba. com.

4. 13. 2. 4　Cambodia Imports by Category

Table 4-52 shows top 10 categories of imported goods in general trade and cross-border e-commerce of Cambodia.

Table 4-52　Top 10 Categories of Imported Goods in General

Trade and Cross-Border E-Commerce of Cambodia

Rank	General Trade (Top 10 Categories of Imported Goods)			Cross-Border E-Commerce (Top 10 Categories of Import Demand)		
	2019	2020	2021	2019	2020	2021
1	Precious metals	Knitwear	Knitted fabric	Consumer electronics	Consumer electronics	Consumer electronics
2	Petroleum & mineral fuels	Vehicles & parts	Petroleum & mineral fuels	Beauty & personal care	Apparel	Toys

Continued

Rank	General Trade (Top 10 Categories of Imported Goods)			Cross-Border E-Commerce (Top 10 Categories of Import Demand)		
	2019	2020	2021	2019	2020	2021
3	Knitwear	Petroleum & mineral fuels	Vehicles & parts	Apparel	Beauty & personal care	Apparel
4	Vehicles & parts	Industrial machinery	Industrial machinery	Cars & motorcycles	Cars & motorcycles	Sports & entertainment
5	Industrial machinery	Electromechanical equipment	Electromechanical equipment	Household supplies	Sports & entertainment	Cars & motorcycles
6	Electromechanical equipment	Man-made fiber	Precious metals	Luggage, bags & cases	Machinery	Home & garden
7	Iron & steel	Plastics	Man-made fiber	Machinery	Security & protection	Beauty & personal care
8	Cotton	Cotton	Plastics	Watches, jewelry & glasses	Medicines & health care	Machinery
9	Plastics	Iron & steel	Paper	Medicines & health care	Toys	Health & medical care
10	Wine	Paper	Cotton	Household appliances	Household supplies	Watches, jewelry & glasses

Source: Data of general trade is from General Department of Customs and Excise of Cambodia, and globalEDGE. Data of cross-border e-commerce is from Alibaba. com.

4. 14　Cross-Border E-Commerce Development of Laos

4. 14. 1　Overview of Social Economy and Cross-Border E-Commerce Development of Laes

In 2020, Laos had a total GDP of $ 19. 136 billion and a GDP per capita of $ 2, 546. The population of Laos was 7. 28 million, an increase of 106,100 over the previous year with the population growth rate of 1. 5%.

With 4% of the population aged 65 and above, Laos has not yet entered an aging society. In terms of gender, the male population is relatively larger than the female. The urbanization rate was 36.3% in 2020, which is steadily increasing year by year.

Laos has weak Internet infrastructure connectivity and the lowest proportion of connections among ASEAN countries. It ranks second to last in the number of mobile broadband users per capita in the ASEAN region. In 2020, the number of Internet users in Laos reached 3.1 million, up 6.5% year-on-year from 2019, and the Internet penetration rate reached 43%. Each year, the Lao government spends more than 60% of its loans and aid, that is, $48-60 million, for road and bridge construction, which will further reduce transportation costs and promote efficient cross-border trade and transportation between Laos and its neighboring countries. Among social media in Laos, Facebook, YouTube and Twitter have the highest user penetration rates of 58.97%, 24.94% and 11.26% respectively, making them the most important new media platforms for Laotians to obtain information. Laotian online shoppers are also more accustomed to shopping on social media platforms.

Internationally, UNCTAD B2C E-Commerce Index and ICT Development Index (IDI) proposed by International Telecommunication Union are commonly used to measure a country's e-commerce development. In 2020, UNCTAD B2C E-Commerce Index in Laos ranked 98th out of the 151 surveyed countries. In the 2020 B2C E-commerce Index, Laos performed excellently in postal reliability despite scoring low in the other indicators. It scored 85 points (out of 100 points) in postal reliability, surpassing China (61 points), India (54 points) and Malaysia (80 points), ranking 5th in the list of the top 10 developing economies. This has given a strong impetus for Laos to strengthen its postal system and improve the performance of the other three indicators in order to prepare for the development of e-commerce in a better way.

The ITU's ICT Development Index (IDI) contains 11 indicators to measure key aspects of ICT access, use and skills. In terms of IDI in 2019, Laos ranked the 139th out of 176 countries. On the whole, the IDI of Laos showed a good development trend, with its ranking climbing from the 144th in 2018 to 139th. However, it still lagged behind India and Myanmar, which ranked the 134th and the 135th respectively. At the invitation of the International Economic and Technical Cooperation Center of the Ministry of Industry and Information Technology of China, representatives from the National Internet Center, Planning and Cooperation Department, and Information and Communication Technology Department of Laos' Ministry of Post and Telecommunication attended the China-ASEAN Digital Economy Development and Cooperation Seminar, and introduced the 2016— 2025 ICT Strategic Development Plan and Development Vision before 2030. This plan is also the ongoing ICT and digital national strategy in Laos.

4.14.2　Comparison between General Trade and Cross-Border E-Commerce of Laos

4.14.2.1　Laos Exports by Country(or Region)

Table 4-53 shows top 10 export countries or regions in general trade and cross-border e-commerce of Laos.

Table 4-53　Top 10 Export Countries or Regions in General

Trade and Cross-Border E-Commerce of Laos

Rank	General Trade (Top 10 Export Countries or Regions)			Cross-Border E-Commerce (Top 10 Countries or Regions of Export Demand)		
	2019	2020	2021	2019	2020	2021
1	Thailand	Thailand	Thailand	US	Panama	US
2	China	China	China	Spain	US	India
3	Vietnam	Vietnam	Vietnam	UK	Algeria	Brazil

Continued

Rank	General Trade (Top 10 Export Countries or Regions)			Cross-Border E-Commerce (Top 10 Countries or Regions of Export Demand)		
	2019	2020	2021	2019	2020	2021
4	Japan	Japan	India	Russia	Thailand	UK
5	India	India	Australia	Kazakhstan	R. O. Korea	Philippines
6	US	Germany	Japan	France	Ukraine	Italy
7	Germany	Hong Kong, China	Germany	Vietnam	Italy	Mexico
8	Switzerland	Switzerland	Hong Kong, China	Portugal	China	Canada
9	Canada	US	Indonesia	Pakistan	Afghanistan	Russia
10	UAE	Italy	Cambodia	Canada	Kazakhstan	Saudi Arabia

Source: Data of general trade is from globalEDGE, OEC and Trading Economics. Data of cross-border e-commerce is from Alibaba.com.

4.14.2.2 Laos Imports by Country(or Region)

Table 4-54 shows top 10 import countries or regions in general trade and cross-border e-commerce of Laos.

Table 4-54 Top 10 Import Countries or Regions in General Trade and Cross-Border E-Commerce of Laos

Rank	General Trade (Top 10 Import Countries or Regions)			Cross-Border E-Commerce (Top 10 Countries or Regions of Import Demand)		
	2019	2020	2021	2019	2020	2021
1	Thailand	Thailand	Thailand	China	China	China
2	China	China	China	Thailand	Thailand	Bangladesh
3	Vietnam	Vietnam	Vietnam	Vietnam	US	Vietnam
4	Japan	Japan	Japan	Hong Kong, China	Denmark	R. O. Korea
5	R. O. Korea	Singapore	US	Philippines	South Africa	Pakistan
6	Singapore	US	Australia	India	Hong Kong, China	UK
7	Russia	R. O. Korea	Singapore	Taiwan, China	R. O. Korea	India

Continued

Rank	General Trade (Top 10 Export Countries or Regions)			Cross-Border E-Commerce (Top 10 Countries or Regions of Export Demand)		
	2019	2020	2021	2019	2020	2021
8	Austria	Australia	R. O. Korea	US	Malaysia	South Africa
9	India	UK	UAE	R. O. Korea	Pakistan	US
10	Indonesia	India	India	UK	Vietnam	Hong Kong, China

Source: Data of general trade is from globalEDGE, OEC and Trading Economics. Data of cross-border e-commerce is from Alibaba. com.

4. 14. 2. 3   Laos Exports by Category

Table 4-55 shows top 10 categories of exported goods in general trade and cross-border e-commerce of Laos.

Table 4-55   Top 10 Categories of Exported Goods in General Trade and Cross-Border E-Commerce of Laos

Rank	General Trade (Top 10 Categories of Exported Goods)			Cross-Border E-Commerce (Top 10 Categories of Export Demand)		
	2019	2020	2021	2019	2020	2021
1	Petroleum & mineral fuels	Petroleum & mineral fuels	Mineral fuels, mineral oils & products of their distillation	Consumer electronics	Cars & motorcycles	Consumer electronics
2	Ores	Ores	Slag & ash	Furniture & home decor	Agriculture	Commercial service equipment
3	Electromechanical equipment	Copper	Pearls, gemstones, metals & coins	Cars & motorcycles	Apparel	Packaging & printing
4	Copper & its products	Electric motors	Edible fruits, nuts, citrus fruit skins & melons	Food & beverage	Packaging & printing	Home textile
5	Beverage & wine	Wood pulp	Living animals	Beauty & personal care	Food & beverage	Agriculture

258

Continued

Rank	General Trade (Top 10 Categories of Exported Goods)			Cross-border E-Commerce(Top 10 Categories of Export Demand)		
	2019	2020	2021	2019	2020	2021
6	Wood pulp	Fruits & nuts	Wood pulp, fibrous cellulose material & waste	Sports & entertainment	Architecture	Food & beverage
7	Precious metals	Beverage	Electrical & electronic equipment	Household supplies	Watches, jewelry & glasses	Home & garden
8	Wood & articles thereof	Living animals	Edible vegetables & certain roots and tubers	Medicines & health care	Rubber raw materials & articles thereof	Health and medical care
9	Rubber	Gemstones & metals	Beverages, spirits & vinegar	Minerals & metals	Minerals & metals	Furniture
10	Fertilizer	Rubber	Rubber	Watches, jewelry & glasses	Furniture	Footwear & accessories

Source: Data of general trade is from globalEDGE, OEC and Trading Economics. Data of cross-border e-commerce is from Alibaba. com.

4. 14. 2. 4　Laos Imports by Category

Table 4-56 shows top 10 categories of imported goods in general trade and cross-border e-commerce of Laos.

Table 4-56　Top 10 Categories of Imported Goods in General

Trade and Cross-Border E-Commerce of Laos

Rank	General Trade (Top 10 Categories of Imported Goods)			Cross-Border E-Commerce (Top 10 Categories of Import Demand)		
	2019	2020	2021	2019	2020	2021
1	Petroleum & mineral fuels	Petroleum & mineral fuels	Mineral fuels, mineral oils & products of their distillation	Cars & motorcycles	Medicines & health care	Consumer electronics

Rank	General Trade (Top 10 Categories of Imported Goods)			Cross-Border E-Commerce (Top 10 Categories of Import Demand)		
	2019	2020	2021	2019	2020	2021
2	Electromechanical equipment	Electric motors	Electrical & electronic equipment	Consumer electronics	Security & protection	Cars & motorcycles
3	Vehicles & parts	Cars & parts	Machinery, nuclear reactors & boilers	Machinery	Machinery	Machinery
4	Iron & steel	Industrial machinery	Vehicles other than railway or tramway	Medicines & health care	Consumer electronics	Toys
5	Articles of iron & steel	Articles of iron & steel	Living animals	Sports & entertainment	Hardware	Apparel
6	Plastics	Iron & steel	Beverages, spirits & vinegar	Watches, jewelry & glasses	Cars & motorcycles	Sports & entertainment
7	Animals	Beverage	Articles of iron & steel	Household supplies	Household supplies	Health & medical care
8	Precious metal	Live animals	Iron & steel	Food & beverage	Apparel	Hardware
9	Beverages & wine	Plastics	Plastics	Packaging & printing	Sports & entertainment	Watches, jewelry & glasses
10	Paper	Sugar & candy	Paper & paperboard, paper pulp & articles thereof	Electrical equipment & articles thereof	Electrical equipment & articles thereof	Home & garden

Source: Data of general trade is from globalEDGE, OEC and Trading Economics. Data of cross-border e-commerce is from Alibaba. com.

4. 15   Cross-Border E-Commerce Development of Brunei

4. 15. 1   Overview of Social Economy and Cross-Border E-Commerce Development of Brunei

According to the World Bank, Brunei's GDP reached $12. 006 billion in 2020, up 1.13% year-on-year, and its GDP per capita reached $27,400, up 0.17% year-on-year. Brunei's population reached 437,500 in 2020. In 2018, Brunei's literacy rate reached 97.21%, with a junior high school dropout rate of merely 0.256% in 2020. In terms of digital economy, Brunei is relatively well underpinned. As of January 2021, Brunei had 418,000 Internet users, up 1.1% year-on-year. With an Internet penetration rate of 95%, Brunei ranked first in Southeast Asia. Brunei's number of mobile phones was 568,000, up 0.2% year-on-year, and the penetration rate of mobile phones reached 129%. According to Janio, in 2020, Brunei's e-commerce market was worth $75 million. Analysts from Statista estimate that Brunei's online retail market boasts great potential, its revenue will reach $170 million in 2022 and will continue to grow at an annual growth rate of 10.14% in 2022—2025. Currently, major e-commerce platforms in Brunei are all from other countries, among which eBay, Zalora and Amazon are the top three.

The development of Brunei's digital economy and e-commerce started late, but its digital economy has a good hardware infrastructure, which is partly due to the government's strong support. In 2019, the Brunei government established the Digital Economy Committee to explore the potential of digital economy. Brunei's Ministry of Transport and Infocommunications also released the country's first master plan for the digital economy in 2025, outlining the strategic plans and key projects for building a smart country.

4.15.2　Comparison between General Trade and Cross-Border E-Commerce of Brunei

4.15.2.1　Brunei Exports by Country(or Region)

Table 4-57 shows top 10 export countries or regions in general trade and cross-border e-commerce of Brunei.

Table 4-57　Top 10 Export Countries or Regions in General

Trade and Cross-Border E-Commerce of Brunei

Rank	General Trade (Top 10 Export Countries or Regions)			Cross-Border E-Commerce (Top 10 Countries or Regions of Export Demand)		
	2018	2019	2020	2019	2020	2021
1	Japan	Japan	Japan	Australia	Malaysia	—
2	Thailand	Singapore	Singapore	Japan	Philippines	—
3	R. O. Korea	Australia	China	Philippines	Australia	—
4	Australia	Malaysia	Malaysia	Malaysia	Japan	—
5	Singapore	India	India	Vietnam	Singapore	—
6	Malaysia	Thailand	Australia	R. O. Korea	Vietnam	—
7	India	China	Thailand	Indonesia	Indonesia	—
8	Other Asian Regions	R. O. Korea	Vietnam	Singapore	Singapore	—
9	China	Vietnam	Philippines	Thailand	Cambodia	—
10	US	Philippines	R. O. Korea	Myanmar	R. O. Korea	—

Source: Data of general trade is from Brunei Bureau of Statistics and data of cross-border e-commerce is from Alibaba. com.

4. 15. 2. 2　Brunei Imports by Country(or Region)

Table 4-58 shows top 10 import countries or regions in general trade and cross-border e-commerce of Brunei.

Table 4-58　Top 10 Import Countries or Regions in General

Trade and Cross-Border E-Commerce of Brunei

Rank	General Trade (Top 10 Import Countries or Regions)			Cross-Border E-Commerce (Top 10 Countries or Regions of Import Demand)		
	2018	2019	2020	2019	2020	2021
1	China	China	Malaysia	China	China	China
2	Singapore	Singapore	Singapore	Malaysia	Thailand	Vietnam
3	Malaysia	Malaysia	China	Thailand	Malaysia	Thailand
4	US	US	UK	R. O. Korea	Vietnam	Malaysia

Continued

Rank	General Trade (Top 10 Import Countries or Regions)			Cross-Border E-Commerce (Top 10 Countries or Regions of Import Demand)		
	2018	2019	2020	2019	2020	2021
5	Japan	Germany	Australia	Vietnam	R. O. Korea	Japan
6	UK	Nigeria	US	Indonesia	Indonesia	R. O. Korea
7	Thailand	UAE	UAE	Philippines	Philippines	Indonesia
8	R. O. Korea	Japan	Russia	Japan	Japan	Singapore
9	Germany	Kazakhstan	Japan	Singapore	Singapore	Philippines
10	Indonesia	Indonesia	Saudi Arabia	Australia	Australia	Myanmar

Source: Data of general trade is from Brunei Bureau of Statistics and data of cross-border e-commerce is from Alibaba. com.

4. 15. 2. 3   Brunei Exports by Category

Table 4-59 shows top 10 categories of exported goods in general trade and cross-border e-commerce of Brunei.

Table 4-59   Top 10 Categories of Exported Goods in General Trade and Cross-Border E-Commerce of Brunei

Rank	General Trade (Top 10 Categories of Exported Goods)			Cross-Border E-Commerce (Top 10 Categories of Export Demand)		
	2019	2020	2021	2019	2020	2021
1	Mineral fuels	Mineral fuels	Mineral fuels	Food & beverage	Food & beverage	—
2	Chemicals	Chemicals	Chemicals	Sports & entertainment	Sports & entertainment	—
3	Machinery and transportation equipment	Machinery and transportation equipment	Machinery and transportation equipment	Beauty & personal care	Agriculture	—
4	Machine & articles thereof	Machine & articles thereof	Machine & articles thereof	Agriculture	Beauty & personal Care	—
5	Industrial products	Industrial products	Food	Medicines & health care	Consumer electronics	—

Continued

Rank	General Trade (Top 10 Categories of Exported Goods)			Cross-Border E-Commerce (Top 10 Categories of Export Demand)		
	2019	2020	2021	2019	2020	2021
6	Inedible materials	Food	Industrial products	Energy	Security & protection	—
7	Food	Inedible materials	Inedible materials	Business services	Health & medical care	—
8	Animal or vegetable oil	Animal or vegetable oil	Animal or vegetable oil	Consumer electronics	Energy	—
9	Beverages & tobacco	Beverages & tobacco	Beverages & tobacco	Cars & motorcycles	Business services	—
10	Fabric	Fabric	Fabric	Sports & entertainment	Household appliances	—

Source: Data of general trade is from Brunei Bureau of Statistics and data of cross-border e-commerce is from Alibaba. com.

4. 15. 2. 4 Brunei Imports by Category

Table 4-60 shows top 10 categories of imported goods in general trade and cross-border e-commerce of Brunei.

Table 4-60   Top 10 Categories of Imported Goods in General Trade and Cross-Border E-Commerce of Brunei

Rank	General Trade (Top 10 Categories of Imported Goods)			Cross-Border E-Commerce (Top 10 Categories of Import Demand)		
	2019	2020	2021	2019	2020	2021
1	Fuels	Fuels	Fuels	Cars & motorcycles	Cars & motorcycles	Horticulture
2	Machinery & transportation equipment	Machinery & transportation equipment	Machinery & transportation equipment	Household supplies	Consumer electronics	Household supplies
3	Industrial products	Industrial products	Food	Consumer electronics	Apparel	Cars & motorcycles
4	Food	Food	Chemicals	Apparel	Packaging & printing	Consumer electronics

Continued

Rank	General Trade (Top 10 Categories of Imported Goods)			Cross-border E-Commerce(Top 10 Categories of Import Demand)		
	2019	2020	2021	2019	2020	2021
5	Chemicals	Chemicals	Industrial products	Machinery	Horticulture	Apparel
6	Machine & articles thereof	Machine & articles thereof	Machine & articles thereof	Packaging & printing	Machinery	Sports & entertainment
7	Beverages & tobacco	Beverages & tobacco	Beverages & tobacco	Sports & entertainment	Furniture & home decor	Toys
8	Inedible materials	Inedible materials	Animal or vegetable oil	Luggage, bags & cases	Household supplies	Furniture & home decor
9	Animal or vegetable oil	Inedible materials	Inedible materials	Furniture & home decor	Architecture	Packaging & printing
10	Fabric	Fabric	Fabric	Gifts & crafts	Security & protection	Machinery

Source: Data of general trade is from Brunei Bureau of Statistics and data of cross-border e-commerce is from Alibaba. com.

5 Summary

The RCEP provides top-level design for a series of specific issues related to cross-border e-commerce, such as cross-border data flow, consumer protection, and the location of computing facilities, etc. This will help reduce development barriers of cross-border e-commerce, promote the interconnection of digital elements in the region, and further unleash the huge potential of the RCEP regional market. Therefore, we expect that with the formal implementation of RCEP, the scale of cross-border e-commerce in the region will continue to maintain rapid growth in the coming years, the digital infrastructure will be further improved, and the corresponding institutional norms will gradually take shape, all of which are important forces to promote regional economic development. Specifically, RCEP will have a profound impact on the cross-border e-commerce industry in the region in the following four aspects.

Firstly, RCEP will provide broader market and development space for enterprises engaged in cross-border e-commerce related industries. The RCEP region covers not only mature markets such as Japan, R. O. Korea, and Australia, but also emerging markets that are still expanding rapidly. With a large number of users, the emerging markets like China and ASEAN have good growth momentum and potential for cross-border e-commerce. As can be seen from the previous chapter of index analysis, from 2019Q1 to 2021Q4, the RCEP B2B Index, the RCEP B2C Index and the RCEP Cross-Border Payment Service Index all showed an obvious upward trend, with the average annual growth rates in 3 years being 28.7%, 33.2% and 21% respectively. The growth rate of the first two is respectively 1.5 times and 2.2 times of the growth rate (19.6%) of the China-ASEAN Trade Index (reflecting the overall trade situation) of the General Administration of Customs in the same period. This reflects the great vitality and resilience of cross-border e-commerce in the RCEP region. At the same time, unlike traditional general trade, cross-border e-commerce is highly inclusive. With the gradual implementation of the zero-tariff policy and the gradual improvement of logistics services, we expect that in the future, a large number of small-, medium- and micro-sized businesses in the RCEP region will participate in the market as micro-multinational companies, and this trend is also reflected in indexes and indicators. On the one hand, the 3-year average annualized growth rate of the indicator of RCEP B2B trade bodies is 11.7%, and after the signing of RCEP in 2020Q4, the growth of the trade body index accelerated, reflecting the positive impact of huge favorable policies on trade bodies. On the other hand, RECP B2C enterprise development indicator grew at an average annual growth rate of 46.7% over the past 3 years. With rapid and stable growth, it is the only one of the 4 primary indirators of RCEP B2C Index that is not affected by seasonality.

Secondly, with the further development of cross-border trade under the **RCEP framework, consumers in the region will be able to enjoy goods of high quality and low price, and logistics services which is faster and more convenient.** According to this book, the average year-on-year growth rate of number of brands on Tmall Global in RCEP from 2020Q1 to 2021Q2 was 31.5%. Thailand and Malaysia are the most significant sources of popular commodities. Thai latex pillows and Malaysian bird's nest have become common in Chinese consumers' shopping carts. Chinese consumers' average satisfaction with brands in the RCEP region has also increased steadily, and their recognition has been continuously improved. In terms of logistics services, with overall decline and occasional repetition, the logistics duration of overseas shipments and bonded warehouses show a good trend under the obstacles of global pandemic spread and rising shipping costs. The average logistics duration of bonded warehouses in 2021Q1 decreased by 42% compared with 2020Q1, and the average logistics time for overseas shipments also fell by 21%. At the same time, with the implementation of the specific provisions of RCEP, members will also provide online consumers with more secure and reliable protection commitments to ease their worries of online consumption.

Thirdly, the prosperity of cross-border e-commerce in RCEP will promote regulatory cooperation and service innovation among governments of members. The ICC TradeFlow Alliance established in 2020, the ASEAN Data Management Framework (DMF) issued in 2021, the ASEAN Model Contract for Cross-Border Data Flow (MCCs) and so on manifest RCEP members' efforts of promoting win-win cooperation at the government level, enforcing the country, and enriching the people. The signing and coming into force of RCEP fully reflects the confidence and determination of members to jointly maintain multilateralism and free trade, and promote regional economic integration, and the development of cross-border e-commerce has also greatly promoted the cooperation between the governments and enterprises of members, intergovernmental cooperation and government innovation management. By widely using digital technology to make scientific decisions, introduce policies and regulations, improve management and service efficiency, and thereby promote regional economic and social development, the governments follow the trend of the digital age to break the traditional shackles of international trade.

Fourthly, the vigorous development of cross-border e-commerce in RCEP will further promote regional economic and trade integration and inclusive common development. On the one hand, RCEP has become the action framework and guideline for economic cooperation and trade exchanges among members in the region. Members are taking practical actions to promote the deep integration of the digital economy and the real economy, and the "dual integration" will support "dual cycle". For example, the eWTP Hangzhou Pilot Zone, which was established in 2017, has become a digital cross-border trade platform connecting the world, and has built multiple e-hubs in the RCEP region to use the dual conveniences of infrastructure interconnection and cross-border e-commerce to promote the integration of regional cross-border e-commerce and the real economy. On the other hand, based on the inclusiveness and importance of cross-border e-commerce, RCEP not only emphasizes the traditional rules of cross-border digital commerce, but also formulates corresponding provisions on consumer rights protection, network security and data privacy, digital trade dialogue and dispute resolution mechanisms, so as to further regulate the organizational form and process system of cross-border e-commerce, bridge the objective digital gap between the RCEP members in the region and promote the inclusive and common development of cross-border e-commerce. By doing so, the inclusive development supported by digital technology is really "on the way". At the same time, cross-border e-commerce is expected to promote the prosperity of green trade through the application of more new technologies and new ideas, and make greater contributions to the cause of sustainable development of mankind.

However, we also need to be aware that due to objective factors such as the lack of detailed and binding provisions on cross-border trade in RCEP, the agreement will also pose greater challenges to Chinese enterprises and governments in cross-border e-commerce. First of all, after the implementation of RCEP, China's cross-border trade-related enterprises will not only gain more market opportunities, but also face more intense competition from overseas enterprises and regulatory risks from different countries. Secondly, in the case of transnational disputes, RCEP can only assume the function of dispute mediation, which will make the protection of the rights and interests of Chinese enterprises uncertain. Moreover, since RCEP does not provide mandatory restrictions on online consumer protection, it remains to be seen whether the rights and interests of online consumers in China can be effectively protected after the implementation of the agreement. Thirdly, RCEP puts forward higher requirements for China's digital supervision. With the in-depth development of cross-border e-commerce, a series of issues such as cross-border information transmission, consumer privacy, and digital taxation will pose risks to China's information security and consumer protection. Finally, the external economic environment and emergencies will have an impact on the development of cross-border e-commerce in RCEP. For example, in recent years, the COVID-19 pandemic has significantly promoted the growth of cross-border e-commerce. However, the interdependence of economic systems, repeated pandemics, tortuous recovery of the world economy, and high shipping costs will also put some pressure on the long-term development of cross-border e-commerce, the RCEP B2B trade bodies indicator saw the largest sequential decline of 19.0% in 2021Q4, which is a wake-up call and needs attention from all parties. In view of the potential problems listed above, this book hopes to promote the healthy development of cross-border e-commerce in China through the following suggestions.

Firstly, strengthening the guidance of enterprises and leveraging RCEP to enhance the core competitiveness of Chinese enterprises. We should encourage Chinese enterprises to give full play to their subjective initiative, fully understand and make good use of the cumulative rules of origin, deeply engage in the regional industrial chain and supply chain, actively adapt to a more open environment and fiercer competition after the implementation of the agreement, improve the management level, improve product quality and enhance the ability to participate in international cooperation and competition. For example, we should encourage technology-intensive enterprises to actively innovate and develop, increase the industrial layout with high added value and large profit margins such as product research and development, management consulting, and professional design. In the meantime, labor-intensive enterprises should be guided to develop in the direction of high-end and refinement, and continuously improve exports product quality and brand influence. At the same time, we should enhance Chinese enterprises' awareness of the potential changes in regional industrial chains and supply chains brought about by RCEP, and plan the development strategy and business strategy to adapt to regional economic integration, invest in high-quality resources, energy and advanced technology industries to enhance the control of important products, resources, technologies and supply channels.

Secondly, actively improving the business environment of local governments and helping enterprises adapt to the high-level rules of RCEP. The first is to encourage local governments to organize teams to deeply analyze the current situation of trade with the RCEP members, and to study the list of key products, key enterprises and key country (or region) markets, so as to provide reference for local enterprises to develop markets. The second is to collect the difficulties encountered by enterprises in conducting trade and investment with the RCEP members in a timely manner through irregular seminars and questionnaires. We should answer relevant questions, and help enterprises better "understand the external situation and understand the internal situation", so as to better cope with the risks and challenges of cooperation with enterprises in the RCEP region. The third is to guide local governments to take the implementation of RCEP as an opportunity, implement higher standards of rules in line with the RCEP, improve local governance capabilities, actively optimize the business environment, and escort enterprises to make good use of new opportunities for investment and business.

Thirdly, actively implementing higher-level cross-border e-commerce rules and improving some important provisions of RCEP in China to protect the rights and interests of enterprises and consumers. Specific measures include but are not limited to: China can first test the cross-border e-commerce rules in high-level free trade agreements such as CPTPP and USMCA in the pilot free trade zone, Hainan free trade port and other open highlands, so as to conduct stress test for China's exploration of cross-border e-commerce rules in higher level, wider scope and broader fields, so as to sum up experience. Besides, we should actively carry out transnational cooperation, jointly explore the formulation of consumer protection measures for cross-border trade, and effectively protect the legitimate rights and interests of online consumers in China. In response to the weak RCEP dispute resolution mechanism, we should accelerate the improvement of relevant laws and regulations to provide related companies engaged in cross-border trade in China with better legal protection.

Fourthly, optimizing the business ecology of enterprises and supporting the construction of cross-border e-commerce platforms and the training of special talents. On the one hand, in view of the characteristic that more than 85% of cross-border e-commerce in the Asia-Pacific region are small enterprises, we should fully affirm the advantages and roles of digital platforms for foreign trade in providing sales, payment, logistics, management and other services for micro multinational companies, innovate the institutional environment, and further support the innovative development of China's digital platforms for foreign trade through policy support and tax incentives, and encourage enterprises to build a better cooperation platform for Chinese enterprises to expand the RCEP market and enterprises from the RCEP members to enter the Chinese market, so as to enable enterprises to fully tap the cooperation potential with RCEP members. On the other hand, around the fact that more than 70% of cross-border e-commerce companies in China believe that "the lack of professional talents is the biggest bottleneck in operation and development", governments at all levels, universities and cross-border e-commerce leading enterprises are encouraged to carry out the training of cross-border e-commerce related talents by jointly building an online learning platform for cross-border e-commerce talents, building an international talent pool for cross-border e-commerce and building an innovation and entrepreneurship ecology for cross-border e-commerce talents.

Fifthly, improving China's digital regulatory legislation and developing a sounder cross-border data flow mechanism. Specific measures include but are not limited to: further improving the existing legal framework, such as The Rules on Counteracting Unjustified Extraterritorial Application of Foreign Legislation and Other Measures; on the basis of drawing on international excellent experience, relevant laws to ensure data network security are introduced in a targeted manner, such as E-Commerce Law, Cross-Border Data Transmission Law, Personal Information Protection Law and so on; speeding up the formulation of laws and regulations related to cross-border data transmission, and classifying and managing cross-border data, such as the prohibition of confidential data flow, restricting the flow of important data, and allowing the free flow of data for non-sensitive data when the overseas receiver meets the legal requirements of China.

Sixthly, comprehensively strengthening the resilience of cross-border e-commerce development, and promoting sustainable development in the same time. On the one hand, we should actively respond to overseas pandemic counter-attacks, high logistics costs and other external economic environment changes and the impact of emergencies, help cross-border e-commerce enterprises improve their resilience, accurately grasp work-from-home, stay-at-home economy and other new ways of life and work changes to cross-border trade demand under the pandemic, help small- and medium-sized cross-border e-commerce enterprises under pressure of the pandemic to turn pressure into opportunities. On the other hand, we should actively seek a new path for sustainable development in the context of cross-border trade of RCEP, such as strengthening multi-party low-carbon cooperation, accelerating the development of green economy and trade, and further strengthening the "double carbon" dialogue between China and developed countries in Europe and the United States on the basis of fully understanding the global economic and social changes of carbon peak and carbon neutrality, paying attention to the study of carbon emission standards and carbon tariffs to prevent the emergence of green trade barriers. In addition, efforts can be made to tap the potential of green and low-carbon industry cooperation between China and other RCEP members. We should learn the advanced green and low-carbon technology and development experience of Japan, R. O. Korea, Singapore and other countries, establish overseas low-carbon R&D centers and innovation centers, adopt diversified methods such as investment and acquisition of advanced low-carbon technology projects to help China's high quality development of related green industry including new energy, new materials, high-end equipment and clean technology.

Postscript

The authors of this book, ordered by contribution, are Zhou Wenyu, Lü Jiamin and Lu Jiajun. Zhou Wenyu contributed 150,000 words. Lü Jiamin contributed 150,000 words. Lu Jiajun contributed 20,000 words.

The writing and publication of this book would not have been possible without the staunch support of all project team members and experts. We would like to express our sincerest gratitude to them. The list is as follows:

Project Team Experts:

Ben Shenglin, Dean of International Business School of Zhejiang University, Dean of the Academy of Internet Finance of Zhejiang University

Ouyang Cheng, Director of Globalization Research Center of AliResearch

Li Zhenhua, Director of Ant Group Research

AliResearch:

Ren Jie, Head of Research Cooperation Project of AliResearch

Li Peng, Data Analysis Expert of AliResearch

Fan Qiuci, Senior Research Expert of Industrial Research Center of AliResearch

Ant Group Research:

Wang Fang, Research Director of Ant Group Research

Ni Dancheng, Research Director of Ant Group Research

Li Yunjing, Expert of Ant Group Research

Cheng Zhiyun, Research Director of Ant Group Research

Research Assistants:

Chen Shengnan, Jia Yue, Gong Jiaowei, Wang Sihan, Cheng Qiyu, Shao Yining, Chen Chutian, Zhao Yunxi, Zhang Huanyu

RCEP Index Weight Scoring Experts:

Yu Jiefang, Associate Professor of School of Economics of Zhejiang University

Zhang Hongsheng, Associate Professor of School of Economics of Zhejiang University

Zhu Zhujun, Director of the Department of International Economics and Trade of Zhejiang Gongshang University

Ma Xiao, Assistant Professor of Peking University HSBC Business School

Luo Dan, Lecturer of Alibaba Business School of Hangzhou Normal University

Gu Yue, Associate Research Fellow of Digital Finance Research Institute of Hangzhou City University

Liang Jie, CEO of Xiajiang Media